Learning RxJava

Build concurrent, maintainable, and responsive Java in less time

Thomas Nield

BIRMINGHAM - MUMBAI

Learning RxJava

First published: June 2017

Production reference: 1140617

Published by Packt Publishing Ltd.
Livery Place
35 Livery Street
Birmingham
B3 2PB, UK.
ISBN 978-1-78712-042-6

www.packtpub.com

Credits

Author

Thomas Nield

Reviewers

David Karnok

David Moten

Commissioning Editor

Aaron Lazar

Acquisition Editor

Denim Pinto

Content Development Editor

Siddhi Chavan

Technical Editor

Pranali Badge

Copy Editor

Stuti Srivastava

Project Coordinator

Prajakta Naik

Proofreader

Safis Editing

Indexer

Tejal Daruwale Soni

Graphics

Abhinash Sahu

Production Coordinator

Shraddha Falebhai

About the Author

Thomas Nield is a business consultant for Southwest Airlines in Schedule Initiatives, and a maintainer for RxJavaFX and RxKotlin. Early in his career, he became fascinated with technology and its role in business analytics. After becoming proficient in Java, Kotlin, Python, SQL, and reactive programming, he became an open source contributor as well as an author/speaker at O'Reilly Media. He is passionate about sharing what he learns and enabling others with new skill sets. He enjoys making technical content relatable and relevant to those unfamiliar with or intimidated by it.

Currently, Thomas is interested in data science, reactive programming, and the Kotlin language. You may find him speaking on these three subjects and how they can interconnect.

He has also authored the book *Getting Started with SQL*, by O'Reilly Media.

Acknowledgements

I am blessed to have great people in my life who have enabled everything I do, including this book. To all my family and friends who saw little of me for 6 months while I wrote this book, thank you for being so patient and understanding.

First, I want to thank my mom and dad. They have worked hard to ensure that I have the opportunities that I have today. My dad did everything he could to provide a better education for my brothers and me. Growing up, my mom always pushed me forward, even when I resisted; she taught me to never settle and always struggle past my limits.

There are so many people at my company, Southwest Airlines, who I have to thank--the leaders and colleagues in ground ops, revenue management, and network planning, who have taken risks to green-light my projects. They have embraced my unconventional approaches in leveraging technology to solve industry challenges. It is amazing to work for a company that continues to be a maverick and support a tradition started by an attorney, a Texas businessman, and a cocktail napkin.

I also want to thank the great folks at O'Reilly Media and Packt who continue to open doors for me to write and speak. Although I was approached by Packt to write this book, they probably would never have found me if it was not for O'Reilly and my previous book, *Getting Started with SQL*.

While he was not involved in this book or ReactiveX, I want to extend my gratitude to Edvin Syse, the creator and maintainer of TornadoFX. I joined his project in early 2016, and it is amazing how far it has come. Edvin's work has helped me save a lot of my time and enabled me to pursue initiatives like this book. If you ever need to build JVM desktop apps quickly, Edvin's work may change how you do so forever. More importantly, he is probably the nicest and most helpful person you will encounter in the open source community.

Finally, I want to thank the open source community for helping me shape this journey and what ultimately became this book. David Karnok and David Moten have been enormously patient with me over the years when I had questions about RxJava. David Karnok seems to have an infinite bandwidth, not only owning and maintaining RxJava, but also answering questions and being the project's ambassador. David Moten also contributes to RxJava and is an Rx advocate for newbies and veterans alike, answering questions and helping anyone at any skill level. It is an honor to have them both review this book. I also want to thank Stepan Goncharov for checking my content on Android and everyone else in the OSS community who has been quick to share their knowledge and insights over the years.

About the Reviewers

David Karnok is the project lead and top contributor of RxJava. He is a PhD candidate in the field of production informatics. He is originally a mechanical engineer by trade who has picked up computer science along the way. He is currently a research assistant at the Engineering and Management Intelligence Research Lab under the Hungarian Academy of Sciences. He was also the first to port the historical Rx.NET library to Java back in 2011 (Reactive4Java)--2 years before Netflix started over again. Starting from late 2013, he contributed more than half of RxJava 1 and then designed, architected, and implemented almost all of RxJava 2 known today. In addition, he is perhaps the only person who does any research and development on reactive flows in terms of architecture, algorithms, and performance, of which, the major contribution to the field is the modern internals in RxJava 2 and Pivotal's Reactor Core 3. If one wants to know the in-depths of RxJava, Reactive-Streams, or reactive programming in general, David is the go-to "guru" worth listening to.

David is also a reviewer of the book, *Learning Reactive Programming With Java 8*, by Packt, and *Reactive Programming with RxJava*, by O'Reilly.

David Moten is a software developer, largely on JVM, who loves creating libraries for others and himself to use. Contributing to open source projects and participating in open source communities has been a source of enjoyment for him and a considerable education in recent years, with some really interesting complex problems in the RxJava project. RxJava itself has proven to be a huge boon, both in his workplace and outside of it, and David sees reactive programming growing in importance in mobile, backend, and frontend applications.

www.PacktPub.com

For support files and downloads related to your book, please visit `www.PacktPub.com`.

Did you know that Packt offers eBook versions of every book published, with PDF and ePub files available? You can upgrade to the eBook version at `www.PacktPub.com`and as a print book customer, you are entitled to a discount on the eBook copy. Get in touch with us at `service@packtpub.com` for more details.

At `www.PacktPub.com`, you can also read a collection of free technical articles, sign up for a range of free newsletters and receive exclusive discounts and offers on Packt books and eBooks.

`https://www.packtpub.com/mapt`

Get the most in-demand software skills with Mapt. Mapt gives you full access to all Packt books and video courses, as well as industry-leading tools to help you plan your personal development and advance your career.

Why subscribe?

- Fully searchable across every book published by Packt
- Copy and paste, print, and bookmark content
- On demand and accessible via a web browser

Customer Feedback

Thanks for purchasing this Packt book. At Packt, quality is at the heart of our editorial process. To help us improve, please leave us an honest review on this book's Amazon page at https://www.amazon.com/dp/1787120422.

If you'd like to join our team of regular reviewers, you can e-mail us at customerreviews@packtpub.com. We award our regular reviewers with free eBooks and videos in exchange for their valuable feedback. Help us be relentless in improving our products!

Table of Contents

Preface   1

Chapter 1: Thinking Reactively   7

  A brief history of ReactiveX and RxJava   8

  Thinking reactively   9

  Why should I learn RxJava?   10

    What we will learn in this book?   11

  Setting up   11

    Navigating the Central Repository   12

      Using Gradle   13

      Using Maven   15

  A quick exposure to RxJava   16

  RxJava 1.0 versus RxJava 2.0 - which one do I use?   20

  When to use RxJava   20

  Summary   21

Chapter 2: Observables and Subscribers   23

  The Observable   23

    How Observables work   23

    Using Observable.create()   24

    Using Observable.just()   28

  The Observer interface   30

    Implementing and subscribing to an Observer   31

    Shorthand Observers with lambdas   32

  Cold versus hot Observables   34

    Cold Observables   35

    Hot Observables   38

    ConnectableObservable   40

  Other Observable sources   42

    Observable.range()   42

    Observable.interval()   44

    Observable.future()   47

    Observable.empty()   48

    Observable.never()   48

    Observable.error()   49

    Observable.defer()   50

Observable.fromCallable()   53
Single, Completable, and Maybe   54
    Single   54
    Maybe   55
    Completable   57
Disposing   58
    Handling a Disposable within an Observer   59
    Using CompositeDisposable   61
    Handling Disposal with Observable.create()   62
Summary   64
Chapter 3: Basic Operators   65
Suppressing operators   65
    filter()   66
    take()   66
    skip()   68
    takeWhile() and skipWhile()   69
    distinct()   70
    distinctUntilChanged()   72
    elementAt()   73
Transforming operators   74
    map()   74
    cast()   75
    startWith()   75
    defaultIfEmpty()   77
    switchIfEmpty()   77
    sorted()   78
    delay()   80
    repeat()   81
    scan()   82
Reducing operators   84
    count()   84
    reduce()   85
    all()   86
    any()   87
    contains()   87
Collection operators   88
    toList()   89
    toSortedList()   90
    toMap() and toMultiMap()   90

collect()   93
Error recovery operators   94
onErrorReturn() and onErrorReturnItem()   95
onErrorResumeNext()   97
retry()   99
Action operators   101
doOnNext(), doOnComplete, and doOnError()   101
doOnSubscribe() and doOnDispose()   103
doOnSuccess()   105
Summary   105
Chapter 4: Combining Observables   107
Merging   108
Observable.merge() and mergeWith()   108
flatMap()   112
Concatenation   117
Observable.concat() and concatWith()   118
concatMap()   120
Ambiguous   121
Zipping   123
Combine latest   125
withLatestFrom()   127
Grouping   128
Summary   130
Chapter 5: Multicasting, Replaying, and Caching   133
Understanding multicasting   134
Multicasting with operators   135
When to multicast   140
Automatic connection   142
autoConnect()   143
refCount() and share()   146
Replaying and caching   148
Replaying   148
Caching   153
Subjects   154
PublishSubject   154
When to use Subjects   155
When Subjects go wrong   157
Serializing Subjects   158

BehaviorSubject   159
ReplaySubject   160
AsyncSubject   161
UnicastSubject   162
Summary   165

Chapter 6: Concurrency and Parallelization
167

Why concurrency is necessary   167
Concurrency in a nutshell   168
Understanding parallelization   169
Introducing RxJava concurrency   169
Keeping an application alive   175
Understanding Schedulers   178
Computation   179
IO   179
New thread   179
Single   180
Trampoline   180
ExecutorService   181
Starting and shutting down Schedulers   182
Understanding subscribeOn()   182
Nuances of subscribeOn()   186
Understanding observeOn()   189
Using observeOn() for UI event threads   193
Nuances of observeOn()   195
Parallelization   196
unsubscribeOn()   201
Summary   204

Chapter 7: Switching, Throttling, Windowing, and Buffering
205

Buffering   206
Fixed-size buffering   206
Time-based buffering   209
Boundary-based buffering   211
Windowing   212
Fixed-size windowing   212
Time-based windowing   214
Boundary-based windowing   215
Throttling   216
throttleLast() / sample()   218

throttleFirst() 219
throttleWithTimeout() / debounce() 219
Switching 221
Grouping keystrokes 226
Summary 229

Chapter 8: Flowables and Backpressure 231

Understanding backpressure 231
An example that needs backpressure 233
Introducing the Flowable 235
When to use Flowables and backpressure 237
Use an Observable If... 237
Use a Flowable If... 238
Understanding the Flowable and Subscriber 239
The Subscriber 240
Creating a Flowable 245
Using Flowable.create() and BackpressureStrategy 246
Turning an Observable into a Flowable (and vice-versa) 248
Using onBackpressureXXX() operators 250
onBackPressureBuffer() 250
onBackPressureLatest() 253
onBackPressureDrop() 254
Using Flowable.generate() 255
Summary 259

Chapter 9: Transformers and Custom Operators 261

Transformers 261
ObservableTransformer 262
FlowableTransformer 266
Avoiding shared state with Transformers 267
Using to() for fluent conversion 270
Operators 273
Implementing an ObservableOperator 273
FlowableOperator 278
Custom Transformers and operators for Singles, Maybes, and Completables 281
Using RxJava2-Extras and RxJava2Extensions 282
Summary 283

Chapter 10: Testing and Debugging 285

Configuring JUnit 286

Blocking subscribers   286
Blocking operators   289
blockingFirst()   290
blockingGet()   291
blockingLast()   292
blockingIterable()   293
blockingForEach()   294
blockingNext()   294
blockingLatest()   295
blockingMostRecent()   296
Using TestObserver and TestSubscriber   297
Manipulating time with the TestScheduler   299
Debugging RxJava code   301
Summary   306

Chapter 11: RxJava on Android   307
Creating the Android project   308
Configuring Retrolambda   314
Configuring RxJava and friends   317
Using RxJava and RxAndroid   318
Using RxBinding   322
Other RxAndroid bindings libraries   325
Life cycles and cautions using RxJava with Android   326
Summary   330

Chapter 12: Using RxJava for Kotlin New   331
Why Kotlin?   332
Configuring Kotlin   332
Configuring Kotlin for Gradle   333
Configuring Kotlin for Maven   333
Configuring RxJava and RxKotlin   335
Kotlin basics   335
Creating a Kotlin file   336
Assigning properties and variables   337
Extension functions   338
Kotlin lambdas   339
Extension operators   341
Using RxKotlin   343
Dealing with SAM ambiguity   344
Using let() and apply()   346

            Using let()   346
            Using apply()   348
        Tuples and data classes   349
        Future of ReactiveX and Kotlin   351
        Summary   352
Appendix   353
        Introducing lambda expressions   353
            Making a Runnable a lambda   353
            Making a Supplier a lambda   355
            Making a Consumer a lambda   357
            Making a Function a lambda   359
        Functional types   361
        Mixing object-oriented and reactive programming   362
        Materializing and Dematerializing   367
        Understanding Schedulers   370
Index   375

Preface

Reactive programming is more than a technology or library specification. It is an entirely new mindset in how we solve problems. The reason it is so effective and revolutionary is it does not structure our world as a series of states, but rather something that is constantly in motion. Being able to quickly capture the complexity and dynamic nature of movement (rather than state) opens up powerful new possibilities in how we represent things with code.

When I first learned Java and object-oriented programming, I felt it was useful, but not effective enough. Although OOP is useful, I believed it needed to be paired with something else to be truly productive, which is why I keep an eye on C# and Scala. Only a few years later, Java 8 came out, and I put functional programming into practice for the first time.

However, something was still missing. I became fascinated with the idea of a value notifying another value of its change, and an event triggering another event in a domino effect. Was there not a way to model events in a fluent and functional way, much like Java 8 Streams? When I voiced this idea one day, somebody introduced me to reactive programming. What I was looking for was the RxJava Observable, which, at first glance, looked a lot like a Java 8 Stream. The two look and feel similar, but the Observable *pushes* not just data but also events. At that moment, I found exactly what I was looking for.

For me, as well as many others, a challenge in learning RxJava is the lack of documentation and literature. I was often left experimenting, asking questions on Stack Overflow, and trawling obscure issues on GitHub to become knowledgeable. As I used RxJava heavily for some business problems at work, I wrote several blog articles, sharing my discoveries on topics such as parallelization and concurrency. To my surprise, these articles exploded with traffic. Perhaps this should not have been surprising since these topics were sparsely documented anywhere else. When Packt approached me to write my second book, *Learning RxJava*, I jumped at the opportunity despite the work involved. Maybe, just maybe, this book can solve the documentation problem once and for all. Every fundamental concept, use case, helpful trick, and "gotcha" can be made accessible, and RxJava will no longer be considered an "advanced topic." I believe RxJava should be made accessible to professional developers of all skill levels, as it effectively makes hard problems easy and easy problems even easier. It may require a bit more abstract understanding, but the immediate productivity gained makes this small hurdle worthwhile.

As far as I know, this is the first published book covering RxJava 2.0, which has many major differences from RxJava 1.0. This book you are reading now is the comprehensive, step-by-step guide that I wish I had. It strives to not cut any corners or present code without thorough explanation. I hope it helps you quickly find value in RxJava, and you become successful in applying it to all your endeavors. If you have any concerns, feedback, or comments, you are welcome to reach out to me at tmnield@outlook.com.

Good luck!

Thomas Nield

What this book covers

Chapter 1, *Thinking Reactively*, introduces you to RxJava.

Chapter 2, *Observables and Subscribers*, talks about the core types in RxJava, including the Observable and Observer.

Chapter 3, *Basic Operators*, gives you a thorough introduction to the core operators that allow you to express logic quickly and make RxJava productive.

Chapter 4, *Combining Observables*, teaches you how to usefully combine multiple Observable sources together in a variety of ways.

Chapter 5, *Multicasting, Replaying, and Caching*, consolidates streams to prevent redundant work with multiple Observers, as well as replay and cache emissions.

Chapter 6, *Concurrency and Parallelization*, helps you discover how RxJava flexibly and powerfully enables concurrency in your application.

Chapter 7, *Switching, Throttling, Windowing, and Buffering*, develops strategies to cope with rapidly-producing Observables without backpressure.

Chapter 8, *Flowables and Backpressure*, utilizes the Flowable to leverage backpressure and keep producers from out-pacing consumers.

Chapter 9, *Transformers and Custom Operators*, teaches you how to reuse reactive logic and create your own RxJava operators.

Chapter 10, *Testing and Debugging*, leverages effective tools to test and debug your RxJava code bases.

Chapter 11, *RxJava on Android*, teaches you how to apply your RxJava knowledge and RxAndroid extensions to streamline your Android apps.

Chapter 12, *Using RxJava for Kotlin New*, takes advantage of Kotlin's language features to enable expressive patterns with RxJava.

What you need for this book

We will be using Java 8, so Oracle's JDK 1.8 will be required. You will need an environment to write and compile your Java code (I recommend Intellij IDEA), and preferably a build automation system such as Gradle or Maven. Later in this book, we will use Android Studio.

Everything you need in this book should be free to use and not require commercial or personal licensing.

Who this book is for

This book is for Java programmers who have a fundamental grasp of object-oriented programing and core Java features. You should be familiar with variables, types, classes, properties, methods, generics, inheritance, interfaces, and static classes/properties/methods. In the Java standard library, you should at least be familiar with collections (including Lists, Sets, and Maps) as well as object equality (`hashcode()`/`equals()`). If any of these topics sound unfamiliar, you may want to read *Java: A Beginner's Guide* by Herbert Schildt to learn the fundamentals of Java. Also, *Effective Java (2nd Edition)* by Joshua Bloch is a classic book that should be on every Java developer's shelf. This book strives to use the best practices cited by Bloch.

You do not need to be familiar with concurrency as a prerequisite. This topic will be covered from an RxJava perspective.

Conventions

In this book, you will find a number of text styles that distinguish between different kinds of information. Here are some examples of these styles and an explanation of their meaning.

Code words in text, database table names, folder names, filenames, file extensions, pathnames, dummy URLs, user input, and Twitter handles are shown as follows: "We can also use several operators between `Observable` and `Observer` to transform each pushed item or manipulate them in some way".

A block of code is set as follows:

```
import io.reactivex.Observable;
public class Launcher {
    public static void main(String[] args) {
       Observable<String> myStrings =
          Observable.just("Alpha", "Beta", "Gamma", "Delta",
"Epsilon");
       }
}
```

Any output is written as follows:

```
Alpha
Beta
Gamma
Delta
Epsilon
```

New terms and **important words** are shown in bold. Words that you see on the screen, for example, in menus or dialog boxes, appear in the text like this: "You also have the option to use Maven, and you can view the appropriate configuration in **The Central Repository** by selecting the **Apache Maven** configuration information."

Warnings or important notes appear in a box like this.

Tips and tricks appear like this.

Reader feedback

Feedback from our readers is always welcome. Let us know what you think about this book-what you liked or disliked. Reader feedback is important for us as it helps us develop titles that you will really get the most out of.

To send us general feedback, simply e-mail feedback@packtpub.com, and mention the book's title in the subject of your message.

If there is a topic that you have expertise in and you are interested in either writing or contributing to a book, see our author guide at www.packtpub.com/authors.

Customer support

Now that you are the proud owner of a Packt book, we have a number of things to help you to get the most from your purchase.

Downloading the example code

You can download the example code files for this book from your account at http://www.packtpub.com. If you purchased this book elsewhere, you can visit http://www.packtpub.com/support and register to have the files e-mailed directly to you.

You can download the code files by following these steps:

1. Log in or register to our website using your e-mail address and password.
2. Hover the mouse pointer on the **SUPPORT** tab at the top.
3. Click on **Code Downloads & Errata**.
4. Enter the name of the book in the **Search** box.
5. Select the book for which you're looking to download the code files.
6. Choose from the drop-down menu where you purchased this book from.
7. Click on **Code Download**.

Once the file is downloaded, please make sure that you unzip or extract the folder using the latest version of:

- WinRAR / 7-Zip for Windows
- Zipeg / iZip / UnRarX for Mac
- 7-Zip / PeaZip for Linux

The code bundle for the book is also hosted on GitHub at https://github.com/PacktPublishing/Learning-RxJava. We also have other code bundles from our rich catalog of books and videos available at https://github.com/PacktPublishing/. Check them out!

Errata

Although we have taken every care to ensure the accuracy of our content, mistakes do happen. If you find a mistake in one of our books-maybe a mistake in the text or the code-we would be grateful if you could report this to us. By doing so, you can save other readers from frustration and help us improve subsequent versions of this book. If you find any errata, please report them by visiting http://www.packtpub.com/submit-errata, selecting your book, clicking on the **Errata Submission Form** link, and entering the details of your errata. Once your errata are verified, your submission will be accepted and the errata will be uploaded to our website or added to any list of existing errata under the Errata section of that title.

To view the previously submitted errata, go to https://www.packtpub.com/books/content/support and enter the name of the book in the search field. The required information will appear under the **Errata** section.

Piracy

Piracy of copyrighted material on the Internet is an ongoing problem across all media. At Packt, we take the protection of our copyright and licenses very seriously. If you come across any illegal copies of our works in any form on the Internet, please provide us with the location address or website name immediately so that we can pursue a remedy.

Please contact us at copyright@packtpub.com with a link to the suspected pirated material.

We appreciate your help in protecting our authors and our ability to bring you valuable content.

Questions

If you have a problem with any aspect of this book, you can contact us at questions@packtpub.com, and we will do our best to address the problem.

1
Thinking Reactively

It is assumed you are fairly comfortable with Java and know how to use classes, interfaces, methods, properties, variables, static/nonstatic scopes, and collections. If you have not done concurrency or multithreading, that is okay. RxJava makes these advanced topics much more accessible.

Have your favorite Java development environment ready, whether it is Intellij IDEA, Eclipse, NetBeans, or any other environment of your choosing. I will be using Intellij IDEA, although it should not matter or impact the examples in this book. I recommend that you have a build automation system as well such as Gradle or Maven, which we will walk through shortly.

Before we dive deep into RxJava, we will cover some core topics first:

- A brief history of Reactive Extensions and RxJava
- Thinking reactively
- Leveraging RxJava
- Setting up your first RxJava project
- Building your first reactive applications
- Differences between RxJava 1.0 and RxJava 2.0

A brief history of ReactiveX and RxJava

As developers, we tend to train ourselves to think in counter-intuitive ways. Modeling our world with code has never been short of challenges. It was not long ago that object-oriented programming was seen as the silver bullet to solve this problem. Making blueprints of what we interact with in real life was a revolutionary idea, and this core concept of classes and objects still impacts how we code today. However, business and user demands continued to grow in complexity. As 2010 approached, it became clear that object-oriented programming only solved part of the problem.

Classes and objects do a great job of representing an entity with properties and methods, but they become messy when they need to interact with each other in increasingly complex (and often unplanned) ways. Decoupling patterns and paradigms emerged, but this yielded an unwanted side effect of growing amounts of boilerplate code. In response to these problems, functional programming began to make a comeback, not to replace object-oriented programming, but rather to complement it and fill this void. Reactive programming, a functional event-driven programming approach, began to receive special attention.

A couple of reactive frameworks emerged ultimately, including **Akka** and **Sodium**. But at Microsoft, a computer scientist named Erik Meijer created a reactive programming framework for .NET called **Reactive Extensions**. In a matter of years, Reactive Extensions (also called **ReactiveX** or **Rx***) was ported to several languages and platforms, including JavaScript, Python, C++, Swift, and Java, of course. ReactiveX quickly emerged as a cross-language standard to bring reactive programming into the industry.

RxJava, the ReactiveX port for Java, was created in large part by Ben Christensen from Netflix and David Karnok. RxJava 1.0 was released in November 2014, followed by RxJava 2.0 in November 2016. RxJava is the backbone to other ReactiveX JVM ports, such as **RxScala**, **RxKotlin**, and **RxGroovy**. It has become a core technology for Android development and has also found its way into Java backend development. Many RxJavaadapter libraries, such as **RxAndroid** (`https://github.com/ReactiveX/RxAndroid`), **RxJava-JDBC** (`https://github.com/davidmoten/rxjava-jdbc`), **RxNetty** (`https://github.com/ReactiveX/RxNetty`), and **RxJavaFX** (`https://github.com/ReactiveX/RxJavaFX`) adapted several Java frameworks to become reactive and work with RxJava out of the box. This all shows that RxJava is more than a library. It is part of a greater ReactiveX ecosystem that represents an entire approach to programming. The fundamental idea of ReactiveX is that *events are data and data are events*. This is a powerful concept that we will explore later in this chapter, but first, let's step back and look at the world through the reactive lens.

Thinking reactively

Suspend everything you know about Java (and programming in general) for a moment, and let's make some observations about our world. These may sound like obvious statements, but as developers, we can easily overlook them. Bring your attention to the fact that everything is in motion. Traffic, weather, people, conversations, financial transactions, and so on are all moving. Technically, even something stationary as a rock is in motion due to the earth's rotation and orbit. When you consider the possibility that everything can be modeled as in motion, you may find it a bit overwhelming as a developer.

Another observation to note is that these different events are happening concurrently. Multiple activities are happening at the same time. Sometimes, they act independently, but other times, they can converge at some point to interact. For instance, a car can drive with no impact on a person jogging. They are two separate streams of events. However, they may converge at some point and the car will stop when it encounters the jogger.

If this is how our world works, why do we not model our code this way?. Why do we not model code as multiple concurrent streams of events or data happening at the same time? It is not uncommon for developers to spend more time managing the states of objects and doing it in an imperative and sequential manner. You may structure your code to execute **Process 1**, **Process 2**, and then **Process 3**, which depends on Process 1 and Process 2. Why not kick-off Process 1 and Process 2 simultaneously, and then the completion of these two events immediately kicks-off Process 3? Of course, you can use callbacks and Java concurrency tools, but RxJava makes this much easier and safer to express.

Let's make one last observation. A book or music CD is static. A book is an unchanging sequence of words and a CD is a collection of tracks. There is nothing dynamic about them. However, when we read a book, we are reading each word one at a time. Those words are effectively put in motion as a stream being consumed by our eyes. It is no different with a music CD track, where each track is put in motion as sound waves and your ears are consuming each track. Static items can, in fact, be put in motion too. This is an abstract but powerful idea because we made each of these static items a series of events. When we level the playing field between data and events by treating them both the same, we unleash the power of functional programming and unlock abilities you previously might have thought impractical.

The fundamental idea behind reactive programming is that *events are data and data are events*. This may seem abstract, but it really does not take long to grasp when you consider our real-world examples. The runner and car both have properties and states, but they are also in motion. The book and CD are put in motion when they are consumed. Merging the event and data to become one allows the code to feel organic and representative of the world we are modeling.

Why should I learn RxJava?

ReactiveX and RxJava paints a broad stroke against many problems programmers face daily, allowing you to express business logic and spend less time engineering code. Have you ever struggled with concurrency, event handling, obsolete data states, and exception recovery? What about making your code more maintainable, reusable, and evolvable so it can keep up with your business? It might be presumptuous to call reactive programming a **silver bullet** to these problems, but it certainly is a progressive leap in addressing them.

There is also growing user demand to make applications real time and responsive. Reactive programming allows you to quickly analyse and work with live data sources such as Twitter feeds or stock prices. It can also cancel and redirect work, scale with concurrency, and cope with rapidly emitting data. Composing events and data as streams that can be mixed, merged, filtered, split, and transformed opens up radically effective ways to compose and evolve code.

In summary, reactive programming makes many hard tasks easy, enabling you to add value in ways you might have thought impractical earlier. If you have a process written reactively and you discover that you need to run part of it on a different thread, you can implement this change in a matter of seconds. If you find network connectivity issues crashing your application intermittently, you can gracefully use reactive recovery strategies that wait and try again. If you need to inject an operation in the middle of your process, it is as simple as inserting a new operator. Reactive programming is broken up into modular chain links that can be added or removed, which can help overcome all the aforementioned problems quickly. In essence, RxJava allows applications to be tactical and evolvable while maintaining stability in production.

What we will learn in this book?

As stated earlier, RxJava is the ReactiveX port for Java. In this book, we will focus primarily on RxJava 2.0, but I will call out significant differences in RxJava 1.0. We will place priority on learning to think reactively and leverage the practical features of RxJava. Starting with a high-level understanding, we will gradually move deeper into how RxJava works. Along the way, we will learn about reactive patterns and tricks to solve common problems programmers encounter.

In Chapter 2, *The Observable and Subscribers*, Chapter 3, *Basic Operators*, and Chapter 4, *Combining Observables*, we will cover core Rx concepts with Observable, Observer, and Operator. These are the three core entities that make up RxJava applications. You will start writing reactive programs immediately and have a solid knowledge foundation to build on for the rest of the book.

Chapter 5, *Multicasting, Replaying, and Caching*, and Chapter 6, *Concurrency and Parallelization*, will explore more of the nuances of RxJava and how to effectively leverage concurrency.

In Chapter 7, *Switching, Throttling, Windowing, and Buffering* and Chapter 8, *Flowables and Backpressure,* we will learn about the different ways to cope with reactive streams that produce data/events faster than they can be consumed.

Finally, Chapter 9, *Transformers and Custom Operators*, Chapter 10, *Testing and Debugging*, Chapter 11, *RxJava on Android*, and Chapter 12, *Using RxJava with Kotlin New*, will touch on several miscellaneous (but essential) topics including custom operators as well as how to use RxJava with testing frameworks, Android, and the Kotlin language.

Setting up

There are two co-existing versions of RxJava currently: 1.0 and 2.0. We will go through some of the major differences later and discuss which version you should use.

RxJava 2.0 is a fairly lightweight library and comes just above 2 **Megabytes** (**MBs**) in size. This makes it practical for Android and other projects that require a low dependency overhead. RxJava 2.0 has only one dependency, called **Reactive Streams** (http://www.reactive-streams.org/), which is a core library (made by the creators of RxJava) that sets a standard for asynchronous stream implementations, one of which is RxJava 2.0.

It may be used in other libraries beyond RxJava and is a critical effort in the standardization of reactive programming on the Java platform. Note that RxJava 1.0 does not have any dependencies, including Reactive Streams, which was realized after 1.0.

If you are starting a project from scratch, try to use RxJava 2.0. This is the version we will cover in this book, but I will call out significant differences in 1.0. While RxJava 1.0 will be supported for a good while due to countless projects using it, innovation will likely only continue onward in RxJava 2.0. RxJava 1.0 will only get maintenance and bug fixes.

Both RxJava 1.0 and 2.0 run on Java 1.6+. In this book, we will use Java 8, and it is recommended that you use a minimum of Java 8 so you can use lambdas out of the box. For Android, there are ways to leverage lambdas in earlier Java versions that will be addressed later. But weighing the fact that Android Nougat uses Java 8 and Java 8 has been out since 2014, hopefully, you will not have to do any workarounds to leverage lambdas.

Navigating the Central Repository

To bring in RxJava as a dependency, you have a few options. The best place to start is to go to **The Central Repository** (search `http://search.maven.org/`) and search for `rxjav`. You should see RxJava 2.0 and RxJava 1.0 as separate repositories at the top of the search results, as shown in the following screenshot:

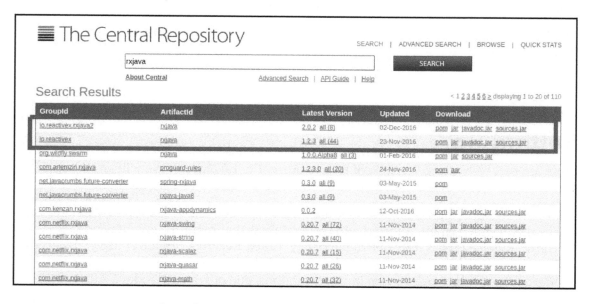

Searching for RxJava in the Central Repository (RxJava 2.0 and 1.0 are highlighted)

At the time of writing, RxJava 2.0.2 is the latest version for RxJava 2.0 and RxJava 1.2.3 is the latest for RxJava 1.0. You can download the latest JAR file for either by clicking the JAR links in the far right under the **Download** column. You can then configure your project to use the JAR file.

However, you might want to consider using Gradle or Maven to automatically import these libraries into your project. This way, you can easily share and store your code project (through GIT or other version control systems) without having to download and configure RxJava manually into it each time. To view the latest configurations for Maven, Gradle, and several other build automation systems, click on the version number for either of the repositories, as highlighted in the following screenshot:

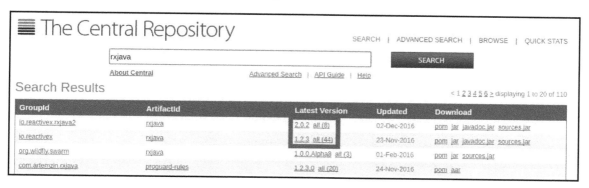

Click the version number under the *Latest Version* column to view the configurations for Maven, Gradle, and other major build automation systems

Using Gradle

There are several automated build systems available, but the two most mainstream options are Gradle and Maven. Gradle is somewhat a successor to Maven and is especially the go-to build automation solution for Android development. If you are not familiar with Gradle and would like to learn how to use it, check out the Gradle **Getting Started** guide (`https ://gradle.org/getting-started-gradle-java/`).

There are also several decent books that cover Gradle in varying degrees of depth, which you can find at `https://gradle.org/books/`. The following screenshot displays the **The Central Repository** page showing how to set up RxJava 2.0.2 for Gradle:

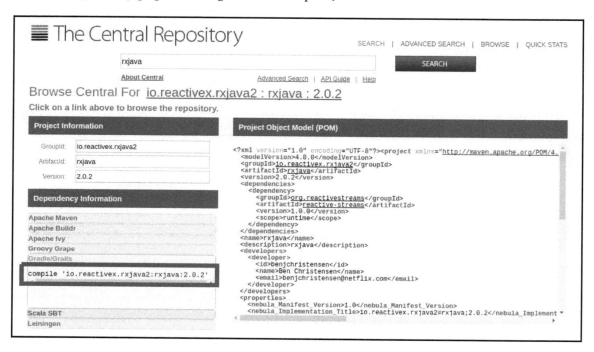

You can find the latest Gradle configuration code and copy it into your Gradle script

In your `build.gradle` script, ensure that you have declared `mavenCentral()` as one of your repositories. Type in or paste that dependency line `compile 'io.reactivex.rxjava2:rxjava:x.y.z'`, where `x.y.z` is the version number you want to use, as shown in the following code snippet:

```
apply plugin: 'java'

sourceCompatibility = 1.8

repositories {
        mavenCentral()
}

dependencies {
        compile 'io.reactivex.rxjava2:rxjava:x.y.z'
}
```

Build your Gradle project and you should be good to go! You will then have RxJava and its types available for use in your project.

Using Maven

You also have the option to use Maven, and you can view the appropriate configuration in **The Central Repository** by selecting the **Apache Maven** configuration information, as shown in the following screenshot:

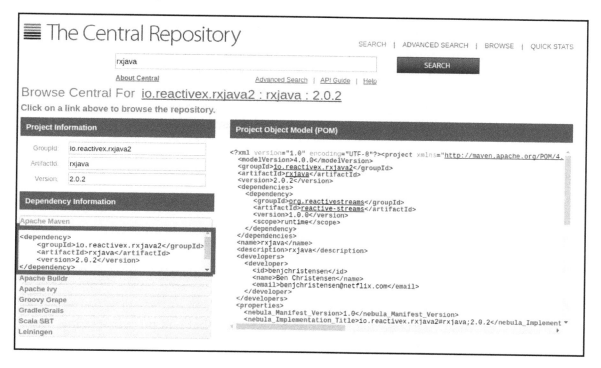

Select and then copy the *Apache Maven* configuration

You can then copy and paste the `<dependency>` block containing the RxJava configuration and paste it inside a `<dependencies>` block in your `pom.xml` file. Rebuild your project, and you should now have RxJava set up as a dependency. The `x.y.z` version number corresponds to the desired RxJava version that you want to use:

```
<project>
  <modelVersion>4.0.0</modelVersion>
    <groupId>org.nield</groupId>
    <artifactId>mavenrxtest</artifactId>
```

```
    <version>1.0</version>
  <dependencies>
    <dependency>
    <groupId>io.reactivex.rxjava2</groupId>
    <artifactId>rxjava</artifactId>
    <version>x.y.z</version>
    </dependency>
  </dependencies>
</project>
```

A quick exposure to RxJava

Before we dive deep into the reactive world of RxJava, here is a quick exposure to get your feet wet first. In ReactiveX, the core type you will work with is the Observable. We will be learning more about the Observable throughout the rest of this book. But essentially, an Observable pushes things. A given Observable<T>pushes things of type T through a series of operators until it arrives at an Observer that consumes the items.

For instance, create a new Launcher.java file in your project and put in the following code:

```
import io.reactivex.Observable;
public class Launcher {
    public static void main(String[] args) {
      Observable<String> myStrings =
        Observable.just("Alpha", "Beta", "Gamma", "Delta",
"Epsilon");
      }
}
```

In our main() method, we have an Observable<String> that will push five string objects. An Observable can push data or events from virtually any source, whether it is a database query or live Twitter feeds. In this case, we are quickly creating an Observable using Observable.just(), which will emit a fixed set of items.

 In RxJava 2.0, most types you will use are contained in the io.reactivex package. In RxJava 1.0, the types are contained in the rx package.

However, running this `main()` method is not going to do anything other than declare `Observable<String>`. To make this `Observable` actually push these five strings (which are called emissions), we need an `Observer` to subscribe to it and receive the items. We can quickly create and connect an `Observer` by passing a lambda expression that specifies what to do with each string it receives:

```java
import io.reactivex.Observable;

public class Launcher {
    public static void main(String[] args)  {
        Observable<String> myStrings =
            Observable.just("Alpha", "Beta", "Gamma", "Delta",
"Epsilon");

        myStrings.subscribe(s -> System.out.println(s));
    }
}
```

When we run this code, we should get the following output:

```
Alpha
Beta
Gamma
Delta
Epsilon
```

What happened here is that our `Observable<String>` pushed each string object one at a time to our `Observer`, which we shorthanded using the lambda expression `s -> System.out.println(s)`. We pass each string through the parameter `s` (which I arbitrarily named) and instructed it to print each one. Lambdas are essentially mini functions that allow us to quickly pass instructions on what action to take with each incoming item. Everything to the left of the arrow `->` are arguments (which in this case is a string we named `s`), and everything to the right is the action (which is `System.out.println(s)`).

If you are unfamiliar with lambda expressions, turn to *Appendix,* to learn more about how they work. If you want to invest extra time in understanding lambda expressions, I highly recommend that you read at least the first few chapters of *Java 8 Lambdas* (O'Reilly) (`http://shop.oreilly.com/product/0636920030713.do`) by Richard Warburton. Lambda expressions are a critical topic in modern programming and have become especially relevant to Java developers since their adoption in Java 8. We will be using lambdas constantly in this book, so definitely take some time getting comfortable with them.

We can also use several operators between `Observable` and `Observer` to transform each pushed item or manipulate them in some way. Each operator returns a new `Observable` derived-off the previous one but reflects that transformation. For example, we can use `map()` to turn each string emission into its `length()`, and each length integer will then be pushed to `Observer` , as shown in the following code snippet:

```
import io.reactivex.Observable;

public class Launcher {
 public static void main(String[] args) {

   Observable<String> myStrings =
     Observable.just("Alpha", "Beta", "Gamma", "Delta",
     "Epsilon");

   myStrings.map(s -> s.length()).subscribe(s ->
   System.out.println(s));
 }
}
```

When we run this code, we should get the following output:

```
5
4
5
5
7
```

If you have used Java 8 Streams or Kotlin sequences, you might be wondering how `Observable` is any different. The key difference is that `Observable` pushes the items while Streams and sequences pull the items. This may seem subtle, but the impact of a push-based iteration is far more powerful than a pull-based one. As we saw earlier, you can push not only data, but also events. For instance, `Observable.interval()` will push a consecutive `Long` at each specified time interval, as shown in the following code snippet. This `Long` emission is not only data, but also an event! Let's take a look:

```
import io.reactivex.Observable;
import java.util.concurrent.TimeUnit;

public class Launcher {
     public static void main(String[] args) {
       Observable<Long> secondIntervals =
         Observable.interval(1, TimeUnit.SECONDS);

       secondIntervals.subscribe(s -> System.out.println(s));
       /* Hold main thread for 5 seconds
```

```
            so Observable above has chance to fire */
            sleep(5000);
        }

        public static void sleep(long millis) {
            try {
                Thread.sleep(millis);
            } catch (InterruptedException e) {
                e.printStackTrace();
            }
        }
    }
```

When we run this code, we should get the following output:

```
0
1
2
3
4
```

When you run the preceding code, you will see that a consecutive emission fires every second. This application will run for about five seconds before it quits, and you will likely see emissions 0 to 4 fired, each separated by a just a second's gap. This simple idea that data is a series of events over time will unlock new possibilities in how we tackle programming.

On a side note, we will get more into concurrency later, but we had to create a sleep() method because this Observable fires emissions on a computation thread when subscribed to. The main thread used to launch our application is not going to wait on this Observable since it fires on a computation thread, not the main thread. Therefore, we use sleep() to pause the main thread for 5000 milliseconds and then allow it to reach the end of the main() method (which will cause the application to terminate). This gives Observable.interval() a chance to fire for a five second window before the application quits.

Throughout this book, we will uncover many mysteries about `Observable` and the powerful abstractions it takes care of for us. If you've conceptually understood what is going on here so far, congrats! You are already becoming familiar with how reactive code works. To emphasize again, emissions are pushed one at a time all the way to `Observer`. Emissions represent both data and an event, which can be emitted over time. Of course, beyond `map()`, there are hundreds of operators in RxJava, and we will learn about the key ones in this book. Learning which operators to use for a situation and how to combine them is the key to mastering RxJava. In the next chapter, we will cover `Observable` and `Observer` much more comprehensively. We will also demystify events and data being represented in `Observable` a bit more.

RxJava 1.0 versus RxJava 2.0 - which one do I use?

As stated earlier, you are encouraged to use RxJava 2.0 if you can. It will continue to grow and receive new features, while RxJava 1.0 will be maintained for bug fixes. However, there are other considerations that may lead you to use RxJava 1.0.

If you inherit a project that is already using RxJava 1.0, you will likely continue using that until it becomes feasible to refactor to 2.0. You can also check out David Akarnokd's *RxJava2Interop* project (`https://github.com/akarnokd/RxJava2Interop`), which converts Rx types from RxJava 1.0 to RxJava 2.0 and vice versa. After you finish this book, you may consider using this library to leverage RxJava 2.0 even if you have the RxJava 1.0 legacy code.

In RxJava, there are several libraries to make several Java APIs reactive and plug into RxJava seamlessly. Just to name a few, these libraries include RxJava-JDBC, RxAndroid, RxJava-Extras, RxNetty, and RxJavaFX. At the time of writing this, only RxAndroid and RxJavaFX have been fully ported to RxJava 2.0 (although many other libraries are following). By the time you are reading this, all major RxJava extension libraries will hopefully be ported to RxJava 2.0.

You will also want to prefer RxJava 2.0 because it was built on much of the hindsight and wisdom gained from RxJava 1.0. It has better performance, simpler APIs, a cleaner approach to backpressure, and a bit more safety when hacking together your own operators.

When to use RxJava

A common question ReactiveX newcomers ask is what circumstances warrant a reactive approach? Do we always want to use RxJava? As someone who has been living and breathing reactive programming for a while, I have learned that there are two answers to this question:

The first answer is when you first start out: *yes!* You always want to take a reactive approach. The only way to truly become a master of reactive programming is to build reactive applications from the ground up. Think of everything as `Observable` and always model your program in terms of data and event flows. When you do this, you will leverage everything reactive programming has to offer and see the quality of your applications go up significantly.

The second answer is that when you become experienced in RxJava, you will find cases where RxJava may not be appropriate. There will occasionally be times where a reactive approach may not be optimal, but usually, this exception applies to only part of your code. Your entire project itself should be reactive. There may be parts that are not reactive and for good reason. These exceptions only stand out to a trained Rx veteran who sees that returning `List<String>` is perhaps better than returning `Observable<String>`.

Rx greenhorns should not worry about when something should be reactive versus something not reactive. Over time, they will start to see cases where the benefits of Rx are marginalized, and this is something that only comes with experience.

So for now, no compromises. Go reactive all the way!

Summary

In this chapter, we learned how to look at the world in a reactive way. As a developer, you may have to retrain yourself from a traditional imperative mindset and develop a reactive one. Especially if you have done imperative, object-oriented programming for a long time, this can be challenging. But the return on investment will be significant as your applications will become more maintainable, scalable, and evolvable. You will also have faster turn around and more legible code.

We also covered how to configure a RxJava project using Gradle or Maven and what decisions should drive whether you should choose RxJava 2.0 versus RxJava 1.0. We also got a brief introduction to reactive code and how `Observable` works through push-based iteration.

By the time you finish this book, you will hopefully find reactive programming intuitive and easy to reason with. I hope you find that RxJava not only makes you more productive, but also helps you take on tasks you hesitated to do earlier. So let's get started!

2
Observables and Subscribers

We already got a glimpse into the `Observable` and how it works in `Chapter 1`, *Thinking Reactively*. You probably have many questions on how exactly it operates and what practical applications it holds. This chapter will provide a foundation for understanding how an `Observable` works as well as the critical relationship it has with the `Observer`. We will also cover several ways to create an `Observable` as well make it useful by covering a few operators. To make the rest of the book flow smoothly, we will also cover all critical nuances head-on to build a solid foundation and not leave you with surprises later.

Here is what we will cover in this chapter:

- The `Observable`
- The `Observer`
- Other `Observable` factories
- `Single`, `Completable`, and `Maybe`
- `Disposable`

The Observable

As introduced in `Chapter 1`, *Thinking Reactively*, the `Observable` is a push-based, composable iterator. For a given `Observable<T>`, it pushes items (called emissions) of type `T` through a series of operators until it finally arrives at a final Observer, which consumes the items. We will cover several ways to create an `Observable`, but first, let's dive into how an `Observable` works through its `onNext()`, `onCompleted()`, and `onError()` calls.

How Observables work

Before we do anything else, we need to study how an Observable sequentially passes items down a chain to an Observer. At the highest level, an Observable works by passing three types of events:

- onNext(): This passes each item one at a time from the source Observable all the way down to the Observer.
- onComplete(): This communicates a completion event all the way down to the Observer, indicating that no more onNext() calls will occur.
- onError(): This communicates an error up the chain to the Observer, where the Observer typically defines how to handle it. Unless a retry() operator is used to intercept the error, the Observable chain typically terminates, and no more emissions will occur.

These three events are abstract methods in the Observer type, and we will cover some of the implementation later. For now, we will focus pragmatically on how they work in everyday usage.

 In RxJava 1.0, the onComplete() event is actually called onCompleted().

Using Observable.create()

Let's start with creating a source Observable using Observable.create(). Relatively speaking, a source Observable is an Observable where emissions originate from and is the starting point of our Observable chain.

The Observable.create() factory allows us to create an Observable by providing a lambda receiving an Observable emitter. We can call the Observable emitter's onNext() method to pass emissions (one a time) up the chain as well as onComplete() to signal completion and communicate that there will be no more items. These onNext() calls will pass these items up the chain towards the Observer, where it will print each item, as shown in the following code snippet:

```
import io.reactivex.Observable;

public class Launcher {
```

```
public static void main(String[] args) {

    Observable<String> source = Observable.create(emitter -> {
        emitter.onNext("Alpha");
        emitter.onNext("Beta");
        emitter.onNext("Gamma");
        emitter.onNext("Delta");
        emitter.onNext("Epsilon");
        emitter.onComplete();
    });

    source.subscribe(s -> System.out.println("RECEIVED: " + s));
  }
}
```

The output is as follows:

```
RECEIVED: Alpha
RECEIVED: Beta
RECEIVED: Gamma
RECEIVED: Delta
RECEIVED: Epsilon
```

In RxJava 1.0, ensure that you use `Observable.fromEmitter()` instead of `Observable.create()`. The latter is something entirely different in RxJava 1.0 and is only for advanced RxJava users.

The `onNext()` method is a way to hand each item, starting with `Alpha`, to the next step in the chain. In this example, the next step is the Observer, which prints the item using the `s -> System.out.println("RECEIVED: " + s)` lambda. This lambda is invoked in the `onNext()` call of `Observer`, and we will look at `Observer` more closely in a moment.

Note that the `Observable` contract (`http://reactivex.io/documentation/contract.html`) dictates that emissions must be passed sequentially and one at a time. Emissions cannot be passed by an `Observable` concurrently or in parallel. This may seem like a limitation, but it does in fact simplify programs and make Rx easier to reason with. We will learn some powerful tricks to effectively leverage concurrency and parallelization in `Chapter 6`, *Concurrency and Parallelization* , without breaking the `Observable` contract.

The onComplete() method is used to communicate up the chain to the Observer that no more items are coming. Observables can indeed be infinite, and if this is the case, the onComplete() event will never be called. Technically, a source could stop emitting onNext() calls and never call onComplete(). This would likely be bad design, though, if the source no longer plans to send emissions.

Although this particular example is unlikely to throw an error, we can catch errors that may occur within our Observable.create() block and emit them through onError(). This way, the error can be pushed up the chain and handled by the Observer. This particular Observer that we have set up does not handle exceptions, but you can do that, as shown here:

```java
import io.reactivex.Observable;

public class Launcher {

public static void main(String[] args) {

  Observable<String> source = Observable.create(emitter -> {
    try {
      emitter.onNext("Alpha");
      emitter.onNext("Beta");
      emitter.onNext("Gamma");
      emitter.onNext("Delta");
      emitter.onNext("Epsilon");
      emitter.onComplete();
    } catch (Throwable e) {
      emitter.onError(e);
    }
  });

    source.subscribe(s -> System.out.println("RECEIVED: " + s),
Throwable::printStackTrace);
    }
  }
```

Note that onNext(), onComplete(), and onError() do not necessarily push directly to the final Observer. They can also push to an operator serving as the next step in the chain. In the following code, we derive new Observables with the map() and filter() operators, which will act between the source Observable and final Observer printing the items:

```java
import io.reactivex.Observable;

public class Launcher {
public static void main(String[] args) {
  Observable<String> source = Observable.create(emitter -> {
```

```
      try {
        emitter.onNext("Alpha");
        emitter.onNext("Beta");
        emitter.onNext("Gamma");
        emitter.onNext("Delta");
        emitter.onNext("Epsilon");
        emitter.onComplete();
      } catch (Throwable e) {
        emitter.onError(e);
      }
    });
    Observable<Integer> lengths = source.map(String::length);

    Observable<Integer> filtered = lengths.filter(i -> i >= 5);

    filtered.subscribe(s -> System.out.println("RECEIVED: " +
    s));
  }
}
```

This is the output after running the code:

```
RECEIVED: 5
RECEIVED: 5
RECEIVED: 5
RECEIVED: 7
```

With the `map()` and `filter()` operators between the source `Observable` and `Observer`, `onNext()` will hand each item to the `map()` operator. Internally, it will act as an intermediary Observer and convert each string to its `length()`. This, in turn, will call `onNext()` on `filter()` to pass that integer, and the lambda condition `i -> i >= 5` will suppress emissions that fail to be at least five characters in length. Finally, the `filter()` operator will call `onNext()` to hand each item to the final `Observer` where they will be printed.

It is critical to note that the `map()` operator will yield a new `Observable<Integer>` derived off the original `Observable<String>`. The `filter()` will also return an `Observable<Integer>` but ignore emissions that fail to meet the criteria. Since operators such as `map()` and `filter()` yield new Observables (which internally use `Observer` implementations to receive emissions), we can chain all our returned Observables with the next operator rather than unnecessarily saving each one to an intermediary variable:

```
import io.reactivex.Observable;

public class Launcher {
```

```
public static void main(String[] args) {
    Observable<String> source = Observable.create(emitter -> {
        try {
            emitter.onNext("Alpha");
            emitter.onNext("Beta");
            emitter.onNext("Gamma");
            emitter.onNext("Delta");
            emitter.onNext("Epsilon");
            emitter.onComplete();
        } catch (Throwable e) {
            emitter.onError(e);
        }
    });
    source.map(String::length)
    .filter(i -> i >= 5)
        .subscribe(s -> System.out.println("RECEIVED: " + s));
    }
}
```

The output is as follows:

```
RECEIVED: 5
RECEIVED: 5
RECEIVED: 5
RECEIVED: 7
```

Chaining operators in this way is common (and encouraged) in reactive programming. It has a nice quality of being readable from left to right and top to bottom much like a book, and this helps in maintainability and legibility.

 In RxJava 2.0, Observables no longer support emitting null values. You will immediately get a non-null exception if you create an `Observable` that attempts to emit a null value. If you need to emit a null, consider wrapping it in a Java 8 or Google Guava Optional.

Using Observable.just()

Before we look at the `subscribe()` method a bit more, note that you likely will not need to use `Observable.create()` often. It can be helpful in hooking into certain sources that are not reactive, and we will see this in a couple of places later in this chapter. But typically, we use streamlined factories to create Observables for common sources.

In our previous example with `Observable.create()`, we could have used `Observable.just()` to accomplish this. We can pass it up to 10 items that we want to emit. It will invoke the `onNext()` call for each one and then invoke `onComplete()` when they all have been pushed:

```java
import io.reactivex.Observable;

public class Launcher {
  public static void main(String[] args) {
    Observable<String> source =
      Observable.just("Alpha", "Beta", "Gamma", "Delta",
      "Epsilon");
source.map(String::length).filter(i -> i >= 5)
      .subscribe(s -> System.out.println("RECEIVED: " + s));
  }
}
```

We can also use `Observable.fromIterable()` to emit the items from any Iterable type, such as a `List`. It also will call `onNext()` for each element and then call `onComplete()` after the iteration is complete. You will likely use this factory frequently since Iterables in Java are common and can easily be made reactive:

```java
import io.reactivex.Observable;
import java.util.Arrays;
import java.util.List;

public class Launcher {
  public static void main(String[] args) {

    List<String> items =
      Arrays.asList("Alpha", "Beta", "Gamma", "Delta", "Epsilon");

    Observable<String> source = Observable.fromIterable(items);
    source.map(String::length).filter(i -> i >= 5)
      .subscribe(s -> System.out.println("RECEIVED: " + s));
  }
}
```

We will explore other factories to create Observables later in this chapter, but for now, let's put that on hold and learn more about Observers.

The Observer interface

The onNext(), onComplete(), and onError() methods actually define the Observer type, an abstract interface implemented throughout RxJava to communicate these events. This is the Observer definition in RxJava shown in the code snippet. Do not bother yourself about onSubscribe() for now, as we will cover it at the end of this chapter. Just bring your attention to the other three methods:

```
package io.reactivex;

import io.reactivex.disposables.Disposable;

public interface Observer<T> {
    void onSubscribe(Disposable d);
    void onNext(T value);
    void onError(Throwable e);
    void onComplete();
}
```

Observers and source Observables are somewhat relative. In one context, a source Observable is where your Observable chain starts and where emissions originate. In our previous examples, you could say that the Observable returned from our Observable.create() method or Observable.just() is the source Observable. But to the filter() operator, the Observable returned from the map() operator is the source. It has no idea where the emissions are originating from, and it just knows that it is receiving emissions from the operator immediately upstream from it, which come from map().

Conversely, each Observable returned by an operator is internally an Observer that receives, transforms, and relays emissions to the next Observer downstream. It does not know whether the next Observer is another operator or the final Observer at the end of the chain. When we talk about the Observer, we are often talking about the final Observer at the end of the Observable chain that consumes the emissions. But each operator, such as map() and filter(), also implements Observer internally.

We will learn in detail about how operators are built in Chapter 9, *Transformers and Custom Operators*. For now, we will focus on using an Observer for the subscribe() method.

 In RxJava 1.0, the Subscriber essentially became a Observer in RxJava 2.0. There is an Observer type in RxJava 1.0 that defines the three event methods, but the Subscriber is what you passed to the subscribe() method, and it is implemented Observer. In RxJava 2.0, a Subscriber only exists when talking about Flowables, which we will discuss in Chapter 8, *Flowables and Backpressure*.

Implementing and subscribing to an Observer

When you call the `subscribe()` method on an `Observable`, an `Observer` is used to consume these three events by implementing its methods. Instead of specifying lambda arguments like we were doing earlier, we can implement an `Observer` and pass an instance of it to the `subscribe()` method. Do not bother yourself about `onSubscribe()` at the moment. Just leave its implementation empty until we discuss it at the end of this chapter:

```java
import io.reactivex.Observable;
import io.reactivex.Observer;
import io.reactivex.disposables.Disposable;

public class Launcher {

  public static void main(String[] args) {

    Observable<String> source =
      Observable.just("Alpha", "Beta", "Gamma", "Delta",
      "Epsilon");

    Observer<Integer> myObserver = new Observer<Integer>() {
      @Override
      public void onSubscribe(Disposable d) {
        //do nothing with Disposable, disregard for now
      }

      @Override
      public void onNext(Integer value) {
        System.out.println("RECEIVED: " + value);
      }

      @Override
      public void onError(Throwable e) {
        e.printStackTrace();
      }

      @Override
      public void onComplete() {
        System.out.println("Done!");
      }
    };

    source.map(String::length).filter(i -> i >= 5)
      .subscribe(myObserver);
  }
}
```

The output is as follows:

```
RECEIVED: 5
RECEIVED: 5
RECEIVED: 5
RECEIVED: 7
Done!
```

We quickly create an `Observer<Integer>` that serves as our `Observer`, and it will receive integer length emissions. Our `Observer` receives emissions at the end of an `Observable` chain and serves as the endpoint where the emissions are consumed. By consumed, this means they reach the end of the process where they are written to a database, text file, a server response, displayed in a UI, or (in this case) just printed to the console.

To further explain this example in detail, we start with string emissions at our source. We declare our `Observer` in advance and pass it to the `subscribe()` method at the end of our `Observable` chain. Note that each string is transformed to its length. The `onNext()` method receives each integer length emission and prints it using `System.out.println("RECEIVED: " + value)`. We will not get any errors running this simple process, but if one did occur anywhere in our `Observable` chain, it will be pushed to our `onError()` implementation on `Observer`, where the stack trace of `Throwable` will be printed. Finally, when the source has no more emissions (after pushing "Epsilon"), it will call `onComplete()` up the chain all the way to the Observer, where its `onComplete()` method will be called and print `Done!` to the console.

Shorthand Observers with lambdas

Implementing an `Observer` is a bit verbose and cumbersome. Thankfully, the `subscribe()` method is overloaded to accept lambda arguments for our three events. This is likely what we will want to use for most cases, and we can specify three lambda parameters separated by commas: the `onNext` lambda, the `onError` lambda, and the `onComplete` lambda. For our previous example, we can consolidate our three method implementations using these three lambdas:

```
Consumer<Integer> onNext = i ->  System.out.println("RECEIVED: "
+ i);

Action onComplete = () -> System.out.println("Done!");

Consumer<Throwable> onError = Throwable::printStackTrace;
```

We can pass these three lambdas as arguments to the `subscribe()` method, and it will use them to implement an `Observer` for us. This is much more concise and requires far less boilerplate code:

```
import io.reactivex.Observable;

public class Launcher {

  public static void main(String[] args) {

    Observable<String> source =
      Observable.just("Alpha", "Beta", "Gamma", "Delta",
      "Epsilon");

    source.map(String::length).filter(i -> i >= 5)
      .subscribe(i -> System.out.println("RECEIVED: " + i),
      Throwable::printStackTrace,
      () ->  System.out.println("Done!"));
    }
  }
```

The output is as follows:

```
RECEIVED:  5
RECEIVED:  5
RECEIVED:  5
RECEIVED:  7
Done!
```

Note that there are other overloads for `subscribe()`. You can omit `onComplete()` and only implement `onNext()` and `onError()`. This will no longer perform any action for `onComplete()`, but there will likely be cases where you do not need one:

```
import io.reactivex.Observable;

public class Launcher {

  public static void main(String[] args) {

    Observable<String> source =
      Observable.just("Alpha", "Beta", "Gamma", "Delta",
      "Epsilon");

    source.map(String::length).filter(i -> i >= 5)
      .subscribe(i -> System.out.println("RECEIVED: " + i),
```

```
                    Throwable::printStackTrace);
        }
    }
```

The output is as follows:

```
RECEIVED: 5
RECEIVED: 5
RECEIVED: 5
RECEIVED: 7
```

As you have seen in earlier examples, you can even omit onError and just specify onNext:

```
import io.reactivex.Observable;

public class Launcher {

    public static void main(String[] args) {

        Observable<String> source =
            Observable.just("Alpha", "Beta", "Gamma", "Delta",
            "Epsilon");

        source.map(String::length).filter(i -> i >= 5)
            .subscribe(i -> System.out.println("RECEIVED: " + i));
    }
}
```

However, not implementing onError() is something you want to avoid doing in production. Errors that happen anywhere in the Observable chain will be propagated to onError() to be handled and then terminate the Observable with no more emissions. If you do not specify an action for onError, the error will go unhandled.

You can use retry() operators to attempt recovery and resubscribe to an Observable if an error occurs. We will cover how to do that in the next chapter.

It is critical to note that most of the subscribe() overload variants (including the shorthand lambda ones we just covered) return a Disposable that we did not do anything with. disposables allow us to disconnect an Observable from an Observer so emissions are terminated early, which is critical for infinite or long-running Observables. We will cover disposables at the end of this chapter.

Cold versus hot Observables

There are subtle behaviors in a relationship between an Observable and an Observer depending on how the Observable is implemented. A major characteristic to be aware of is cold versus hot Observables, which defines how Observables behave when there are multiple Observers. First, we will cover cold Observables.

Cold Observables

Cold Observables are much like a music CD that can be replayed to each listener, so each person can hear all the tracks at any time. In the same manner, cold Observables will replay the emissions to each Observer, ensuring that all Observers get all the data. Most data-driven Observables are cold, and this includes the Observable.just() and Observable.fromIterable() factories.

In the following example, we have two Observers subscribed to one Observable. The Observable will first play all the emissions to the first Observer and then call onComplete(). Then, it will play all the emissions again to the second Observer and call onComplete(). They both receive the same datasets by getting two separate streams each, which is typical behavior for a cold Observable:

```
import io.reactivex.Observable;

public class Launcher {
public static void main(String[] args) {

  Observable<String> source =
    Observable.just("Alpha","Beta","Gamma","Delta","Epsilon");

  //first observer
  source.subscribe(s -> System.out.println("Observer 1 Received:
    " + s));

  //second observer
  source.subscribe(s -> System.out.println("Observer 2 Received:
    " + s));

  }
}
```

The output is as follows:

```
Observer 1 Received: Alpha
Observer 1 Received: Beta
Observer 1 Received: Gamma
Observer 1 Received: Delta
Observer 1 Received: Epsilon
Observer 2 Received: Alpha
Observer 2 Received: Beta
Observer 2 Received: Gamma
Observer 2 Received: Delta
Observer 2 Received: Epsilon
```

Even if the second `Observer` transforms its emissions with operators, it will still get its own stream of emissions. Using operators such as `map()` and `filter()` against a cold `Observable` will still maintain the cold nature of the yielded Observables:

```java
import io.reactivex.Observable;

public class Launcher {
    public static void main(String[] args) {

        Observable<String> source =
            Observable.just("Alpha","Beta","Gamma","Delta","Epsilon");

        //first observer
        source.subscribe(s -> System.out.println("Observer 1 Received:
            " + s));

        //second observer
        source.map(String::length).filter(i -> i >= 5)
            .subscribe(s -> System.out.println("Observer 2 Received: " +
        s));

    }
}
```

The output is as follows:

```
Observer 1 Received: Alpha
Observer 1 Received: Beta
Observer 1 Received: Gamma
Observer 1 Received: Delta
Observer 1 Received: Epsilon
Observer 2 Received: 5
Observer 2 Received: 5
Observer 2 Received: 5
Observer 2 Received: 7
```

As stated earlier, `Observable` sources that emit finite datasets are usually cold.

Here is a more real-world example: Dave Moten's RxJava-JDBC (`https://github.com/dav idmoten/rxjava-jdbc`) allows you to create cold Observables built off of SQL database queries. We will not digress into this library for too long, but if you want to query a SQLite database, for instance, include the **SQLite JDBC** driver and **RxJava-JDBC** libraries in your project. You can then query a database table reactively, as shown in the following code snippet:

```
import com.github.davidmoten.rx.jdbc.ConnectionProviderFromUrl;
import com.github.davidmoten.rx.jdbc.Database;
import rx.Observable;
import java.sql.Connection;

public class Launcher {
  public static void main(String[] args) {
    Connection conn =
  new ConnectionProviderFromUrl("jdbc:sqlite:/home/thomas
      /rexon_metals.db").get();
  Database db = Database.from(conn);

    Observable<String> customerNames =
      db.select("SELECT NAME FROM CUSTOMER")
      .getAs(String.class);

    customerNames.subscribe(s -> System.out.println(s));
  }
}
```

The output is as follows:

```
LITE Industrial
Rex Tooling Inc
Re-Barre Construction
Prairie Construction
Marsh Lane Metal Works
```

This SQL-driven `Observable` is cold. Many Observables emitting from finite data sources such as databases, text files, or JSON are cold. It is still important to note how the source `Observable` is architected. RxJava-JDBC will run the query each time for each `Observer`. This means that if the data changes in between two subscriptions, the second `Observer` will get different emissions than the first one. But the `Observable` is still cold since it is replaying the query even if the resulting data changes from the underlying tables.

Again, cold Observables will, in some shape or form, repeat the operation to generate these emissions to each `Observer`. Next, we will cover **hot Observables** that resemble events more than data.

Hot Observables

You just learned about the cold `Observable`, which works much like a music CD. A hot `Observable` is more like a radio station. It broadcasts the same emissions to all Observers at the same time. If an `Observer` subscribes to a hot `Observable`, receives some emissions, and then another `Observer` comes in afterwards, that second `Observer` will have missed those emissions. Just like a radio station, if you tune in too late, you will have missed that song.

Logically, hot Observables often represent events rather than finite datasets. The events can carry data with them, but there is a time-sensitive component where late observers can miss previously emitted data.

For instance, a JavaFX or Android UI event can be represented as a hot `Observable`. In JavaFX, you can create an `Observable<Boolean>` off a `selectedProperty()` operator of a `ToggleButton` using `Observable.create()`. You can then transform the Boolean emissions into strings indicating whether the `ToggleButton` is UP or DOWN and then use an `Observer` to display them in `Label`, as shown in the following code snippet:

```
import io.reactivex.Observable;
import javafx.application.Application;
import javafx.beans.value.ChangeListener;
import javafx.beans.value.ObservableValue;
import javafx.scene.Scene;
import javafx.scene.control.Label;
import javafx.scene.control.ToggleButton;
import javafx.scene.layout.VBox;
import javafx.stage.Stage;

public class MyJavaFxApp extends Application {
```

```
  @Override
public void start(Stage stage) throws Exception {

  ToggleButton toggleButton = new ToggleButton("TOGGLE ME");
  Label label = new Label();

  Observable<Boolean> selectedStates =
    valuesOf(toggleButton.selectedProperty());

  selectedStates.map(selected -> selected ? "DOWN" : "UP")
    .subscribe(label::setText);

  VBox vBox = new VBox(toggleButton, label);

  stage.setScene(new Scene(vBox));
  stage.show();
}

private static <T> Observable<T> valuesOf(final
ObservableValue<T> fxObservable) {
  return Observable.create(observableEmitter -> {

    //emit initial state
    observableEmitter.onNext(fxObservable.getValue());

    //emit value changes uses a listener
    final ChangeListener<T> listener = (observableValue, prev,
    current) -> observableEmitter.onNext(current);

    fxObservable.addListener(listener);
  });
}
}
```

A JavaFX app backed by a hot **Observable<Boolean>** created off a **ToggleButton**'s selection state

Note that if you are using OpenJDK, you will need to get the JavaFX library separately. It is easiest to use Oracle's official JDK, which includes JavaFX and is available at `http://www.oracle.com/technetwork/java/javase/downloads/index.html`.

A JavaFX `ObservableValue` has nothing to do with an RxJava `Observable`. It is proprietary to JavaFX, but we can easily turn it into an RxJava `Observable` using the `valuesOf()` factory implemented earlier to hook `ChangeListener` as an `onNext()` call. Every time you click on the `ToggleButton`, the `Observable<Boolean>` will emit a `true` or `false` reflecting the selection state. This is a simple example, showing that this `Observable` is emitting events but is also emitting data in the form of `true` or `false`. It will transform that boolean into a string and have an Observer modify a text of `Label`.

We only have one Observer in this JavaFX example. If we were to bring in more Observers to this `ToggleButton`'s events after emissions have occurred, those new Observers will have missed these emissions.

UI events on JavaFX and Android are prime examples of hot Observables, but you can also use hot Observables to reflect server requests. If you created an `Observable` off a live Twitter stream emitting tweets for a certain topic, that also would be a hot `Observable`. All of these sources are likely infinite, and while many hot Observables are indeed infinite, they do not have to be. They just have to share emissions to all Observers simultaneously and not replay missed emissions for tardy Observers.

Note that RxJavaFX (as well as RxAndroid, covered in `Chapter 11`, *RxJava on Android*) has factories to turn various UI events into Observables and bindings for you. Using RxJavaFX, you can simplify the previous example using the `valuesOf()` factory.

Note that we did leave a loose end with this JavaFX example, as we never handled disposal. We will revisit this when we cover Disposables at the end of this chapter.

ConnectableObservable

A helpful form of hot `Observable` is `ConnectableObservable`. It will take any `Observable`, even if it is cold, and make it hot so that all emissions are played to all Observers at once. To do this conversion, you simply need to call `publish()` on any `Observable`, and it will yield a `ConnectableObservable`. But subscribing will not start the emissions yet. You need to call its `connect()` method to start firing the emissions. This allows you to set up all your Observers beforehand. Take a look at the following code snippet:

```
import io.reactivex.Observable;
import io.reactivex.observables.ConnectableObservable;

public class Launcher {
  public static void main(String[] args) {

    ConnectableObservable<String> source =
     Observable.just("Alpha","Beta","Gamma","Delta","Epsilon")
     .publish();

    //Set up observer 1
    source.subscribe(s -> System.out.println("Observer 1: " + s));

    //Set up observer 2
    source.map(String::length)
      .subscribe(i -> System.out.println("Observer 2: " + i));

    //Fire!
    source.connect();
  }
}
```

Take a look at the following code:

```
Observer 1: Alpha
Observer 2: 5
Observer 1: Beta
Observer 2: 4
Observer 1: Gamma
Observer 2: 5
Observer 1: Delta
Observer 2: 5
Observer 1: Epsilon
Observer 2: 7
```

Note how one Observer is receiving the string while the other is receiving the length and the two are printing them in an interleaved fashion. Both subscriptions are set up beforehand, and then `connect()` is called to fire the emissions. Rather than `Observer 1` processing all the emissions before `Observer 2`, each emission goes to each Observer simultaneously. `Observer 1` receives `Alpha` and `Observer 2` receives 5 and then `Beta` and 4, and so on. Using `ConnectableObservable` to force each emission to go to all Observers simultaneously is known as **multicasting**, which we will cover in detail in `Chapter 5`, *Multicasting*.

`ConnectableObservable` is helpful in preventing the replay of data to each Observer. You may want to do this if replaying emissions is expensive and you would rather emit them to all Observers at once. You may also do it simply to force the operators upstream to use a single stream instance even if there are multiple Observers downstream. Multiple Observers normally result in multiple stream instances upstream, but using `publish()` to return `ConnectableObservable` consolidates all the upstream operations before `publish()` into a single stream. Again, these nuances will be covered more in Chapter 5, *Multicasting*.

For now, remember that `ConnectableObservable` is hot, and therefore, if new subscriptions occur after `connect()` is called, they will miss emissions that were fired previously.

Other Observable sources

We already covered a few factories to create `Observable` sources, including `Observable.create()`, `Observable.just()`, and `Observable.fromIterable()`. After our detour covering Observers and their nuances, let's pick up where we left off and cover a few more `Observable` factories.

Observable.range()

To emit a consecutive range of integers, you can use `Observable.range()`. This will emit each number from a start value and increment each emission until the specified count is reached. These numbers are all passed through the `onNext()` event, followed by the `onComplete()` event:

```
import io.reactivex.Observable;

public class Launcher {
  public static void main(String[] args) {
    Observable.range(1,10)
      .subscribe(s -> System.out.println("RECEIVED: " + s));

  }
}
```

The output is as follows:

```
RECEIVED: 1
RECEIVED: 2
RECEIVED: 3
RECEIVED: 4
RECEIVED: 5
RECEIVED: 6
RECEIVED: 7
RECEIVED: 8
RECEIVED: 9
RECEIVED: 10
```

Note closely that the two arguments for `Observable.range()` are not lower/upper bounds. The first argument is the starting value. The second argument is the total count of emissions, which will include both the initial value and incremented values. Try emitting `Observable.range(5,10)`, and you will notice that it emits 5 followed by the next nine consecutive integers following it (for a grand total of 10 emissions):

```java
import io.reactivex.Observable;

public class Launcher {
  public static void main(String[] args) {
    Observable.range(5,10)
    .subscribe(s -> System.out.println("RECEIVED: " + s));

  }
}
```

The output is as follows:

```
RECEIVED: 5
RECEIVED: 6
RECEIVED: 7
RECEIVED: 8
RECEIVED: 9
RECEIVED: 10
RECEIVED: 11
RECEIVED: 12
RECEIVED: 13
RECEIVED: 14
```

 Note that there is also a long equivalent called `Observable.rangeLong()` if you need to emit larger numbers.

Observable.interval()

As we have seen, Observables have a concept of emissions over time. Emissions are handed from the source up to the Observer sequentially. But these emissions can be spaced out over time depending on when the source provides them. Our JavaFX example with `ToggleButton` demonstrated this, as each click resulted in an emission of `true` or `false`.

But let's look at a simple example of a time-based `Observable` using `Observable.interval()`. It will emit a consecutive long emission (starting at 0) at every specified time interval. Here, we have an `Observable<Long>` that emits every second:

```
import io.reactivex.Observable;

import java.util.concurrent.TimeUnit;

 public class Launcher {
  public static void main(String[]args) {

    Observable.interval(1, TimeUnit.SECONDS)
      .subscribe(s -> System.out.println(s + " Mississippi"));
    sleep(5000);

  }
  public static void sleep(int millis) {
    try {
      Thread.sleep(millis);
    } catch (InterruptedException e) {
      e.printStackTrace();
    }
  }
}
```

The output is as follows:

```
0 Mississippi
1 Mississippi
2 Mississippi
3 Mississippi
4 Mississippi
```

`Observable.interval()` will emit infinitely at the specified interval (which is 1 second in this case). However, because it operates on a timer, it needs to run on a separate thread and will run on the computation **Scheduler** by default. We will cover concurrency in `Chapter 6`, *Concurrency and Parallelization* and learn about schedulers. For now, just note that our `main()` method is going to kick off this `Observable`, but it will not wait for it to finish. It is now emitting on a separate thread. To keep our `main()` method from finishing and exiting the application before our `Observable` has a chance to fire, we use a `sleep()` method to keep this application alive for five seconds. This gives our `Observable` five seconds to fire emissions before the application quits. When you create production applications, you likely will not run into this issue often as non-daemon threads for tasks such as web services, Android apps, or JavaFX will keep the application alive.

Trick question: does `Observable.interval()` return a hot or a cold `Observable`? Because it is event-driven (and infinite), you may be tempted to say it is hot. But put a second `Observer` on it, wait for five seconds, and then add another Observer. What happens? Let's take a look:

```
import io.reactivex.Observable;
import java.util.concurrent.TimeUnit;

public class Launcher {

  public static void main(String[] args) {

    Observable<Long> seconds = Observable.interval(1,
    TimeUnit.SECONDS);

    //Observer 1
    seconds.subscribe(l -> System.out.println("Observer 1: " + l));

    //sleep 5 seconds
    sleep(5000);

    //Observer 2
    seconds.subscribe(l -> System.out.println("Observer 2: " + l));

    //sleep 5 seconds
    sleep(5000);
  }

  public static void sleep(int millis) {
    try {
      Thread.sleep(millis);
    } catch (InterruptedException e) {
      e.printStackTrace();
```

```
        }
      }
  }
```

The output is as follows:

```
Observer 1: 0
Observer 1: 1
Observer 1: 2
Observer 1: 3
Observer 1: 4
Observer 1: 5
Observer 2: 0
Observer 1: 6
Observer 2: 1
Observer 1: 7
Observer 2: 2
Observer 1: 8
Observer 2: 3
Observer 1: 9
Observer 2: 4
```

Look what happened after five seconds elapsed, when Observer 2 came in. Note that it is on its own separate timer and starting at 0! These two observers are actually getting their own emissions, each starting at 0. So this Observable is actually cold. To put all observers on the same timer with the same emissions, you will want to use ConnectableObservable to force these emissions to become hot:

```java
import io.reactivex.Observable;
import io.reactivex.observables.ConnectableObservable;
import java.util.concurrent.TimeUnit;

public class Launcher {

  public static void main(String[] args) {
    ConnectableObservable<Long> seconds =
      Observable.interval(1, TimeUnit.SECONDS).publish();

    //observer 1
    seconds.subscribe(l -> System.out.println("Observer 1: " + l));
    seconds.connect();

    //sleep 5 seconds
    sleep(5000);

    //observer 2
    seconds.subscribe(l -> System.out.println("Observer 2: " + l));
```

```
        //sleep 5 seconds
        sleep(5000);

    }

    public static void sleep(int millis) {
      try {
        Thread.sleep(millis);
      } catch (InterruptedException e) {
        e.printStackTrace();
      }
    }
  }
}
```

The output is as follows:

```
Observer 1: 0
Observer 1: 1
Observer 1: 2
Observer 1: 3
Observer 1: 4
Observer 1: 5
Observer 2: 5
Observer 1: 6
Observer 2: 6
Observer 1: 7
Observer 2: 7
Observer 1: 8
Observer 2: 8
Observer 1: 9
Observer 2: 9
```

Now Observer 2, although 5 seconds late and having missed the previous emissions, will at least be completely in sync with Observer 1 and receive the same emissions.

Observable.future()

RxJava Observables are much more robust and expressive than Futures, but if you have existing libraries that yield Futures, you can easily turn them into Observables via Observable.future():

```
import io.reactivex.Observable;
import java.util.concurrent.Future;

public class Launcher {
  public static void main(String[] args) {
```

```
Future<String> futureValue = ...;
Observable.fromFuture(futureValue)
  .map(String::length)
  .subscribe(System.out::println);
}
}
```

Observable.empty()

Although this may not seem useful yet, it is sometimes helpful to create an Observable that emits nothing and calls onComplete():

```
import io.reactivex.Observable;

public class Launcher {
  public static void main(String[] args) {

    Observable<String> empty = Observable.empty();

    empty.subscribe(System.out::println,
      Throwable::printStackTrace,
      () -> System.out.println("Done!"));
  }
}
```

The output is as follows:

```
Done!
```

Note that no emissions were printed because there were none. It went straight to calling onComplete, which printed the **Done!** message in the Observer. Empty observables are common to represent empty datasets. They can also result from operators such as filter() when all emissions fail to meet a condition. Sometimes, you will deliberately create empty Observables using Observable.empty(), and we will see examples of this in a few places throughout this book.

An empty Observable is essentially RxJava's concept of null. It is the absence of a value (or technically, "values"). Empty Observables are much more elegant than nulls because operations will simply continue empty rather than throw NullPointerExceptions. But when things go wrong in RxJava programs, sometimes it is because observers are receiving no emissions. When this happens, you have to trace through your Observable's chain of operators to find which one caused emissions to become empty.

Observable.never()

A close cousin of `Observable.empty()` is `Observable.never()`. The only difference between them is that it never calls `onComplete()`, forever leaving observers waiting for emissions but never actually giving any:

```
import io.reactivex.Observable;

public class Launcher {
  public static void main(String[] args) {

    Observable<String> empty = Observable.never();

    empty.subscribe(System.out::println,
      Throwable::printStackTrace,
        () -> System.out.println("Done!"));

    sleep(5000);

  }

  public static void sleep(int millis) {
    try {
      Thread.sleep(millis);
    } catch (InterruptedException e) {
      e.printStackTrace();
    }
  }
}
```

This `Observable` is primarily used for testing and not that often in production. We have to use `sleep()` here just like `Observable.interval()` because the main thread is not going to wait for it after kicking it off. In this case, we just use `sleep()` for five seconds to prove that no emissions are coming from it. Then, the application will quit.

Observable.error()

This too is something you likely will only do with testing, but you can create an `Observable` that immediately calls `onError()` with a specified exception:

```
import io.reactivex.Observable;

public class Launcher {
  public static void main(String[] args) {
    Observable.error(new Exception("Crash and burn!"))
```

```
      .subscribe(i -> System.out.println("RECEIVED: " + i),
        Throwable::printStackTrace,
          () -> System.out.println("Done!"));
  }
}
```

The output is as follows:

```
java.lang.Exception: Crash and burn!
at Launcher.lambda$main$0(Launcher.java:7)
at io.reactivex.internal.operators.observable.
  ObservableError.subscribeActual(ObservableError.java:32)
at io.reactivex.Observable.subscribe(Observable.java:10514)
at io.reactivex.Observable.subscribe(Observable.java:10500)
...
```

You can also provide the exception through a lambda so that it is created from scratch and separate exception instances are provided to each Observer:

```
import io.reactivex.Observable;

public class Launcher {
  public static void main(String[] args) {

    Observable.error(() -> new Exception("Crash and burn!"))
      .subscribe(i -> System.out.println("RECEIVED: " + i),
        Throwable::printStackTrace,
        () -> System.out.println("Done!"));
  }
}
```

Observable.defer()

`Observable.defer()` is a powerful factory due to its ability to create a separate state for each `Observer`. When using certain `Observable` factories, you may run into some nuances if your source is stateful and you want to create a separate state for each `Observer`. Your source `Observable` may not capture something that has changed about its parameters and send emissions that are obsolete. Here is a simple example: we have an `Observable.range()` built off two static `int` properties, `start` and `count`.

If you subscribe to this `Observable`, modify the count, and then subscribe again, you will find that the second `Observer` does not see this change:

```java
import io.reactivex.Observable;

public class Launcher {

  private static int start = 1;
  private static int count = 5;
  public static void main(String[] args) {
    Observable<Integer> source = Observable.range(start,count);

    source.subscribe(i -> System.out.println("Observer 1: " + i));

    //modify count
    count = 10;

    source.subscribe(i -> System.out.println("Observer 2: " + i));
  }
}
```

The output is as follows:

```
Observer 1: 1
Observer 1: 2
Observer 1: 3
Observer 1: 4
Observer 1: 5
Observer 2: 1
Observer 2: 2
Observer 2: 3
Observer 2: 4
Observer 2: 5
```

To remedy this problem of `Observable` sources not capturing state changes, you can create a fresh `Observable` for each subscription. This can be achieved using `Observable.defer()`, which accepts a lambda instructing how to create an `Observable` for every subscription. Because this creates a new `Observable` each time, it will reflect any changes driving its parameters:

```java
import io.reactivex.Observable;

public class Launcher {

  private static int start = 1;
  private static int count = 5;
```

```java
public static void main(String[] args) {

    Observable<Integer> source = Observable.defer(() ->
    Observable.range(start,count));

    source.subscribe(i -> System.out.println("Observer 1: " + i));

    //modify count
    count = 10;

    source.subscribe(i -> System.out.println("Observer 2: " + i));
  }
}
```

The output is as follows:

```
Observer 1: 1
Observer 1: 2
Observer 1: 3
Observer 1: 4
Observer 1: 5
Observer 2: 1
Observer 2: 2
Observer 2: 3
Observer 2: 4
Observer 2: 5
Observer 2: 6
Observer 2: 7
Observer 2: 8
Observer 2: 9
Observer 2: 10
```

That's better! When your `Observable` source is not capturing changes to the things driving it, try putting it in `Observable.defer()`. If your Observable source was implemented naively and behaves brokenly with more than one Observer (for example, it reuses an Iterator that only iterates data once), `Observable.defer()` provides a quick workaround for this as well.

Observable.fromCallable()

If you need to perform a calculation or action and then emit it, you can use
`Observable.just()` (or `Single.just()` or `Maybe.just()`, which we will learn about
later). But sometimes, we want to do this in a lazy or deferred manner. Also, if that
procedure throws an error, we want it to be emitted up the `Observable` chain through
`onError()` rather than throw the error at that location in traditional Java fashion. For
instance, if you try to wrap `Observable.just()` around an expression that divides 1 by
0, the exception will be thrown, not emitted up to `Observer`:

```
import io.reactivex.Observable;
public class Launcher {
  public static void main(String[] args) {

    Observable.just(1 / 0)
    .subscribe(i -> System.out.println("RECEIVED: " + i),
    e -> System.out.println("Error Captured: " + e));
  }
}
```

The output is as follows:

```
Exception in thread "main" java.lang.ArithmeticException: / by zero
at Launcher.main(Launcher.java:6)
at sun.reflect.NativeMethodAccessorImpl.invoke0(Native Method)
at sun.reflect.NativeMethodAccessorImpl.invoke
  (NativeMethodAccessorImpl.java:62)
at sun.reflect.DelegatingMethodAccessorImpl.
  invoke(DelegatingMethodAccessorImpl.java:43)
at java.lang.reflect.Method.invoke(Method.java:498)
at com.intellij.rt.execution.
  application.AppMain.main(AppMain.java:147)
```

If we are going to be reactive in our error handling, this may not be desirable. Perhaps you
would like the error to be emitted down the chain to the `Observer` where it will be
handled. If that is the case, use `Observable.fromCallable()` instead, as it accepts a
lambda `Supplier<T>` and it will emit any error that occurs down to `Observer`:

```
import io.reactivex.Observable;

public class Launcher {
public static void main(String[] args) {

    Observable.fromCallable(() -> 1 / 0)
    .subscribe(i -> System.out.println("Received: " + i),
```

```
          e -> System.out.println("Error Captured: " + e));
      }
   }
```

The output is as follows:

```
Error Captured: java.lang.ArithmeticException: / by zero
```

That is better! The error was emitted to the `Observer` rather than being thrown where it occurred. If initializing your emission has a likelihood of throwing an error, you should use `Observable.fromCallable()` instead of `Observable.just()`.

Single, Completable, and Maybe

There are a few specialized flavors of `Observable` that are explicitly set up for one or no emissions: `Single`, `Maybe`, and `Completable`. These all follow the `Observable` closely and should be intuitive to use in your reactive coding workflow. You can create them in similar ways as the `Observable` (for example, they each have their own `create()` factory), but certain `Observable` operators may return them too.

Single

`Single<T>` is essentially an `Observable<T>` that will only emit one item. It works just like an Observable, but it is limited only to operators that make sense for a single emission. It has its own `SingleObserver` interface as well:

```
interface SingleObserver<T> {
void onSubscribe(Disposable d);
void onSuccess(T value);
void onError(Throwable error);
}
```

The `onSuccess()` essentially consolidates `onNext()` and `onComplete()` into a single event that accepts the one emission. When you call `subscribe()` against a Single, you provide the lambdas for `onSuccess()` as well as an optional `onError()`:

```
import io.reactivex.Single;

public class Launcher {
  public static void main(String[] args) {
    Single.just("Hello")
      .map(String::length)
```

```
        .subscribe(System.out::println,
      Throwable::printStackTrace);
  }
}
```

Certain RxJava Observable operators will yield a Single, as we will see in the next chapter. For instance, the `first()` operator will return a Single since that operator is logically concerned with a single item. However, it accepts a default value as a parameter (which I specified as `Nil` in the following example) if the Observable comes out empty:

```
import io.reactivex.Observable;

public class Launcher {
  public static void main(String[] args) {
    Observable<String> source =
    Observable.just("Alpha","Beta","Gamma");

    source.first("Nil") //returns a Single
      .subscribe(System.out::println);
  }
}
```

The output is as follows:

```
Alpha
```

The `Single` must have one emission, and you should prefer it if you only have one emission to provide. This means that instead of using `Observable.just("Alpha")`, you should try to use `Single.just("Alpha")` instead. There are operators on `Single` that will allow you to turn it into an `Observable` when needed, such as `toObservable()`.

If there are 0 or 1 emissions, you will want to use `Maybe`.

Maybe

`Maybe` is just like a `Single` except that it allows no emission to occur at all (hence `Maybe`). `MaybeObserver` is much like a standard Observer, but `onNext()` is called `onSuccess()` instead:

```
public interface MaybeObserver<T> {
void onSubscribe(Disposable d);
void onSuccess(T value);
void onError(Throwable e);
void onComplete();
}
```

A given `Maybe<T>` will only emit 0 or 1 emissions. It will pass the possible emission to `onSuccess()`, and in either case, it will call `onComplete()` when done. `Maybe.just()` can be used to create a `Maybe` emitting the single item. `Maybe.empty()` will create a `Maybe` that yields no emission:

```
import io.reactivex.Maybe;

public class Launcher {

  public static void main(String[] args) {

    // has emission
    Maybe<Integer> presentSource = Maybe.just(100);

    presentSource.subscribe(s -> System.out.println("Process 1
      received: " + s),
    Throwable::printStackTrace,
    () -> System.out.println("Process 1 done!"));

    //no emission
    Maybe<Integer> emptySource = Maybe.empty();

    emptySource.subscribe(s -> System.out.println("Process 2
      received: " + s),
    Throwable::printStackTrace,
    () -> System.out.println("Process 2 done!"));
  }
}
```

The output is as follows:

```
Process 1 received: 100
Process 2 done!
```

Certain `Observable` operators that we will learn about later yield a `Maybe`. One example is the `firstElement()` operator, which is similar to `first()`, but it returns an empty result if no elements are emitted:

```
import io.reactivex.Observable;

public class Launcher {

  public static void main(String[] args) {

    Observable<String> source =
      Observable.just("Alpha","Beta","Gamma","Delta","Epsilon");
```

```
        source.firstElement().subscribe(
          s -> System.out.println("RECEIVED " + s),
        Throwable::printStackTrace,
        () -> System.out.println("Done!"));
    }
  }
```

The output is as follows:

```
    RECEIVED Alpha
```

Completable

`Completable` is simply concerned with an action being executed, but it does not receive any emissions. Logically, it does not have `onNext()` or `onSuccess()` to receive emissions, but it does have `onError()` and `onComplete()`:

```
    interface CompletableObserver<T> {
    void onSubscribe(Disposable d);
    void onComplete();
    void onError(Throwable error);
    }
```

Completable is something you likely will not use often. You can construct one quickly by calling `Completable.complete()` or `Completable.fromRunnable()`. The former will immediately call `onComplete()` without doing anything, while `fromRunnable()` will execute the specified action before calling `onComplete()`:

```
    import io.reactivex.Completable;

    public class Launcher {

      public static void main(String[] args) {

        Completable.fromRunnable(() -> runProcess())
        .subscribe(() -> System.out.println("Done!"));

      }
      public static void runProcess() {
        //run process here
      }
    }
```

The output is as follows:

```
    Done!
```

Disposing

When you `subscribe()` to an Observable to receive emissions, a stream is created to process these emissions through the Observable chain. Of course, this uses resources. When we are done, we want to dispose of these resources so that they can be garbage-collected. Thankfully, the finite Observables that call `onComplete()` will typically dispose of themselves safely when they are done. But if you are working with infinite or long-running Observables, you likely will run into situations where you want to explicitly stop the emissions and dispose of everything associated with that subscription. As a matter of fact, you cannot trust the garbage collector to take care of active subscriptions that you no longer need, and explicit disposal is necessary in order to prevent memory leaks.

The Disposable is a link between an Observable and an active Observer, and you can call its `dispose()` method to stop emissions and dispose of all resources used for that Observer. It also has an `isDisposed()` method, indicating whether it has been disposed of already:

```
package io.reactivex.disposables;

public interface Disposable {
  void dispose();
  boolean isDisposed();
}
```

When you provide `onNext()`, `onComplete()`, and/or `onError()` lambdas as arguments to the `subscribe()` method, it will actually return a `Disposable`. You can use this to stop emissions at any time by calling its `dispose()` method. For instance, we can stop receiving emissions from an `Observable.interval()` after five seconds:

```
import io.reactivex.Observable;
import io.reactivex.disposables.Disposable;
import java.util.concurrent.TimeUnit;

public class Launcher {

  public static void main(String[] args) {

    Observable<Long> seconds =
      Observable.interval(1, TimeUnit.SECONDS);

    Disposable disposable =
      seconds.subscribe(l -> System.out.println("Received: " + l));

    //sleep 5 seconds
    sleep(5000);
```

```
    //dispose and stop emissions
    disposable.dispose();

    //sleep 5 seconds to prove
    //there are no more emissions
    sleep(5000);

  }

  public static void sleep(int millis) {
    try {
      Thread.sleep(millis);
    } catch (InterruptedException e) {
      e.printStackTrace();
    }
  }
}
```

Here, we let `Observable.interval()` run for five seconds with an Observer, but we save the Disposable returned from the `subscribe()` method. Then we call the Disposable's `dispose()` method to stop the process and free any resources that were being used. Then, we sleep for another five seconds just to prove that no more emissions are happening.

Handling a Disposable within an Observer

Earlier, I shied away from talking about the `onSubscribe()` method in the `Observer`, but now we will address it. You may have noticed that `Disposable` is passed in the implementation of an `Observer` through the `onSubscribe()` method. This method was added in RxJava 2.0, and it allows the `Observer` to have the ability to dispose of the subscription at any time.

For instance, you can implement your own `Observer` and use `onNext()`, `onComplete()`, or `onError()` to have access to the `Disposable`. This way, these three events can call `dispose()` if, for whatever reason, the `Observer` does not want any more emissions:

```
Observer<Integer> myObserver = new Observer<Integer>() {
  private Disposable disposable;

  @Override
  public void onSubscribe(Disposable disposable) {
    this.disposable = disposable;
  }

  @Override
```

```
public void onNext(Integer value) {
  //has access to Disposable
}

@Override
public void onError(Throwable e) {
  //has access to Disposable
}

@Override
public void onComplete() {
  //has access to Disposable
  }
};
```

The `Disposable` is sent from the source all the way up the chain to the Observer, so each step in the `Observable` chain has access to the Disposable.

Note that passing an `Observer` to the `subscribe()` method will be void and not return a `Disposable` since it is assumed that the `Observer` will handle it. If you do not want to explicitly handle the `Disposable` and want RxJava to handle it for you (which is probably a good idea until you have reason to take control), you can extend `ResourceObserver` as your Observer, which uses a default `Disposable` handling. Pass this to `subscribeWith()` instead of `subscribe()`, and you will get the default `Disposable` returned:

```
import io.reactivex.Observable;
import io.reactivex.disposables.Disposable;
import io.reactivex.observers.ResourceObserver;
import java.util.concurrent.TimeUnit;

public class Launcher {
  public static void main(String[] args) {

    Observable<Long> source =
    Observable.interval(1, TimeUnit.SECONDS);

    ResourceObserver<Long> myObserver = new
    ResourceObserver<Long>() {
     @Override
     public void onNext(Long value) {
       System.out.println(value);
     }

     @Override
     public void onError(Throwable e) {
       e.printStackTrace();
     }
```

```
    @Override
    public void onComplete() {
      System.out.println("Done!");
    }
  };

  //capture Disposable
  Disposable disposable = source.subscribeWith(myObserver);
  }
}
```

Using CompositeDisposable

If you have several subscriptions that need to be managed and disposed of, it can be helpful to use CompositeDisposable. It implements Disposable, but it internally holds a collection of disposables, which you can add to and then dispose all at once:

```java
import io.reactivex.Observable;
import io.reactivex.disposables.CompositeDisposable;
import io.reactivex.disposables.Disposable;
import java.util.concurrent.TimeUnit;

public class Launcher {

  private static final CompositeDisposable disposables
    = new CompositeDisposable();

  public static void main(String[] args) {

    Observable<Long> seconds =
    Observable.interval(1, TimeUnit.SECONDS);

    //subscribe and capture disposables
    Disposable disposable1 =
      seconds.subscribe(l -> System.out.println("Observer 1: " +
      l));

    Disposable disposable2 =
      seconds.subscribe(l -> System.out.println("Observer 2: " +
      l));

    //put both disposables into CompositeDisposable
    disposables.addAll(disposable1, disposable2);

    //sleep 5 seconds
```

```
              sleep(5000);

              //dispose all disposables
              disposables.dispose();

              //sleep 5 seconds to prove
              //there are no more emissions
              sleep(5000);

          }

          public static void sleep(int millis) {
              try {
                  Thread.sleep(millis);
              } catch (InterruptedException e) {
                  e.printStackTrace();
              }
          }
      }
```

CompositeDisposable is a simple but helpful utility to maintain a collection of disposables that you can add to by calling add() or addAll(). When you no longer want these subscriptions, you can call dispose() to dispose of all of them at once.

Handling Disposal with Observable.create()

If your Observable.create() is returning a long-running or infinite Observable, you should ideally check the isDisposed() method of ObservableEmitter regularly, to see whether you should keep sending emissions. This prevents unnecessary work from being done if the subscription is no longer active.

In this case, you should use Observable.range(), but for the sake of the example, let's say we are emitting integers in a for loop in Observable.create(). Before emitting each integer, you should make sure that ObservableEmitter does not indicate that a disposal was called:

```
      import io.reactivex.Observable;

      public class Launcher {
          public static void main(String[] args) {
              Observable<Integer> source =
              Observable.create(observableEmitter -> {
                  try {
                      for (int i = 0; i < 1000; i++) {
                          while (!observableEmitter.isDisposed()) {
```

```
        observableEmitter.onNext(i);
      }
      if (observableEmitter.isDisposed())
        return;
    }
    observableEmitter.onComplete();
  } catch (Throwable e) {
    observableEmitter.onError(e);
  }
});
  }
}
```

If your `Observable.create()` is wrapped around some resource, you should also handle the disposal of that resource to prevent leaks. `ObservableEmitter` has the `setCancellable()` and `setDisposable()` methods for that. In our earlier JavaFX example, we should remove the `ChangeListener` from our JavaFX `ObservableValue` when a disposal occurs. We can provide a lambda to `setCancellable()`, which will execute the following action for us, which will occur when `dispose()` is called:

```
private static <T> Observable<T> valuesOf(final ObservableValue<T>
fxObservable) {
  return Observable.create(observableEmitter -> {

    //emit initial state
    observableEmitter.onNext(fxObservable.getValue());

    //emit value changes uses a listener
    final ChangeListener<T> listener =
      (observableValue, prev, current) ->
       observableEmitter.onNext(current);

    //add listener to ObservableValue
    fxObservable.addListener(listener);

    //Handle disposing by specifying cancellable
    observableEmitter.setCancellable(() ->
   fxObservable.removeListener(listener));
  });
  }
```

Summary

This was an intense chapter, but it will provide a solid foundation as you learn how to use RxJava to tackle real-world work. RxJava, with all of its expressive power, has some nuances that are entirely due to the change of mindset it demands. It has done an impressive amount of work taking an imperative language like Java and adapting it to become reactive and functional. But this interoperability requires some understanding of the implementations between an `Observable` and a `Observer`. We touched on various ways to create Observables as well as how they interact with Observers.

Take your time trying to digest all this information but do not let it stop you from moving on to the next two chapters, where the usefulness of RxJava starts to take formation. In the next chapters, the pragmatic usefulness of RxJava will start to become clear.

3
Basic Operators

In the previous chapter, you learned a lot about the Observable and Observer. We also covered a small number of operators, particularly map() and filter(), to understand the role of operators as well. But there are hundreds of RxJava operators we can leverage to express business logic and behaviors. We will cover operators comprehensively throughout much of this book, so you know which ones to use and when. Being aware of the operators available and combining them is critical to being successful using ReactiveX. You should strive to use operators to express business logic so your code stays as reactive as possible.

It should be noted that operators themselves are Observers to the Observable they are called on. If you call map() on an Observable, the returned Observable will subscribe to it. It will then transform each emission and in turn be a producer for Observers downstream, including other operators and the terminal Observer itself.

You should strive to execute as much logic as possible using RxJava operators, and you should use an Observer to receive the end product emissions that are ready to be consumed. Try not to cheat or get creative by extracting values out of the Observable chain, or resort to blocking processes or imperative programming tactics. When you keep algorithms and processes reactive, you can easily leverage the benefits of reactive programming such as lower memory usage, flexible concurrency, and disposability.

In this chapter, we will cover the following topics:

- Suppressing operators
- Transforming operators
- Reducing operators
- Error-recovery operators
- Action operators

Suppressing operators

There are a number of operators that will suppress emissions that fail to meet a specified criterion. These operators work by simply not calling the `onNext()` function downstream for a disqualified emission, and therefore does not go down the chain to `Observer`. We have already seen the `filter()` operator, which is probably the most common suppressing operator. We will start with this one.

filter()

The `filter()` operator accepts `Predicate<T>` for a given `Observable<T>`. This means that you provide it a lambda that qualifies each emission by mapping it to a Boolean value, and emissions with false will not go forward.

For instance, you can use `filter()` to only allow string emissions that are not five characters in length:

```
import io.reactivex.Observable;

public class Launcher {
    public static void main(String[] args) {

        Observable.just("Alpha", "Beta", "Gamma", "Delta", "Epsilon")
        .filter(s -> s.length() != 5)
        subscribe(s -> System.out.println("RECEIVED: " + s));
    }
}
```

The output of the preceding code snippet is as follows:

```
RECEIVED: Beta
RECEIVED: Epsilon
```

The `filter()` function is probably the most commonly used operator to suppress emissions.

 Note that if all emissions fail to meet your criteria, the returned `Observable` will be empty, with no emissions occurring before `onComplete()` is called.

take()

The `take()` operator has two overloads. One will take a specified number of emissions and then call `onComplete()` after it captures all of them. It will also dispose of the entire subscription so that no more emissions will occur. For instance, `take(3)` will emit the first three emissions and then call the `onComplete()` event:

```java
import io.reactivex.Observable;

public class Launcher {
    public static void main(String[] args) {

        Observable.just("Alpha", "Beta", "Gamma", "Delta", "Epsilon")
        .take(3)
        .subscribe(s -> System.out.println("RECEIVED: " + s));
    }
}
```

The output of the preceding code snippet is as follows:

```
RECEIVED: Alpha
RECEIVED: Beta
RECEIVED: Gamma
```

Note that if you receive fewer emissions than you specify in your `take()` function, it will simply emit what it does get and then call the `onComplete()` function.

The other overload will take emissions within a specific time duration and then call `onComplete()`. Of course, our cold `Observable` here will emit so quickly that it would serve as a bad example for this case. Maybe a better example would be to use an `Observable.interval()` function. Let's emit every 300 milliseconds, but `take()` emissions for only 2 seconds in the following code snippet:

```java
import io.reactivex.Observable;
import java.util.concurrent.TimeUnit;

public class Launcher {
    public static void main(String[] args) {

        Observable.interval(300, TimeUnit.MILLISECONDS)
          .take(2, TimeUnit.SECONDS)
          .subscribe(i -> System.out.println("RECEIVED: " + i));

        sleep(5000);
    }
```

```
public static void sleep(long millis) {
  try {
    Thread.sleep(millis);
  } catch (InterruptedException e) {
    e.printStackTrace();
  }
}
}
```

The output of the preceding code snippet is as follows:

```
RECEIVED: 0
RECEIVED: 1
RECEIVED: 2
RECEIVED: 3
RECEIVED: 4
RECEIVED: 5
```

You will likely get the output that's shown here (each print happening every 300 milliseconds). You can only get six emissions in 2 seconds if they are spaced out by 300 milliseconds.

Note that there is also a takeLast() operator, which will take the last specified number of emissions (or time duration) before the onComplete() function is called. Just keep in mind that it will internally queue emissions until its onComplete() function is called, and then it can logically identify and emit the last emissions.

skip()

The skip() operator does the opposite of the take() operator. It will ignore the specified number of emissions and then emit the ones that follow. If I wanted to skip the first 90 emissions of an Observable, I could use this operator, as shown in the following code snippet:

```
import io.reactivex.Observable;

public class Launcher {
    public static void main(String[] args) {

      Observable.range(1,100)
        .skip(90)
        .subscribe(i -> System.out.println("RECEIVED: " + i));
    }
}
```

The output of the following code snippet is as follows:

```
RECEIVED: 91
RECEIVED: 92
RECEIVED: 93
RECEIVED: 94
RECEIVED: 95
RECEIVED: 96
RECEIVED: 97
RECEIVED: 98
RECEIVED: 99
RECEIVED: 100
```

Just like the `take()` operator, there is also an overload accepting a time duration. There is also a `skipLast()` operator, which will skip the last specified number of items (or time duration) before the `onComplete()` event is called. Just keep in mind that the `skipLast()` operator will queue and delay emissions until it confirms the last emissions in that scope.

takeWhile() and skipWhile()

Another variant of the `take()` operator is the `takeWhile()` operator, which takes emissions while a condition derived from each emission is true. The following example will keep taking emissions while emissions are less than 5. The moment it encounters one that is not, it will call the `onComplete()` function and dispose of this:

```java
import io.reactivex.Observable;

public class Launcher {
    public static void main(String[] args) {

        Observable.range(1,100)
            .takeWhile(i -> i < 5)
            .subscribe(i -> System.out.println("RECEIVED: " + i));
    }
}
```

The output of the preceding code snippet is as follows:

```
RECEIVED: 1
RECEIVED: 2
RECEIVED: 3
RECEIVED: 4
```

Just like the `takeWhile()` function, there is a `skipWhile()` function. It will keep skipping emissions while they qualify with a condition. The moment that condition no longer qualifies, the emissions will start going through. In the following code, we skip emissions as long as they are less than or equal to 95. The moment an emission is encountered that does not meet this condition, it will allow all subsequent emissions going forward:

```
import io.reactivex.Observable;

public class Launcher {
    public static void main(String[] args) {

      Observable.range(1,100)
        .skipWhile(i -> i <= 95)
        .subscribe(i -> System.out.println("RECEIVED: " + i));
    }
}
```

The output of the preceding code snippet is as follows:

```
RECEIVED: 96
RECEIVED: 97
RECEIVED: 98
RECEIVED: 99
RECEIVED: 100
```

The `takeUntil()` operator is similar to `takeWhile()`, but it accepts another `Observable` as a parameter. It will keep taking emissions until that other `Observable` pushes an emission.
The `skipUntil()` operator has similar behavior. It also accepts another `Observable` as an argument but it will keep skipping until the other `Observable` emits something.

distinct()

The `distinct()` operator will emit each unique emission, but it will suppress any duplicates that follow. Equality is based on `hashCode()`/`equals()` implementation of the emitted objects. If we wanted to emit the distinct lengths of a string sequence, it could be done as follows:

```
import io.reactivex.Observable;

public class Launcher {
    public static void main(String[] args) {
```

```
        Observable.just("Alpha", "Beta", "Gamma", "Delta",
"Epsilon")
            .map(String::length)
            .distinct()
            .subscribe(i -> System.out.println("RECEIVED: " + i));
        }
    }
```

The output of the preceding code snippet is as follows:

```
RECEIVED: 5
RECEIVED: 4
RECEIVED: 7
```

Keep in mind that if you have a wide, diverse spectrum of unique values, distinct() can use a bit of memory. Imagine that each subscription results in a HashSet that tracks previously captured unique values.

You can also add a lambda argument that maps each emission to a key used for equality logic. This allows the emissions, but not the key, to go forward while using the key for distinct logic. For instance, we can key off each string's length and use it for uniqueness, but emit the strings rather than their lengths:

```
import io.reactivex.Observable;

public class Launcher {
    public static void main(String[] args) {

        Observable.just("Alpha", "Beta", "Gamma", "Delta",
"Epsilon")
            .distinct(String::length)
            .subscribe(i -> System.out.println("RECEIVED: " + i));
        }
    }
```

The output of the preceding code snippet is as follows:

```
RECEIVED: Alpha
RECEIVED: Beta
RECEIVED: Epsilon
```

Alpha is five characters, and Beta is four. Gamma and Delta were ignored because Alpha was already emitted and is 5 characters. Epsilon is seven characters, and because no seven-character string was emitted yet, it was emitted forward.

distinctUntilChanged()

The `distinctUntilChanged()` function will ignore duplicate consecutive emissions. It is a helpful way to ignore repetitions until they change. If the same value is being emitted repeatedly, all the duplicates will be ignored until a new value is emitted. Duplicates of the next value will be ignored until it changes again, and so on. Observe the output for the following code to see this behavior in action:

```java
import io.reactivex.Observable;

public class Launcher {
    public static void main(String[] args) {

      Observable.just(1, 1, 1, 2, 2, 3, 3, 2, 1, 1)
        .distinctUntilChanged()
        .subscribe(i -> System.out.println("RECEIVED: " + i));
    }
}
```

The output of the preceding code snippet is as follows:

```
RECEIVED: 1
RECEIVED: 2
RECEIVED: 3
RECEIVED: 2
RECEIVED: 1
```

We first receive an emission of 1, which is allowed forward. But the next two 1 are ignored because they are consecutive duplicates. When it switches to 2, that initial 2 is emitted, but the following duplicate is ignored. A 3 is emitted and its following duplicate is ignored as well. Finally, we switch back to a 2 that emits and then a 1 whose duplicate is ignored.

Just like `distinct()`, you can provide an optional argument for a key through a lambda mapping. In the following code snippet, we execute the `distinctUntilChanged()` operation with strings keyed on their lengths:

```java
import io.reactivex.Observable;

public class Launcher {
    public static void main(String[] args) {

        Observable.just("Alpha", "Beta", "Zeta", "Eta", "Gamma",
"Delta")
            .distinctUntilChanged(String::length)
```

```
                    .subscribe(i -> System.out.println("RECEIVED: " + i));
            }
    }
```

The output of the preceding code snippet is as follows:

```
RECEIVED: Alpha
RECEIVED: Beta
RECEIVED: Eta
RECEIVED: Gamma
```

Note that `Zeta` was skipped because it comes right after `Beta`, which also is four characters. `Delta` is ignored as well because it follows `Gamma`, which is five characters as well.

elementAt()

You can get a specific emission by its index specified by a Long, starting at 0. After that item is found and emitted, `onComplete()` will be called and the subscription will be disposed of.

If you want to get the fourth emission coming from an `Observable`, you can do it as shown in the following code snippet:

```
import io.reactivex.Observable;

public class Launcher {
        public static void main(String[] args) {

            Observable.just("Alpha", "Beta", "Zeta", "Eta", "Gamma",
    "Delta")
                    .elementAt(3)
                    .subscribe(i -> System.out.println("RECEIVED: " + i));
        }
    }
```

The output of the following code snippet is as follows:

```
RECEIVED: Eta
```

You may not have noticed, but `elementAt()` returns `Maybe<T>` instead of `Observable<T>`. This is because it will yield one emission, but if there are fewer emissions than the sought index, it will be empty.

There are other flavors of elementAt(), such as elementAtOrError(), which return a Single and will emit an error if an element at that index is not found. singleElement() will turn an Observable into a Maybe, but will produce an error if there is anything beyond one element. Finally, firstElement() and lastElement() will yield, maybe emitting the first or last emission, respectively.

Transforming operators

Next, we will cover various common operators that transform emissions. A series of operators in an Observable chain is a stream of transformations. You have already seen map(), which is the most obvious operator in this category. We will start with that one.

map()

For a given Observable<T>, the map() operator will transform a T emission into an R emission using the provided Function<T, R> lambda. We have already used this operator many times, turning strings into lengths. Here is a new example: we can take raw date strings and use the map() operator to turn each one into a LocalDate emission, as shown in the following code snippet:

```
import io.reactivex.Observable;
import java.time.LocalDate;
import java.time.format.DateTimeFormatter;

public class Launcher {
    public static void main(String[] args) {

        DateTimeFormatter dtf = DateTimeFormatter.ofPattern("M/d
        /yyyy");

        Observable.just("1/3/2016", "5/9/2016", "10/12/2016")
            .map(s -> LocalDate.parse(s, dtf))
            .subscribe(i -> System.out.println("RECEIVED: " + i));
    }
}
```

The output of the preceding code snippet is as follows:

```
RECEIVED: 2016-01-03
RECEIVED: 2016-05-09
RECEIVED: 2016-10-12
```

We passed a lambda that turns each string into a `LocalDate` object. We created a `DateTimeFormatter` in advance in order to assist with the `LocalDate.parse()` operation, which returns a `LocalDate`. In turn, we pushed each `LocalDate` emission to our `Observer` to be printed.

The `map()` operator does a one-to-one conversion for each emission. If you need to do a one-to-many conversion (turn one emission into several emissions), you will likely want to use `flatMap()` or `concatMap()`, which we will cover in the next chapter.

cast()

A simple, map-like operator to cast each emission to a different type is `cast()`. If we want to take `Observable<String>` and cast each emission to an object (and return an `Observable<Object>`), we could use the `map()` operator like this:

```
Observable<Object> items =
    Observable.just("Alpha", "Beta", "Gamma").map(s -> (Object) s);
```

But a shorthand we can use instead is `cast()`, and we can simply pass the class type we want to cast to, as shown in the following code snippet:

```
Observable<Object> items =
    Observable.just("Alpha", "Beta", "Gamma").cast(Object.class);
```

If you find that you are having typing issues due to inherited or polymorphic types being mixed, this is an effective brute-force way to cast everything down to a common base type. But strive to properly use generics and type wildcards appropriately first.

startWith()

For a given `Observable<T>`, the `startWith()` operator allows you to insert a `T` emission that precedes all the other emissions. For instance, if we have an `Observable<String>`that emits items on a menu we want to print, we can use `startWith()` to append a title header first:

```
import io.reactivex.Observable;

public class Launcher {
    public static void main(String[] args) {

        Observable<String> menu =
            Observable.just("Coffee", "Tea", "Espresso", "Latte");
```

```
        //print menu
        menu.startWith("COFFEE SHOP MENU")
            .subscribe(System.out::println);


    }
}
```

The output of the preceding code snippet is as follows:

```
COFFEE SHOP MENU
Coffee
Tea
Espresso
Latte
```

If you want to start with more than one emission, use `startWithArray()` to accept `varargs` parameters. If we want to add a divider between our header and menu items, we can start with both the header and divider as emissions:

```java
import io.reactivex.Observable;

public class Launcher {
    public static void main(String[] args) {

        Observable<String> menu =
            Observable.just("Coffee", "Tea", "Espresso", "Latte");

        //print menu
        menu.startWithArray("COFFEE SHOP MENU","----------------")
            .subscribe(System.out::println);


    }
}
```

The output of the preceding code snippet is as follows:

```
COFFEE SHOP MENU
----------------
Coffee
Tea
Espresso
Latte
```

The `startWith()` operator is helpful for cases like this, where we want to seed an initial value or precede our emissions with one or more emissions.

If you want an entire emissions of `Observable` to precede emissions of another `Observable`, you will want to use `Observable.concat()` or `concatWith()`, which we will cover in the next chapter.

defaultIfEmpty()

If we want to resort to a single emission if a given `Observable` comes out empty, we can use `defaultIfEmpty()`. For a given `Observable<T>`, we can specify a default `T` emission if no emissions occur when `onComplete()` is called.

If we have an `Observable<String>` and filter for items that start with `Z` but no items meet this criteria, we can resort to emitting `None`:

```
import io.reactivex.Observable;

public class Launcher {
    public static void main(String[] args) {

        Observable<String> items =
Observable.just("Alpha","Beta","Gamma","Delta","Epsilon");

        items.filter(s -> s.startsWith("Z"))
          .defaultIfEmpty("None")
          .subscribe(System.out::println);
    }
}
```

The output of the preceding code snippet is as follows:

```
None
```

Of course, if emissions were to occur, we would never see `None` emitted. It will only happen if the preceding `Observable` is empty.

switchIfEmpty()

Similar to `defaultIfEmpty()`, `switchIfEmpty()` specifies a different `Observable` to emit values from if the source `Observable` is empty. This allows you specify a different sequence of emissions in the event that the source is empty rather than emitting just one value.

We could choose to emit three additional strings, for example, if the preceding `Observable` came out empty due to a `filter()` operation:

```
import io.reactivex.Observable;

public class Launcher {
    public static void main(String[] args) {

        Observable.just("Alpha", "Beta", "Gamma", "Delta",
"Epsilon")
            .filter(s -> s.startsWith("Z"))
            .switchIfEmpty(Observable.just("Zeta", "Eta", "Theta"))
            .subscribe(i -> System.out.println("RECEIVED: " + i),
            e -> System.out.println("RECEIVED ERROR: " + e)
            );
    }
}
```

The output of the preceding code snippet is as follows:

```
RECEIVED: Zeta
RECEIVED: Eta
RECEIVED: Theta
```

Of course, if the preceding `Observable` is not empty, then `switchIfEmpty()` will have no effect and not use that specified `Observable`.

sorted()

If you have a finite `Observable<T>` emitting items that implement `Comparable<T>`, you can use `sorted()` to sort the emissions. Internally, it will collect all the emissions and then re-emit them in their sorted order. In the following code snippet, we sort emissions from `Observable<Integer>`so that they are emitted in their natural order:

```
import io.reactivex.Observable;

public class Launcher {
    public static void main(String[] args) {

        Observable.just(6, 2, 5, 7, 1, 4, 9, 8, 3)
            .sorted()
            .subscribe(System.out::println);
    }
}
```

The output of the preceding code snippet is as follows:

```
1
2
3
4
5
6
7
8
9
```

Of course, this can have some performance implications as it will collect all emissions in memory before emitting them again. If you use this against an infinite `Observable`, you may get an `OutOfMemory` error.

You can also provide `Comparator` as an argument to specify an explicit sorting criterion. We can provide `Comparator` to reverse the sorting order, such as the one shown as follows:

```java
import io.reactivex.Observable;
import java.util.Comparator;

public class Launcher {
    public static void main(String[] args) {

        Observable.just(6, 2, 5, 7, 1, 4, 9, 8, 3)
            .sorted(Comparator.reverseOrder())
            .subscribe(System.out::println);
    }
}
```

The output of the preceding code snippet is as follows:

```
9
8
7
6
5
4
3
2
1
```

Since `Comparator` is a single-abstract-method interface, you can implement it quickly with a lambda. Specify the two parameters representing two emissions, and then map them to their comparison operation. We can use this to sort string emissions by their lengths, for instance. This also allows us to sort items that do not implement Comparable:

```
import io.reactivex.Observable;

public class Launcher {
    public static void main(String[] args) {

        Observable.just("Alpha", "Beta", "Gamma" ,"Delta",
"Epsilon")
            .sorted((x,y) -> Integer.compare(x.length(), y.length()))
            .subscribe(System.out::println);
    }
}
```

The output of the preceding code snippet is as follows:

```
Beta
Alpha
Gamma
Delta
Epsilon
```

delay()

We can postpone emissions using the `delay()` operator. It will hold any received emissions and delay each one for the specified time period. If we wanted to delay emissions by three seconds, we could do it like this:

```
import io.reactivex.Observable;
import java.util.concurrent.TimeUnit;

public class Launcher {
    public static void main(String[] args) {

        Observable.just("Alpha", "Beta", "Gamma" ,"Delta",
"Epsilon")
            .delay(3, TimeUnit.SECONDS)
            .subscribe(s -> System.out.println("Received: " + s));

        sleep(5000);
    }
    public static void sleep(long millis) {
      try {
```

```
            Thread.sleep(millis);
        } catch (InterruptedException e) {
            e.printStackTrace();
        }
    }
}
```

The output of the preceding code snippet is as follows:

```
Received: Alpha
Received: Beta
Received: Gamma
Received: Delta
Received: Epsilon
```

Because delay() operates on a different scheduler (such as Observable.interval()), we need to leverage a sleep() method to keep the application alive long enough to see this happen. Each emission will be delayed by three seconds. You can pass an optional third Boolean argument indicating whether you want to delay error notifications as well.

For more advanced cases, you can pass another Observable as your delay() argument, and this will delay emissions until that other Observable emits something.

 Note that there is a delaySubscription() operator, which will delay subscribing to the Observable preceding it rather than delaying each individual emission.

repeat()

The repeat() operator will repeat subscription upstream after onComplete() a specified number of times.

For instance, we can repeat the emissions twice for a given Observable by passing a long 2 as an argument for repeat(), as shown in the following code snippet:

```
import io.reactivex.Observable;

public class Launcher {
    public static void main(String[] args) {

        Observable.just("Alpha", "Beta", "Gamma" ,"Delta",
"Epsilon")
```

```
            .repeat(2)
            .subscribe(s -> System.out.println("Received: " + s));
        }
    }
```

The output of the preceding code snippet is as follows:

```
Received: Alpha
Received: Beta
Received: Gamma
Received: Delta
Received: Epsilon
Received: Alpha
Received: Beta
Received: Gamma
Received: Delta
Received: Epsilon
```

If you do not specify a number, it will repeat infinitely, forever re-subscribing after every onComplete(). There is also a repeatUntil() operator that accepts a Boolean Supplier lambda argument and will continue repeating until it yields true.

scan()

The scan() method is a rolling aggregator. For every emission, you add it to an accumulation. Then, it will emit each incremental accumulation.

For instance, you can emit the rolling sum for each emission by passing a lambda to thescan() method that adds each next emission to the accumulator:

```
import io.reactivex.Observable;

public class Launcher {
  public static void main(String[] args) {

    Observable.just(5, 3, 7, 10, 2, 14)
      .scan((accumulator, next) -> accumulator + next)
      .subscribe(s -> System.out.println("Received: " + s));

    }
}
```

The output of the preceding code snippet is as follows:

```
Received: 5
Received: 8
Received: 15
Received: 25
Received: 27
Received: 41
```

It emitted the initial value of 5, which was the first emission it received. Then, it received 3 and added it to 5, emitting 8. After that, 7 was received, which was added to 8, emitting 15, and so on. This does not have to be used just for rolling sums. You can create many kinds of accumulations (even non-math ones such as string concatenations or Boolean reductions).

Note that `scan()` is very similar to `reduce()`, which we will learn about shortly. Be careful to not confuse the two. The `scan()` method emits the rolling accumulation for each emission, whereas `reduce()` yields a single emission reflecting the final accumulation once `onComplete()` is called. `scan()` can be used on infinite Observables safely since it does not require an `onComplete()` call.

You can also provide an initial value for the first argument and aggregate into a different type than what is being emitted. If we wanted to emit the rolling count of emissions, we can provide an initial value of 0 and just add 1 to it for every emission. Keep in mind that the initial value will be emitted first, so use `skip(1)` after `scan()` if you do not want that initial emission:

```
import io.reactivex.Observable;

public class Launcher {
    public static void main(String[] args) {

        Observable.just("Alpha", "Beta", "Gamma", "Delta",
"Epsilon")
            .scan(0, (total, next) -> total + 1)
            .subscribe(s -> System.out.println("Received: " + s));

    }
}
```

The output of the preceding code snippet is as follows:

```
Received: 0
Received: 1
Received: 2
Received: 3
Received: 4
Received: 5
```

Reducing operators

You will likely have moments where you want to take a series of emissions and consolidate them into a single emission (usually emitted through a `Single`). We will cover a few operators that accomplish this. Note that nearly all of these operators only work on a finite `Observable` that calls `onComplete()` because typically, we can consolidate only finite datasets. We will explore this behavior as we cover these operators.

count()

The simplest operator to consolidate emissions into a single one is `count()`. It will count the number of emissions and emit through a Single once `onComplete()` is called, shown as follows:

```java
import io.reactivex.Observable;

public class Launcher {
        public static void main(String[] args) {

            Observable.just("Alpha", "Beta", "Gamma", "Delta",
"Epsilon")
                .count()
                .subscribe(s -> System.out.println("Received: " + s));

        }
}
```

The output of the preceding code snippet is as follows:

```
Received: 5
```

Like most reduction operators, this should not be used on an infinite `Observable`. It will hang up and work infinitely, never emitting a count or calling `onComplete()`. You should consider using `scan()` to emit a rolling count instead.

reduce()

The `reduce()` operator is syntactically identical to `scan()`, but it only emits the final accumulation when the source calls `onComplete()`. Depending on which overload you use, it can yield `Single` or `Maybe`. If you want to emit the sum of all integer emissions, you can take each one and add it to the rolling total. But it will only emit once it is finalized:

```
import io.reactivex.Observable;

public class Launcher {
    public static void main(String[] args) {

      Observable.just(5, 3, 7, 10, 2, 14)
        .reduce((total, next) -> total + next)
        .subscribe(s -> System.out.println("Received: " + s));
    }
}
```

The output of the preceding code snippet is as follows:

```
Received: 41
```

Similar to `scan()`, there is a seed argument that you can provide that will serve as the initial value to accumulate on. If we wanted to turn our emissions into a single comma-separated value string, we could use `reduce()` like this, shown as follows:

```
import io.reactivex.Observable;

public class Launcher {
    public static void main(String[] args) {

      Observable.just(5, 3, 7, 10, 2, 14)
        .reduce("", (total, next) -> total + (total.equals("") ?
"" :
          ",") + next)
          .subscribe(s -> System.out.println("Received: " +
s));
    }
}
```

The output of the preceding code snippet is as follows:

```
Received: 5,3,7,10,2,14
```

We provided an empty string as our seed value, and we maintain a rolling concatenation total and keep adding to it. We prevent a preceding comma using a ternary operator to check whether the `total` is the seed value and returning an empty string instead of a comma if it is.

Your seed value should be immutable, such as an integer or string. Bad side-effects can happen if it is mutable, and you should use `collect()` (or `seedWith()`) for these cases, which we will cover in a moment. For instance, if you want to reduce `T` emissions into a collection, such as `List<T>`, use `collect()` instead of `reduce()`. Using `reduce()` will have an undesired side-effect of using the same list for each subscription, rather than creating a fresh, empty one each time.

all()

The `all()` operator verifies that each emission qualifies with a specified condition and return a `Single<Boolean>`. If they all pass, it will emit `True`. If it encounters one that fails, it will immediately emit `False`. In the following code snippet, we emit a test against six integers, verifying that they all are less than `10`:

```
import io.reactivex.Observable;

public class Launcher {
    public static void main(String[] args) {

        Observable.just(5, 3, 7, 11, 2, 14)
            .all(i -> i < 10)
            .subscribe(s -> System.out.println("Received: " + s));
    }
}
```

The output of the preceding code snippet is as follows:

```
Received: false
```

When the `all()` operator encountered 11, it immediately emitted `False` and called `onComplete()`. It did not even get to 2 or 14 because that would be unnecessary work. It already found an element that fails the entire test.

If you call `all()` on an empty `Observable`, it will emit true due to the principle of vacuous truth. You can read more about vacuous truth on Wikipedia at `https://en.wikipedia.org/wiki/Vacuous_truth`.

any()

The `any()` method will check whether at least one emission meets a specific criterion and return a `Single<Boolean>`. The moment it finds an emission that qualifies, it will emit true and then call `onComplete()`. If it processes all emissions and finds that they all are false, it will emit false and call `onComplete()`.

In the following code snippet, we emit four date strings, convert them into `LocalDate` emissions, and test for any that are in the month of June or later:

```
import io.reactivex.Observable;
import java.time.LocalDate;

public class Launcher {
    public static void main(String[] args) {

        Observable.just("2016-01-01", "2016-05-02", "2016-09-12",
"2016-04-03")
            .map(LocalDate::parse)
            .any(dt -> dt.getMonthValue() >= 6)
            .subscribe(s -> System.out.println("Received: " + s));
    }
}
```

The output of the preceding code snippet is as follows:

```
Received: true
```

When it encountered the `2016-09-12` date, it immediately emitted true and called `onComplete()`. It did not proceed to process `2016-04-03`.

If you call `any()` on an empty `Observable`, it will emit false due to the principle of vacuous truth. You can read more about vacuous truth on Wikipedia at `https://en.wikipedia.org/wiki/Vacuous_truth`.

contains()

The `contains()` operator will check whether a specific element (based on the `hashCode()`/`equals()` implementation) ever emits from an `Observable`. It will return a `Single<Boolean>` that will emit true if it is found and false if it is not.

In the following code snippet, we emit the integers `1` through `10000`, and we check whether the number `9563` is emitted from it using `contains()`:

```
import io.reactivex.Observable;

public class Launcher {
        public static void main(String[] args) {

            Observable.range(1,10000)
                .contains(9563)
                .subscribe(s -> System.out.println("Received: " + s));
        }
}
```

The output of the preceding code snippet is as follows:

```
Received: true
```

As you can probably guess, the moment the element is found, it will emit true and call `onComplete()` and dispose of the operation. If the source calls `onComplete()` and the element was not found, it will emit `false`.

Collection operators

Collection operators will accumulate all emissions into a collection such as a list or map and then emit that entire collection as a single emission. Collection operators are another form of reducing operators since they consolidate emissions into a single one. We will cover them separately since they are a significant category on their own, though.

Note that you should avoid reducing emissions into collections for the sake of it. It can undermine the benefits of reactive programming where items are processed in a beginning-to-end, one-at-a-time sequence. You only want to consolidate emissions into collections when you are logically grouping them in some way.

toList()

A common collection operator is `toList()`. For a given `Observable<T>`, it will collect incoming emissions into a `List<T>` and then push that entire `List<T>` as a single emission (through `Single<List<T>>`). In the following code snippet, we collect string emissions into a `List<String>`. After the preceding `Observable` signals `onComplete()`, that list is pushed forward to the `observer` to be printed:

```
import io.reactivex.Observable;

public class Launcher {
    public static void main(String[] args) {

        Observable.just("Alpha", "Beta", "Gamma", "Delta",
"Epsilon")
            .toList()
            .subscribe(s -> System.out.println("Received: " + s));
    }
}
```

The output of the preceding code snippet is as follows:

```
Received: [Alpha, Beta, Gamma, Delta, Epsilon]
```

By default, `toList()` will use a standard `ArrayList` implementation. You can optionally specify an integer argument to serve as the `capacityHint`, and that will optimize the initialization of ArrayList to expect roughly that number of items:

```
import io.reactivex.Observable;

public class Launcher {
    public static void main(String[] args) {

        Observable.range(1,1000)
            .toList(1000)
            .subscribe(s -> System.out.println("Received: " + s));
    }
}
```

If you want to specify a different list implementation besides `ArrayList`, you can provide a `Callable` lambda as an argument to construct one. In the following code snippet, I provide a `CopyOnWriteArrayList` instance to serve as my list:

```
import io.reactivex.Observable;
import java.util.concurrent.CopyOnWriteArrayList;
```

```
public class Launcher {
    public static void main(String[] args) {

        Observable.just("Alpha", "Beta", "Gamma", "Delta",
"Epsilon")
            .toList(CopyOnWriteArrayList::new)
            .subscribe(s -> System.out.println("Received: " + s));
    }
}
```

If you want to use Google Guava's immutable list, this is a little trickier since it is immutable and uses a builder. We will show you how to do this with `collect()` later in this section.

toSortedList()

A different flavor of `toList()` is `toSortedList()`. This will collect the emissions into a list that sorts the items naturally based on their `Comparator` implementation. Then, it will emit that sorted `List<T>` forward to the `Observer`:

```
import io.reactivex.Observable;

public class Launcher {
    public static void main(String[] args) {

        Observable.just(6, 2, 5, 7, 1, 4, 9, 8, 3)
            .toSortedList()
            .subscribe(s -> System.out.println("Received: " + s));
    }
}
```

The output of the preceding code snippet is as follows:

```
Received: [1, 2, 3, 4, 5, 6, 7, 8, 9]
```

Like `sorted()`, you can provide a `Comparator` as an argument to apply a different sorting logic. You can also specify an initial capacity for the backing `ArrayList` just like `toList()`.

toMap() and toMultiMap()

For a given `Observable<T>`, the `toMap()` operator will collect emissions into `Map<K, T>`, where `K` is the key type derived off a lambda `Function<T, K>` argument producing the key for each emission.

If we want to collect strings into Map<Char, String>, where each string is keyed off their first character, we can do it like this:

```java
import io.reactivex.Observable;

public class Launcher {
    public static void main(String[] args) {

        Observable.just("Alpha", "Beta", "Gamma", "Delta",
"Epsilon")
            .toMap(s -> s.charAt(0))
            .subscribe(s -> System.out.println("Received: " + s));
    }
}
```

The output of the preceding code snippet is as follows:

```
Received: {A=Alpha, B=Beta, D=Delta, E=Epsilon, G=Gamma}
```

The s -> s.charAt(0) lambda argument takes each string and derives the key to pair it with. In this case, we are making the first character of that string the key.

If we wanted to yield a different value other than the emission to associate with the key, we can provide a second lambda argument that maps each emission to a different value. We can, for instance, map each first letter key with the length of that string:

```java
import io.reactivex.Observable;

public class Launcher {
    public static void main(String[] args) {

        Observable.just("Alpha", "Beta", "Gamma", "Delta",
"Epsilon")
            .toMap(s -> s.charAt(0), String::length)
            .subscribe(s -> System.out.println("Received: " + s));
    }
}
```

The output of the preceding code snippet is as follows:

```
Received: {A=5, B=4, D=5, E=7, G=5}
```

By default, `toMap()` will use `HashMap`. You can also provide a third lambda argument that provides a different map implementation. For instance, I can provide `ConcurrentHashMap` instead of `HashMap`:

```
import io.reactivex.Observable;
import java.util.concurrent.ConcurrentHashMap;

public class Launcher {
    public static void main(String[] args) {
        Observable.just("Alpha", "Beta", "Gamma", "Delta",
"Epsilon")
            .toMap(s -> s.charAt(0), String::length,
ConcurrentHashMap::new)
            .subscribe(s -> System.out.println("Received: " + s));
        }
    }
```

Note that if I have a key that maps to multiple emissions, the last emission for that key is going to replace subsequent ones. If I make the string length the key for each emission, `Alpha` is going to be replaced by `Gamma`, which is going to be replaced by `Delta`:

```
import io.reactivex.Observable;

public class Launcher {
    public static void main(String[] args) {

        Observable.just("Alpha", "Beta", "Gamma", "Delta",
"Epsilon")
            .toMap(String::length)
            .subscribe(s -> System.out.println("Received: " + s));
        }
    }
```

The output of the preceding code snippet is as follows:

```
Received: {4=Beta, 5=Delta, 7=Epsilon}
```

If you want a given key to map to multiple emissions, you can use `toMultiMap()` instead, which will maintain a list of corresponding values for each key. `Alpha`, `Gamma`, and `Delta` will then all be put in a list that is keyed off the length five:

```
import io.reactivex.Observable;

public class Launcher {
    public static void main(String[] args) {
```

```
            Observable.just("Alpha", "Beta", "Gamma", "Delta",
"Epsilon")
                    .toMultimap(String::length)
                    .subscribe(s -> System.out.println("Received: " + s));
        }
    }
```

The output of the preceding code snippet is as follows:

```
    Received: {4=[Beta], 5=[Alpha, Gamma, Delta], 7=[Epsilon]}
```

collect()

When none of the collection operators have what you need, you can always use the `collect()` operator to specify a different type to collect items into. For instance, there is no `toSet()` operator to collect emissions into a `Set<T>`, but you can quickly use `collect()` to effectively do this. You will need to specify two arguments that are built with lambda expressions: `initialValueSupplier`, which will provide a new `HashSet`for a new `Observer`, and `collector`, which specifies how each emission is added to that `HashSet`:

```
        import io.reactivex.Observable;
        import java.util.HashSet;

        public class Launcher {
            public static void main(String[] args) {

                Observable.just("Alpha", "Beta", "Gamma", "Delta",
        "Epsilon")
                    .collect(HashSet::new, HashSet::add)
                    .subscribe(s -> System.out.println("Received: " + s));
            }
        }
```

The output of the preceding code snippet is as follows:

```
    Received: [Gamma, Delta, Alpha, Epsilon, Beta]
```

Now our `collect()` operator will emit a single `HashSet<String>` containing all the emitted values.

Use `collect()` instead of `reduce()` when you are putting emissions into a mutable object, and you need a new mutable object seed each time. We can also use `collect()` for trickier cases that are not straightforward collection implementations.

Say you added Google Guava as a dependency (`https://github.com/google/guava`) and you want to collect emissions into an `ImmutableList`. To create an `ImmutableList`, you have to call its `builder()` factory to yield an `ImmutableList.Builder<T>`. You then call its `add()` method to put items in the builder, followed by a call to `build()`, which returns a sealed, final `ImmutableList<T>` that cannot be modified.

To collect emissions into `ImmutableList`, you can supply an `ImmutableList.Builder<T>` for your first lambda argument and then add each element through its `add()` method in the second argument. This will emit `ImmutableList.Builder<T>` once it is fully populated, and you can `map()` it to its `build()` call in order to emit an `ImmutableList<T>`:

```
import com.google.common.collect.ImmutableList;
import io.reactivex.Observable;

public class Launcher {
    public static void main(String[] args) {
        Observable.just("Alpha", "Beta", "Gamma", "Delta",
"Epsilon")
            .collect(ImmutableList::builder,
ImmutableList.Builder::add)
            .map(ImmutableList.Builder::build)
            .subscribe(s -> System.out.println("Received: " + s));
    }
}
```

The output of the preceding code snippet is as follows:

```
Received: [Alpha, Beta, Gamma, Delta, Epsilon]
```

Again, the `collect()` operator is helpful to collect emissions into any arbitrary type that RxJava does not provide out of the box.

Error recovery operators

Exceptions can occur in your `Observable` chain across many operators depending on what you are doing. We already know about the `onError()` event that is communicated down the `Observable` chain to the `Observer`. After that, the subscription terminates and no more emissions will occur. But sometimes, we want to intercept exceptions before they get to the `Observer` and attempt some form of recovery. We cannot necessarily pretend that the error never happened and expect emissions to resume, but we can attempt re-subscribing or switch to an alternate source `Observable`.

We can still do the former, just not with RxJava operators, which we will see shortly. If you find that the error recovery operators do not meet your needs, chances are you can compose them creatively.

For these examples, let's divide each integer emission by 10, where one of the emissions is 0. This will result in a "/ by zero" exception being emitted to the Observer, as shown in the following code snippet:

```
import io.reactivex.Observable;

public class Launcher {
    public static void main(String[] args) {

        Observable.just(5, 2, 4, 0, 3, 2, 8)
            .map(i -> 10 / i)
            .subscribe(i -> System.out.println("RECEIVED: " + i),
            e -> System.out.println("RECEIVED ERROR: " + e)
            );
    }
}
```

The output of the preceding code snippet is as follows:

```
RECEIVED: 2
RECEIVED: 5
RECEIVED: 2
RECEIVED ERROR: java.lang.ArithmeticException: / by zero
```

onErrorReturn() and onErrorReturnItem()

When you want to resort to a default value when an exception occurs, you can use
onErrorReturnItem(). If we want to emit −1 when an exception occurs, we can do it like this:

```
import io.reactivex.Observable;

public class Launcher {
    public static void main(String[] args) {

        Observable.just(5, 2, 4, 0, 3, 2, 8)
            .map(i -> 10 / i)
            .onErrorReturnItem(-1)
            .subscribe(i -> System.out.println("RECEIVED: " + i),
```

```
        e -> System.out.println("RECEIVED ERROR: " + e)
      );
  }
}
```

The output of the preceding code snippet is as follows:

```
RECEIVED: 2
RECEIVED: 5
RECEIVED: 2
RECEIVED: -1
```

You can also supply `Function<Throwable, T>` to dynamically produce the value using a lambda. This gives you access to `Throwable`, which you can use to determine the returned value as shown in the following code snippet:

```
import io.reactivex.Observable;

public class Launcher {
    public static void main(String[] args) {

        Observable.just(5, 2, 4, 0, 3, 2, 8)
          .map(i -> 10 / i)
          .onErrorReturn(e -> - 1)
          .subscribe(i -> System.out.println("RECEIVED: " + i),
          e -> System.out.println("RECEIVED ERROR: " + e)
          );
    }
}
```

The placement of `onErrorReturn()` matters. If we put it before the `map()` operator, the error would not be caught because it happened after `onErrorReturn()`. To intercept the emitted error, it must be downstream from where the error occurred.

Note that even though we emitted -1 to handle the error, the sequence still terminated after that. We did not get the 3, 2, or 8 that was supposed to follow. If you want to resume emissions, you will just want to handle the error within the `map()` operator where the error can occur. You would do this in lieu of `onErrorReturn()` or `onErrorReturnItem()`:

```
import io.reactivex.Observable;

public class Launcher {
    public static void main(String[] args) {

        Observable.just(5, 2, 4, 0, 3, 2, 8)
          .map(i -> {
            try {
```

```
                        return 10 / i;
                    } catch (ArithmeticException e) {
                    return -1;
                    }
                })
                .subscribe(i -> System.out.println("RECEIVED: " +
i),

                    e -> System.out.println("RECEIVED ERROR: " + e)
                );
        }
    }
```

The output of the preceding code snippet is as follows:

```
RECEIVED: 2
RECEIVED: 5
RECEIVED: 2
RECEIVED: -1
RECEIVED: 3
RECEIVED: 5
RECEIVED: 1
```

onErrorResumeNext()

Similar to onErrorReturn() and onErrorReturnItem(), onErrorResumeNext() is very similar. The only difference is that it accepts another Observable as a parameter to emit potentially multiple values, not a single value, in the event of an exception.

This is somewhat contrived and likely has no business use case, but we can emit three -1 emissions in the event of an error:

```
import io.reactivex.Observable;

public class Launcher {
public static void main(String[] args) {

    Observable.just(5, 2, 4, 0, 3, 2, 8)
        .map(i -> 10 / i)
        .onErrorResumeNext(Observable.just(-1).repeat(3))
        .subscribe(i -> System.out.println("RECEIVED: " + i),
        e -> System.out.println("RECEIVED ERROR: " + e)
        );
    }
}
```

The output of the preceding code snippet is as follows:

```
RECEIVED: 2
RECEIVED: 5
RECEIVED: 2
RECEIVED: -1
RECEIVED: -1
RECEIVED: -1
```

We can also pass it `Observable.empty()` to quietly stop emissions in the event that there is an error and gracefully call the `onComplete()` function:

```
import io.reactivex.Observable;

public class Launcher {
    public static void main(String[] args) {

      Observable.just(5, 2, 4, 0, 3, 2, 8)
        .map(i -> 10 / i)
        .onErrorResumeNext(Observable.empty())
        .subscribe(i -> System.out.println("RECEIVED: " + i),
        e -> System.out.println("RECEIVED ERROR: " + e)
        );
    }
}
```

The output of the preceding code snippet is as follows:

```
RECEIVED: 2
RECEIVED: 5
RECEIVED: 2
```

Similar to `onErrorReturn()`, you can provide a `Function<Throwable,Observable<T>>` lambda to produce an `Observable` dynamically from the emitted `Throwable`, as shown in the code snippet:

```
import io.reactivex.Observable;

public class Launcher {
    public static void main(String[] args) {

      Observable.just(5, 2, 4, 0, 3, 2, 8)
        .map(i -> 10 / i)
        .onErrorResumeNext((Throwable e) ->
Observable.just(-1).repeat(3))
            .subscribe(i -> System.out.println("RECEIVED: " + i),
```

```
            e -> System.out.println("RECEIVED ERROR: " + e)
        );
    }
}
```

The output of the preceding code is as follows:

```
RECEIVED: 2
RECEIVED: 5
RECEIVED: 2
RECEIVED: -1
RECEIVED: -1
RECEIVED: -1
```

retry()

Another way to attempt recovery is to use the `retry()` operator, which has several parameter overloads. It will re-subscribe to the preceding `Observable` and, hopefully, not have the error again.

If you call `retry()` with no arguments, it will resubscribe an infinite number of times for each error. You need to be careful with `retry()` as it can have chaotic effects. Using it with our example will cause it to emit these integers infinitely and repeatedly:

```
import io.reactivex.Observable;

public class Launcher {
    public static void main(String[] args) {

        Observable.just(5, 2, 4, 0, 3, 2, 8)
        .map(i -> 10 / i)
        .retry()
        .subscribe(i -> System.out.println("RECEIVED: " + i),
        e -> System.out.println("RECEIVED ERROR: " + e)
        );
    }
}
```

The output of the preceding code snippet is as follows:

```
RECEIVED: 5
RECEIVED: 2
RECEIVED: 2
RECEIVED: 5
RECEIVED: 2
RECEIVED: 2
RECEIVED: 5
RECEIVED: 2
...
```

It might be safer to specify a fixed number of times to retry() before it gives up and just emits the error to the Observer. In the following code snippet, we will only retry two times:

```java
import io.reactivex.Observable;

public class Launcher {
    public static void main(String[] args) {

        Observable.just(5, 2, 4, 0, 3, 2, 8)
            .map(i -> 10 / i)
            .retry(2)
            .subscribe(i -> System.out.println("RECEIVED: " + i),
            e -> System.out.println("RECEIVED ERROR: " + e)
            );
        }
    }
```

The output of the preceding code snippet is as follows:

```
RECEIVED: 2
RECEIVED: 5
RECEIVED: 2
RECEIVED: 2
RECEIVED: 5
RECEIVED: 2
RECEIVED: 2
RECEIVED: 5
RECEIVED: 2
RECEIVED ERROR: java.lang.ArithmeticException: / by zero
```

You can also provide `Predicate<Throwable>` or `BiPredicate<Integer,Throwable>` to conditionally control when `retry()` is attempted. The `retryUntil()` operator will allow retries while a given `BooleanSupplier` lambda is false. There is also an advanced `retryWhen()` operator that supports advanced composition for tasks such as delaying retries.

Action operators

To close this chapter, we will cover some helpful operators that can assist in debugging as well as getting visibility into an `Observable` chain. These are the action or `doOn` operators.

doOnNext(), doOnComplete(), and doOnError()

These three operators: `doOnNext()`, `doOnComplete()`, and `doOnError()` are like putting a mini `Observer` right in the middle of the `Observable` chain.

The `doOnNext()` operator allows you to peek at each emission coming out of an operator and going into the next. This operator does not affect the operation or transform the emissions in any way. We just create a side-effect for each event that occurs at that point in the chain. For instance, we can perform an action with each string before it is mapped to its length. In this case, we will just print them by providing a `Consumer<T>` lambda:

```
import io.reactivex.Observable;

public class Launcher {
    public static void main(String[] args) {

        Observable.just("Alpha", "Beta", "Gamma", "Delta",
"Epsilon")
            .doOnNext(s -> System.out.println("Processing: " + s))
            .map(String::length)
            .subscribe(i -> System.out.println("Received: " + i));
    }
}
```

The output of the preceding code snippet is as follows:

```
Processing: Alpha
Received: 5
Processing: Beta
Received: 4
Processing: Gamma
Received: 5
Processing: Delta
Received: 5
Processing: Epsilon
Received: 7
```

 You can also leverage `doAfterNext()`, which performs the action after the emission is passed downstream rather than before.

The `onComplete()` operator allows you to fire off an action when `onComplete()` is called at the point in the `Observable` chain. This can be helpful in seeing which points of the `Observable` chain have completed, as shown in the following code snippet:

```
import io.reactivex.Observable;

public class Launcher {
        public static void main(String[] args) {

            Observable.just("Alpha", "Beta", "Gamma", "Delta",
"Epsilon")
                .doOnComplete(() -> System.out.println("Source is done
                    emitting!"))
                .map(String::length)
                .subscribe(i -> System.out.println("Received: " + i));
        }
}
```

The output of the preceding code snippet is as follows:

```
Received: 5
Received: 4
Received: 5
Received: 5
Received: 7
Source is done emitting!
```

And, of course, `onError()` will peek at the error being emitted up the chain, and you can perform an action with it. This can be helpful to put between operators to see which one is to blame for an error:

```
import io.reactivex.Observable;

public class Launcher {
    public static void main(String[] args) {

        Observable.just(5, 2, 4, 0, 3, 2, 8)
            .doOnError(e -> System.out.println("Source failed!"))
            .map(i -> 10 / i)
            .doOnError(e -> System.out.println("Division failed!"))
            .subscribe(i -> System.out.println("RECEIVED: " + i),
            e -> System.out.println("RECEIVED ERROR: " + e)
            );
    }
}
```

The output of the preceding code snippet is as follows:

```
RECEIVED: 2
RECEIVED: 5
RECEIVED: 2
Division failed!
RECEIVED ERROR: java.lang.ArithmeticException: / by zero
```

We used `doOnError()` in two places to see where the error first appeared. Since we did not see `Source failed!` printed but we saw `Division failed!`, we can deduct that the error occurred in the `map()` operator.

Use these three operators together to get an insight into what your `Observable` operation is doing or to quickly create side-effects.

 You can specify all three actions for `onNext()`, `onComplete()`, and `onError()` using `doOnEach()` as well. The `subscribe()` method accepts these three actions as lambda arguments or an entire `Observer<T>`. It is like putting `subscribe()` right in the middle of your Observable chain! There is also a `doOnTerminate()` operator, which fires for an `onComplete()` or `onError()` event.

doOnSubscribe() and doOnDispose()

Two other helpful action operators are doOnSubscribe() and doOnDispose(). The doOnSubscribe() fires a specific Consumer<Disposable> the moment subscription occurs at that point in the Observable chain. It provides access to the Disposable in case you want to call dispose() in that action. The doOnDispose() operator will perform a specific action when disposal is executed at that point in the Observable chain.

We use both operators to print when subscription and disposal occur, as shown in the following code snippet. As you can predict, we see the subscribe event fire off first. Then, the emissions go through, and then disposal is finally fired:

```java
import io.reactivex.Observable;

public class Launcher {
    public static void main(String[] args) {

        Observable.just("Alpha", "Beta", "Gamma", "Delta",
"Epsilon")
            .doOnSubscribe(d -> System.out.println("Subscribing!"))
            .doOnDispose(() -> System.out.println("Disposing!"))
            .subscribe(i -> System.out.println("RECEIVED: " + i));
    }
}
```

The output of the preceding code snippet is as follows:

```
Subscribing!
RECEIVED: Alpha
RECEIVED: Beta
RECEIVED: Gamma
RECEIVED: Delta
RECEIVED: Epsilon
Disposing!
```

Note that doOnDispose() can fire multiple times for redundant disposal requests or not at all if it is not disposed of in some form or another. Another option is to use the doFinally() operator, which will fire after either onComplete() or onError() is called or disposed of by the downstream.

doOnSuccess()

Remember that `Maybe` and `Single` types do not have an `onNext()` event but rather an `onSuccess()` operator to pass a single emission. Therefore, there is no `doOnNext()` operator on either of these types, as observed in the following code snippet, but rather a `doOnSuccess()` operator. Its usage should effectively feel like `doOnNext()`:

```
import io.reactivex.Observable;

public class Launcher {

    public static void main(String[] args) {
        Observable.just(5, 3, 7, 10, 2, 14)
          .reduce((total, next) -> total + next)
          .doOnSuccess(i -> System.out.println("Emitting: " + i))
          .subscribe(i -> System.out.println("Received: " + i));
    }
}
```

The output of the preceding code snippet is as follows:

```
Emitting: 41
Received: 41
```

Summary

We covered a lot of ground in this chapter, and hopefully by now, you are starting to see that RxJava has a lot of practical use. We covered various operators that suppress and transform emissions as well as reduce them to a single emission in some form. You learned how RxJava provides robust ways to recover from errors as well as get visibility into what `Observable` chains are doing with action operators.

If you want to learn more about RxJava operators, there are many resources online. Marble diagrams are a popular form of Rx documentation, visually showing how each operator works. The *rxmarbles.com* (http://rxmarbles.com) site is a popular, interactive web app that allows you to drag marble emissions and see the affected behavior with each operator. There is also an *RxMarbles* Android App (https://play.google.com/store/apps/details?id=com.moonfleet.rxmarbles) that you can use on your Android device. Of course, you can also see a comprehensive list of operators on the ReactiveX website (http://reactivex.io/documentation/operators.html).

Believe it or not, we have barely gotten started. This chapter only covered the basic operators. In the coming chapters, we will cover operators that perform powerful behaviors, such as concurrency and multicasting. But before we do that, let's move on to operators that combine Observables.

4
Combining Observables

We have covered many operators that suppress, transform, reduce, and collect emissions. These operators can do a lot of work, but what about combining multiple Observables and consolidating them into one? If we want to accomplish more with ReactiveX, we need to take multiple streams of data and events and make them work together, and there are operators and factories to achieve this. These combining operators and factories also work safely with Observables occurring on different threads (discussed in `Chapter 6`, *Concurrency and Parallelization*).

This is where we start to transition from making RxJava useful to making it powerful. We will cover the following operations to combine Observables:

- Merging
- Concatenating
- Ambiguous
- Zipping
- Combine latest
- Grouping

Merging

A common task done in ReactiveX is taking two or more `Observable<T>` instances and merging them into one `Observable<T>`. This merged `Observable<T>` will subscribe to all of its merged sources simultaneously, making it effective for merging both finite and infinite Observables. There are a few ways that we can leverage this merging behavior using factories as well as operators.

Observable.merge() and mergeWith()

The `Observable.merge()` operator will take two or more `Observable<T>` sources emitting the same type `T` and then consolidate them into a single `Observable<T>`.

If we have only two to four `Observable<T>` sources to merge, you can pass each one as an argument to the `Observable.merge()` factory. In the following code snippet, I have merged two `Observable<String>` instances into one `Observable<String>`:

```java
import io.reactivex.Observable;

public class Launcher {
    public static void main(String[] args) {

        Observable<String> source1 =
            Observable.just("Alpha", "Beta", "Gamma", "Delta",
"Epsilon");

        Observable<String> source2 =
            Observable.just("Zeta", "Eta", "Theta");

        Observable.merge(source1, source2)
            .subscribe(i -> System.out.println("RECEIVED: " + i));
    }
}
```

The output of the preceding program is as follows:

```
RECEIVED: Alpha
RECEIVED: Beta
RECEIVED: Gamma
RECEIVED: Delta
RECEIVED: Epsilon
RECEIVED: Zeta
RECEIVED: Eta
RECEIVED: Theta
```

Alternatively, you can use `mergeWith()`, which is the operator version of `Observable.merge()`:

```
source1.mergeWith(source2)
    .subscribe(i -> System.out.println("RECEIVED: " + i));
```

The `Observable.merge()` factory and the `mergeWith()` operator will subscribe to all the specified sources simultaneously, but will likely fire the emissions in order if they are cold and on the same thread. This is just an implementation detail, and you should use `Observable.concat()` if you explicitly want to fire elements of each `Observable` sequentially and keep their emissions in a sequential order.

You should not rely on ordering when using merge factories and operators even if ordering seems to be preserved. Having said that, the order of emissions from each source Observable is maintained. The way the sources are merged is an implementation detail, so use concatenation factories and operators if you want to guarantee order.

If you have more than four `Observable<T>` sources, you can use the `Observable.mergeArray()` to pass a varargs of `Observable[]` instances that you want to merge, as shown in the following code snippet. Since RxJava 2.0 was written for JDK 6+ and has no access to a `@SafeVarargs` annotation, you will likely get some type safety warnings:

```
import io.reactivex.Observable;

public class Launcher {
    public static void main(String[] args) {

        Observable<String> source1 =
            Observable.just("Alpha", "Beta");

        Observable<String> source2 =
            Observable.just("Gamma", "Delta");

        Observable<String> source3 =
            Observable.just("Epsilon", "Zeta");

        Observable<String> source4 =
            Observable.just("Eta", "Theta");

        Observable<String> source5 =
            Observable.just("Iota", "Kappa");

        Observable.mergeArray(source1, source2, source3, source4,
source5)
```

```
                                .subscribe(i -> System.out.println("RECEIVED: " + i));
                }
        }
```

The output of the preceding code is as follows:

```
RECEIVED: Alpha
RECEIVED: Beta
RECEIVED: Gamma
RECEIVED: Delta
RECEIVED: Epsilon
RECEIVED: Zeta
RECEIVED: Eta
RECEIVED: Theta
RECEIVED: Iota
RECEIVED: Kappa
```

You can pass Iterable<Observable<T>> to Observable.merge() as well. It will merge all the Observable<T> instances in that Iterable. I could achieve the preceding example in a more type-safe way by putting all these sources in List<Observable<T>> and passing them to Observable.merge():

```
import io.reactivex.Observable;
import java.util.Arrays;
import java.util.List;

public class Launcher {
        public static void main(String[] args) {

            Observable<String> source1 =
                Observable.just("Alpha", "Beta");

            Observable<String> source2 =
                Observable.just("Gamma", "Delta");

            Observable<String> source3 =
                Observable.just("Epsilon", "Zeta");

            Observable<String> source4 =
                Observable.just("Eta", "Theta");

            Observable<String> source5 =
                Observable.just("Iota", "Kappa");

            List<Observable<String>> sources =
                Arrays.asList(source1, source2, source3, source4,
        source5);
```

```
Observable.merge(sources)
    .subscribe(i -> System.out.println("RECEIVED: " + i));
}
}
```

 The reason `mergeArray()` gets its own method and is not a `merge()` overload instead is to avoid ambiguity with the Java 8 compiler and its treatment with functional types. This is true for all the `xxxArray()` operators.

The `Observable.merge()` works with infinite Observables. Since it will subscribe to all Observables and fire their emissions as soon as they are available, you can merge multiple infinite sources into a single stream. Here, we merge two `Observable.interval()` sources that emit at one second and 300 millisecond intervals, respectively. But before we merge, we do some math with the emitted index to figure out how much time has elapsed and emit it with the source name in a string. We let this process run for three seconds:

```
import io.reactivex.Observable;
import java.util.concurrent.TimeUnit;

public class Launcher {
    public static void main(String[] args) {

        //emit every second
        Observable<String> source1 = Observable.interval(1,
TimeUnit.SECONDS)
            .map(l -> l + 1) // emit elapsed seconds
            .map(l -> "Source1: " + l + " seconds");

        //emit every 300 milliseconds
        Observable<String> source2 =
            Observable.interval(300, TimeUnit.MILLISECONDS)
            .map(l -> (l + 1) * 300) // emit elapsed milliseconds
            .map(l -> "Source2: " + l + " milliseconds");

        //merge and subscribe
        Observable.merge(source1, source2)
.subscribe(System.out::println);
        //keep alive for 3 seconds
        sleep(3000);
    }

    public static void sleep(long millis) {
      try {
        Thread.sleep(millis);
      } catch (InterruptedException e) {
        e.printStackTrace();
```

```
                }
            }
        }
```

The output of the preceding code is as follows:

```
Source2: 300 milliseconds
Source2: 600 milliseconds
Source2: 900 milliseconds
Source1: 1 seconds
Source2: 1200 milliseconds
Source2: 1500 milliseconds
Source2: 1800 milliseconds
Source1: 2 seconds
Source2: 2100 milliseconds
Source2: 2400 milliseconds
Source2: 2700 milliseconds
Source1: 3 seconds
Source2: 3000 milliseconds
```

To summarize, `Observable.merge()` will combine multiple `Observable<T>` sources emitting the same type `T` and consolidate into a single `Observable<T>`. It works on infinite Observables and does not necessarily guarantee that the emissions come in any order. If you care about the emissions being strictly ordered by having each `Observable` source fired sequentially, you will likely want to use `Observable.concat()`, which we will cover shortly.

flatMap()

One of the most powerful and critical operators in RxJava is `flatMap()`. If you have to invest time in understanding any RxJava operator, this is the one. It is an operator that performs a dynamic `Observable.merge()` by taking each emission and mapping it to an `Observable`. Then, it merges the emissions from the resulting Observables into a single stream.

The simplest application of `flatMap()` is to map *one emission to many emissions*. Say, we want to emit the characters from each string coming from `Observable<String>`. We can use `flatMap()` to specify a `Function<T, Observable<R>>` lambda that maps each string to an `Observable<String>`, which will emit the letters. Note that the mapped `Observable<R>` can emit any type `R`, different from the source `T` emissions. In this example, it just happened to be `String`, like the source:

```
import io.reactivex.Observable;
```

```
public class Launcher {
    public static void main(String[] args) {

        Observable<String> source =
            Observable.just("Alpha", "Beta", "Gamma", "Delta",
"Epsilon");

        source.flatMap(s -> Observable.fromArray(s.split("")))
            .subscribe(System.out::println);
    }
}
```

The output of the preceding code is as follows:

```
A
l
p
h
a
B
e
t
a
G
a
m
m
...
```

We have taken those five string emissions and mapped them (through `flatMap()`) to emit the letters from each one. We did this by calling each string's `split()` method, and we passed it an empty `String` argument `""`, which will separate on every character. This returns an array `String[]` containing all the characters, which we pass to `Observable.fromArray()` to emit each one. The `flatMap()` expects each emission to yield an `Observable`, and it will merge all the resulting Observables and emit their values in a single stream.

Here is another example: let's take a sequence of `String` values (each a concatenated series of values separated by `"/"`), use `flatMap()` on them, and filter for only numeric values before converting them into `Integer` emissions:

```
import io.reactivex.Observable;

public class Launcher {
    public static void main(String[] args) {
```

```
Observable<String> source =
    Observable.just("521934/2342/FOXTROT", "21962/12112/78886
        /TANGO",
"283242/4542/WHISKEY/2348562");

source.flatMap(s -> Observable.fromArray(s.split("/")))
    .filter(s -> s.matches("[0-9]+")) //use regex to filter
        integers
    .map(Integer::valueOf)
    .subscribe(System.out::println);
    }
}
```

The output of the preceding code is as follows:

```
521934
2342
21962
12112
78886
283242
4542
2348562
```

We broke up each `String` by the / character, which yielded an array. We turned that into an `Observable` and used `flatMap()` on it to emit each `String`. We filtered only for String values that are numeric using a regular expression `[0-9]+` (eliminating FOXTROT, TANGO, and WHISKEY) and then turned each emission into an `Integer`.

Just like `Observable.merge()`, you can also map emissions to infinite `Observables` and merge them. For instance, we can emit simple `Integer` values from `Observable<Integer>` but use `flatMap()` on them to drive an `Observable.interval()`, where each one serves as the period argument. In the following code snippet, we emit the values 2, 3, 10, and 7, which will yield interval Observables that emit at 2 seconds, 3 seconds, 10 seconds, and 7 seconds, respectively. These four Observables will be merged into a single stream:

```
import io.reactivex.Observable;
import java.util.concurrent.TimeUnit;

public class Launcher {
    public static void main(String[] args) {

        Observable<Integer> intervalArguments =
            Observable.just(2, 3, 10, 7);
```

```
                   intervalArguments.flatMap(i ->
          Observable.interval(i, TimeUnit.SECONDS)
                    .map(i2 -> i + "s interval: " + ((i + 1) * i) + "
          seconds
                       elapsed")
                  ).subscribe(System.out::println);

                  sleep(12000);
          }
          public static void sleep(long millis) {
            try {
              Thread.sleep(millis);
            } catch (InterruptedException e) {
              e.printStackTrace();
            }
          }
        }
```

The output of the preceding code is as follows:

```
2s interval: 2 seconds elapsed
3s interval: 3 seconds elapsed
2s interval: 4 seconds elapsed
2s interval: 6 seconds elapsed
3s interval: 6 seconds elapsed
7s interval: 7 seconds elapsed
2s interval: 8 seconds elapsed
3s interval: 9 seconds elapsed
2s interval: 10 seconds elapsed
10s interval: 10 seconds elapsed
2s interval: 12 seconds elapsed
3s interval: 12 seconds elapsed
```

The `Observable.merge()` operator will accept a fixed number of `Observable` sources. But `flatMap()` will dynamically keep adding new `Observable` sources for each emission that comes in. This means that you can keep merging new incoming Observables over time.

Another quick note about `flatMap()` is it can be used in many clever ways. To this day, I keep finding new ways to use it. But another way you can get creative is to evaluate each emission within `flatMap()` and figure out what kind of `Observable` you want to return. For example, if my previous example emitted an emission of 0 to `flatMap()`, this will break the resulting `Observable.interval()`. But I can use an `if` statement to check whether it is 0 and return `Observable.empty()` instead, as used in the following code snippet:

```
Observable<Integer> secondIntervals =
Observable.just(2, 0, 3, 10, 7);
```

```
secondIntervals.flatMap(i -> {
if (i == 0)
return Observable.empty();
else
return Observable.interval(i, TimeUnit.SECONDS)
.map(l -> i + "s interval: " + ((l + 1) * i) + " seconds
elapsed");
}).subscribe(System.out::println);
```

Of course, this is probably too clever as you can just put `filter()` before `flatMap()` and filter out emissions that are equal to 0. But the point is that you can evaluate an emission in `flatMap()` and determine what kind of `Observable` you want to return.

The `flatMap()` is also a great way to take a hot Observable UI event stream (such as JavaFX or Android button clicks) and `flatMap()` each of those events to an entire process within `flatMap()`. The failure and error recovery can be handled entirely within that `flatMap()`, so each instance of the process does not disrupt future button clicks.

If you do not want rapid button clicks to produce several redundant instances of a process, you can disable the button using `doOnNext()` or leverage `switchMap()` to kill previous processes, which we will discuss in Chapter 7, *Switching, Throttling, Windowing, and Buffering.*

Note that there are many flavors and variants of `flatMap()`, accepting a number of overloads that we will not get into deeply for the sake of brevity. We can pass a second combiner argument, which is a `BiFunction<T,U,R>` lambda, to associate the originally emitted `T` value with each flat-mapped `U` value and turn both into an `R` value. In our earlier example of emitting letters from each string, we can associate each letter with the original string emission it was mapped from:

```
import io.reactivex.Observable;

public class Launcher {
    public static void main(String[] args) {
        Observable<String> source =
            Observable.just("Alpha", "Beta", "Gamma", "Delta",
"Epsilon");

        source.flatMap(s -> Observable.fromArray(s.split("")),
(s,r) ->
s + "-" + r)
            .subscribe(System.out::println);
    }
```

```
}
```

The output of the preceding code is as follows:

```
Alpha-A
Alpha-l
Alpha-p
Alpha-h
Alpha-a
Beta-B
Beta-e
Beta-t
Beta-a
Gamma-G
. . .
```

We can also use `flatMapIterable()` to map each `T` emission into an `Iterable<R>` instead of an `Observable<R>`. It will then emit all the `R` values for each `Iterable<R>`, saving us the step and overhead of converting it into an `Observable`. There are also `flatMap()` variants that map to Singles (`flatMapSingle()`), Maybes (`flatMapMaybe()`), and Completables (`flatMapCompletable()`). A lot of these overloads also apply to `concatMap()`, which we will cover next.

Concatenation

Concatenation is remarkably similar to merging, but with an important nuance: it will fire elements of each provided `Observable` sequentially and in the order specified. It will not move on to the next `Observable` until the current one calls `onComplete()`. This makes it great to ensure that merged Observables fire their emissions in a guaranteed order. However, it is often a poor choice for infinite Observables, as an infinite `Observable` will indefinitely hold up the queue and forever leave subsequent Observables waiting.

We will cover the factories and operators used for concatenation. You will find that they are much like the merging ones except that they have the sequential behavior.

 You should prefer concatenation when you want to guarantee that Observables fire their emissions in order. If you do not care about ordering, prefer merging instead.

Observable.concat() and concatWith()

The `Observable.concat()` factory is the concatenation equivalent to `Observable.merge()`. It will combine the emissions of multiple Observables, but will fire each one sequentially and only move to the next after `onComplete()` is called.

In the following code, we have two source Observables emitting strings. We can use `Observable.concat()` to fire the emissions from the first one and then fire the emissions from the second one:

```java
import io.reactivex.Observable;

public class Launcher {
    public static void main(String[] args) {

        Observable<String> source1 =
            Observable.just("Alpha", "Beta", "Gamma", "Delta",
"Epsilon");

        Observable<String> source2 =
            Observable.just("Zeta", "Eta", "Theta");

        Observable.concat(source1, source2)
            .subscribe(i -> System.out.println("RECEIVED: " + i));
    }
}
```

The output of the preceding code is as follows:

```
RECEIVED: Alpha
RECEIVED: Beta
RECEIVED: Gamma
RECEIVED: Delta
RECEIVED: Epsilon
RECEIVED: Zeta
RECEIVED: Eta
RECEIVED: Theta
```

This is the same output as our `Observable.merge()` example earlier. But as discussed in the merging section, we should use `Observable.concat()` to guarantee emission ordering, as merging does not guarantee it. You can also use the `concatWith()` operator to accomplish the same thing, as shown in the following code line:

```java
source1.concatWith(source2)
    .subscribe(i -> System.out.println("RECEIVED: " + i));
```

If we use `Observable.concat()` with infinite Observables, it will forever emit from the first one it encounters and prevent any following Observables from firing. If we ever want to put an infinite `Observable` anywhere in a concatenation operation, it would likely be specified last. This ensures that it does not hold up any Observables following it because there are none. We can also use `take()` operators to make infinite Observables finite.

Here, we fire an `Observable` that emits every second, but only take two emissions from it. After that, it will call `onComplete()` and dispose it. Then, a second `Observable` concatenated after it will emit forever (or in this case, when the application quits after five seconds). Since this second `Observable` is the last one specified in `Observable.concat()`, it will not hold up any subsequent Observables by being infinite:

```
import io.reactivex.Observable;
import java.util.concurrent.TimeUnit;

public class Launcher {
    public static void main(String[] args) {

        //emit every second, but only take 2 emissions
        Observable<String> source1 =
          Observable.interval(1, TimeUnit.SECONDS)
            .take(2)
            .map(l -> l + 1) // emit elapsed seconds
            .map(l -> "Source1: " + l + " seconds");

        //emit every 300 milliseconds
        Observable<String> source2 =
          Observable.interval(300, TimeUnit.MILLISECONDS)
            .map(l -> (l + 1) * 300) // emit elapsed milliseconds
            .map(l -> "Source2: " + l + " milliseconds");

        Observable.concat(source1, source2)
          .subscribe(i -> System.out.println("RECEIVED: " + i));

        //keep application alive for 5 seconds
        sleep(5000);
    }

    public static void sleep(long millis) {
      try {
        Thread.sleep(millis);
      } catch (InterruptedException e) {
        e.printStackTrace();
      }
    }
}
```

The output of the preceding code is as follows:

```
RECEIVED: Source1: 1 seconds
RECEIVED: Source1: 2 seconds
RECEIVED: Source2: 300 milliseconds
RECEIVED: Source2: 600 milliseconds
RECEIVED: Source2: 900 milliseconds
RECEIVED: Source2: 1200 milliseconds
RECEIVED: Source2: 1500 milliseconds
```

There are concatenation counterparts for arrays and `Iterable<Observable<T>>` inputs as well, just like there is for merging. The `Observable.concatArray()` factory will fire off each `Observable` sequentially in an `Observable[]` array. The `Observable.concat()` factory will also accept an `Iterable<Observable<T>>` and fire off each `Observable<T>` in the same manner.

Note there are a few variants of `concatMap()`. Use `concatMapIterable()` when you want to map each emission to an `Iterable<T>` instead of an `Observable<T>`. It will emit all `T` values for each `Iterable<T>`, saving you the step and overhead of turning each one into an `Observable<T>`. There is also a `concatMapEager()` operator that will eagerly subscribe to all `Observable` sources it receives and will cache the emissions until it is their turn to emit.

concatMap()

Just as there is `flatMap()`, which dynamically merges Observables derived off each emission, there is a concatenation counterpart called `concatMap()`. You should prefer this operator if you care about ordering and want each `Observable` mapped from each emission to finish before starting the next one. More specifically, `concatMap()` will merge each mapped `Observable` sequentially and fire it one at a time. It will only move to the next Observable when the current one calls `onComplete()`. If source emissions produce Observables faster than `concatMap()` can emit from them, those Observables will be queued.

Our earlier `flatMap()` examples would be better suited for `concatMap()` if we explicitly cared about emission order. Although our example here has the same output as the `flatMap()` example, we should use `concatMap()` when we explicitly care about maintaining ordering and want to process each mapped `Observable` sequentially:

```
import io.reactivex.Observable;
```

```
public class Launcher {
    public static void main(String[] args) {

        Observable<String> source =
                Observable.just("Alpha", "Beta", "Gamma", "Delta",
"Epsilon");

        source.concatMap(s -> Observable.fromArray(s.split("")))
                .subscribe(System.out::println);
    }
}
```

The output will be as follows:

```
A
l
p
h
a
B
e
t
a
G
a
m
m
...
```

Again, it is unlikely that you will ever want to use `concatMap()` to map to infinite Observables. As you can guess, this would result in subsequent Observables never firing. You will likely want to use `flatMap()` instead, and we will see it used in concurrency examples in `Chapter 6`, *Concurrency and Parallelization*.

Ambiguous

After covering merging and concatenation, let's get an easy combine operation out of the way. The `Observable.amb()` factory (**amb** stands for **ambiguous**) will accept an `Iterable<Observable<T>>` and emit the emissions of the first `Observable` that emits, while the others are disposed of. The first `Observable` with an emission is the one whose emissions go through. This is helpful when you have multiple sources for the same data or events and you want the fastest one to win.

Here, we have two interval sources and we combine them with the `Observable.amb()` factory. If one emits every second while the other every 300 milliseconds, the latter is going to win because it will emit first:

```java
import io.reactivex.Observable;
import java.util.Arrays;
import java.util.concurrent.TimeUnit;

public class Launcher {
    public static void main(String[] args) {

        //emit every second
        Observable<String> source1 =
                Observable.interval(1, TimeUnit.SECONDS)
                        .take(2)
                        .map(l -> l + 1) // emit elapsed seconds
                        .map(l -> "Source1: " + l + " seconds");


        //emit every 300 milliseconds
        Observable<String> source2 =
                Observable.interval(300, TimeUnit.MILLISECONDS)
                        .map(l -> (l + 1) * 300) // emit elapsed
milliseconds
                        .map(l -> "Source2: " + l + "
milliseconds");


        //emit Observable that emits first
        Observable.amb(Arrays.asList(source1, source2))
                .subscribe(i -> System.out.println("RECEIVED: " +
i));

        //keep application alive for 5 seconds
        sleep(5000);
    }

    public static void sleep(long millis) {
        try {
            Thread.sleep(millis);
        } catch (InterruptedException e) {
            e.printStackTrace();
        }
    }
}
```

The output is as follows:

```
RECEIVED: Source2: 300 milliseconds
RECEIVED: Source2: 600 milliseconds
RECEIVED: Source2: 900 milliseconds
RECEIVED: Source2: 1200 milliseconds
RECEIVED: Source2: 1500 milliseconds
RECEIVED: Source2: 1800 milliseconds
RECEIVED: Source2: 2100 milliseconds
...
```

You can also use an `ambWith()` operator, which will accomplish the same result:

```
//emit Observable that emits first
source1.ambWith(source2)
        .subscribe(i -> System.out.println("RECEIVED: " + i));
```

You can also use `Observable.ambArray()` to specify a `varargs` array rather than `Iterable<Observable<T>>`.

Zipping

Zipping allows you to take an emission from each `Observable` source and combine it into a single emission. Each `Observable` can emit a different type, but you can combine these different emitted types into a single emission. Here is an example, If we have an `Observable<String>` and an `Observable<Integer>`, we can zip each `String` and `Integer` together in a one-to-one pairing and concatenate it with a lambda:

```java
import io.reactivex.Observable;

public class Launcher {
    public static void main(String[] args) {

        Observable<String> source1 =
                Observable.just("Alpha", "Beta", "Gamma", "Delta",
"Epsilon");

        Observable<Integer> source2 = Observable.range(1,6);

        Observable.zip(source1, source2, (s,i) -> s + "-" + i)
                .subscribe(System.out::println);
    }
}
```

The output is as follows:

```
Alpha-1
Beta-2
Gamma-3
Delta-4
Epsilon-5
```

The `zip()` function received both `Alpha` and a `1` and then paired them up into a concatenated string separated by a dash – and pushed it forward. Then, it received `Beta` and `2` and emitted them forward as a concatenation, and so on. An emission from one `Observable` must wait to get paired with an emission from the other `Observable`. If one `Observable` calls `onComplete()` and the other still has emissions waiting to get paired, those emissions will simply drop, since they have nothing to couple with. This happened to the `6` emission since we only had five string emissions.

You can also accomplish this using a `zipWith()` operator, as shown here:

```
source1.zipWith(source2, (s,i) -> s + "-" + i)
```

You can pass up to nine `Observable` instances to the `Observable.zip()` factory. If you need more than that, you can pass an `Iterable<Observable<T>>` or use `zipArray()` to provide an `Observable[]` array. Note that if one or more sources are producing emissions faster than another, `zip()` will queue up those rapid emissions as they wait on the slower source to provide emissions. This could cause undesirable performance issues as each source queues in memory. If you only care about zipping the latest emission from each source rather than catching up an entire queue, you will want to use `combineLatest()`, which we will cover later in this section.

 Use `Observable.zipIterable()` to pass a Boolean `delayError` argument to delay errors until all sources terminate and an int `bufferSize` to hint an expected number of elements from each source for queue size optimization. You may specify the latter to increase performance in certain scenarios by buffering emissions before they are zipped.

Zipping can also be helpful in slowing down emissions using `Observable.interval()`. Here, we zip each string with a 1-second interval. This will slow each string emission by one second, but keep in mind the five string emissions will likely be queued as they wait for an interval emission to pair with:

```
import io.reactivex.Observable;
import java.time.LocalTime;
import java.util.concurrent.TimeUnit;
```

```
public class Launcher {
    public static void main(String[] args) {

        Observable<String> strings =
                Observable.just("Alpha", "Beta", "Gamma", "Delta",
"Epsilon");

        Observable<Long> seconds =
                Observable.interval(1, TimeUnit.SECONDS);

        Observable.zip(strings, seconds, (s,l) -> s)
                .subscribe(s ->
System.out.println("Received " + s +
                                " at " + LocalTime.now())
                );

        sleep(6000);
    }
    public static void sleep(long millis) {
        try {
            Thread.sleep(millis);
        } catch (InterruptedException e) {
            e.printStackTrace();
        }
    }
}
```

The output is as follows:

```
Received Alpha at 13:28:28.428
Received Beta at 13:28:29.388
Received Gamma at 13:28:30.389
Received Delta at 13:28:31.389
Received Epsilon at 13:28:32.389
```

Combine latest

The Observable.combineLatest() factory is somewhat similar to zip(), but for every emission that fires from one of the sources, it will immediately couple up with the latest emission from every other source. It will not queue up unpaired emissions for each source, but rather cache and pair the latest one.

Here, let's use `Observable.combineLatest()` between two interval Observables, the first emitting at 300 milliseconds and the other every one second:

```java
import io.reactivex.Observable;
import java.util.concurrent.TimeUnit;

public class Launcher {
    public static void main(String[] args) {

        Observable<Long> source1 =
                Observable.interval(300, TimeUnit.MILLISECONDS);

        Observable<Long> source2 =
                Observable.interval(1, TimeUnit.SECONDS);

        Observable.combineLatest(source1, source2,
                (l1,l2) -> "SOURCE 1: " + l1 + "  SOURCE 2: " + l2)
                .subscribe(System.out::println);


        sleep(3000);
    }
    public static void sleep(long millis) {
        try {
            Thread.sleep(millis);
        } catch (InterruptedException e) {
            e.printStackTrace();
        }
    }
}
```

The output is as follows:

```
SOURCE 1: 2   SOURCE 2: 0
SOURCE 1: 3   SOURCE 2: 0
SOURCE 1: 4   SOURCE 2: 0
SOURCE 1: 5   SOURCE 2: 0
SOURCE 1: 5   SOURCE 2: 1
SOURCE 1: 6   SOURCE 2: 1
SOURCE 1: 7   SOURCE 2: 1
SOURCE 1: 8   SOURCE 2: 1
SOURCE 1: 9   SOURCE 2: 1
SOURCE 1: 9   SOURCE 2: 2
```

There is a lot going on here, but let's try to break it down. `source1` is emitting every 300 milliseconds, but the first two emissions do not yet have anything to pair with from `source2`, which emits every second, and no emission has occurred yet. Finally, after one second, `source2` pushes its first emission 0, and it pairs with the latest emission 2 (the third emission) from `source1`. Note that the two previous emissions 0 and 1 from `source1` were completely forgotten because the third emission 2 is now the latest emission. `source1` then pushes 3, 4, and then 5 at 300 millisecond intervals, but 0 is still the latest emission from `source2`, so all three pair with it. Then, `source2` emits its second emission 1, and it pairs with 5, the latest emission from `source2`.

In simpler terms, when one source fires, it couples with the latest emissions from the others. `Observable.combineLatest()` is especially helpful in combining UI inputs, as previous user inputs are frequently irrelevant and only the latest is of concern.

withLatestFrom()

Similar to `Observable.combineLatest()`, but not exactly the same, is the `withLatestfrom()` operator. It will map each `T` emission with the latest values from other Observables and combine them, but it will only take *one* emission from each of the other Observables:

```java
import io.reactivex.Observable;
import java.util.concurrent.TimeUnit;

public class Launcher {
    public static void main(String[] args) {

        Observable<Long> source1 =
                Observable.interval(300, TimeUnit.MILLISECONDS);

        Observable<Long> source2 =
                Observable.interval(1, TimeUnit.SECONDS);

        source2.withLatestFrom(source1,
            (l1,l2) -> "SOURCE 2: " + l1 + "  SOURCE 1: " + l2
        ) .subscribe(System.out::println);


        sleep(3000);
    }
    public static void sleep(long millis) {
        try {
            Thread.sleep(millis);
```

```
            } catch (InterruptedException e) {
                e.printStackTrace();
            }
        }
    }
```

The output is as follows:

```
SOURCE 2: 0   SOURCE 1: 2
SOURCE 2: 1   SOURCE 1: 5
SOURCE 2: 2   SOURCE 1: 9
```

As you can see here, `source2` emits every one second while `source1` emits every 300 milliseconds. When you call `withLatestFrom()` on `source2` and pass it `source1`, it will combine with the latest emission from `source1` but it does not care about any previous or subsequent emissions.

You can pass up to four `Observable` instances of any varying types to `withLatestFrom()`. If you need more than that, you can pass it an `Iterable<Observable<T>>`.

Grouping

A powerful operation that you can achieve with RxJava is to group emissions by a specified key into separate Observables. This can be achieved by calling the `groupBy()` operator, which accepts a lambda mapping each emission to a key. It will then return an `Observable<GroupedObservable<K, T>>`, which emits a special type of `Observable` called `GroupedObservable`. `GroupedObservable<K, T>` is just like any other `Observable`, but it has the key `K` value accessible as a property. It will emit the `T` emissions that are mapped for that given key.

For instance, we can use the `groupBy()` operator to group emissions for an `Observable<String>` by each String's length. We will subscribe to it in a moment, but here is how we declare it:

```
import io.reactivex.Observable;
import io.reactivex.observables.GroupedObservable;

public class Launcher {
    public static void main(String[] args) {

        Observable<String> source =
Observable.just("Alpha", "Beta", "Gamma", "Delta", "Epsilon");
```

```
        Observable<GroupedObservable<Integer,String>> byLengths =
                source.groupBy(s -> s.length());
    }
}
```

We will likely need to use `flatMap()` on each `GroupedObservable`, but within that `flatMap()` operation, we may want to reduce or collect those common-key emissions (since this will return a `Single`, we will need to use `flatMapSingle()`). Let's call `toList()` so that we can emit the emissions as lists grouped by their lengths:

```java
import io.reactivex.Observable;
import io.reactivex.observables.GroupedObservable;

public class Launcher {
    public static void main(String[] args) {

        Observable<String> source =
                Observable.just("Alpha", "Beta", "Gamma", "Delta",
"Epsilon");

        Observable<GroupedObservable<Integer,String>> byLengths =
                source.groupBy(s -> s.length());

        byLengths.flatMapSingle(grp -> grp.toList())
                .subscribe(System.out::println);
    }
}
```

The output is as follows:

```
[Beta]
[Alpha, Gamma, Delta]
[Epsilon]
```

`Beta` is the only emission with length four, so it is the only element in the list for that length key. `Alpha`, `Beta`, and `Gamma` all have lengths of five, so they were emitted from the same `GroupedObservable` emitting items for the length five and were collected into the same list. `Epsilon` was the only emission with length seven so it was the only element in its list.

Keep in mind that `GroupedObservable` also has a `getKey()` method, which returns the key value identified with that `GroupedObservable`. If we wanted to simply concatenate the `String` emissions for each `GroupedObservable` and then concatenate the `length` key in form of it, we could do it like this:

```java
import io.reactivex.Observable;
import io.reactivex.observables.GroupedObservable;
```

```
public class Launcher {
    public static void main(String[] args) {

        Observable<String> source =
                Observable.just("Alpha", "Beta", "Gamma", "Delta",
"Epsilon");

        Observable<GroupedObservable<Integer,String>> byLengths =
                source.groupBy(s -> s.length());

        byLengths.flatMapSingle(grp ->
grp.reduce("",(x,y) -> x.equals("") ? y : x + ", " + y)
                            .map(s -> grp.getKey() + ": " + s)
        ).subscribe(System.out::println);
    }
}
```

The output is as follows:

```
4: Beta
5: Alpha, Gamma, Delta
7: Epsilon
```

Note closely that `GroupedObservables` are a weird combination of a hot and cold `Observable`. They are not cold in that they will not replay missed emissions to a second `Observer`, but they will cache emissions and flush them to the first `Observer`, ensuring none are missed. If you need to replay the emissions, collect them into a list, like we did earlier, and perform your operations against that list. You can also use caching operators, which we will learn about in the next chapter.

Summary

In this chapter, we covered combining Observables in various useful ways. Merging is helpful in combining and simultaneously firing multiple Observables and combining their emissions into a single stream. The `flatMap()` operator is especially critical to know, as dynamically merging Observables derived from emissions opens a lot of useful functionality in RxJava. Concatenation is similar to merging, but it fires off the source Observables sequentially rather than all at once. Combining with ambiguous allows us to select the first `Observable` to emit and fire its emissions. Zipping allows you to combine emissions from multiple Observables, whereas combine latest combines the latest emissions from each source every time one of them fires. Finally, grouping allows you to split up an `Observable` into several `GroupedObservables`, each with emissions that have a common key.

Take time to explore combining Observables and experiment to see how they work. They are critical to unlock functionalities in RxJava and quickly express event and data transformations. We will look at some powerful applications with `flatMap()` when we cover concurrency in `Chapter 6`, *Concurrency and Parallelization,* where we will also cover how to multitask and parallelize.

5
Multicasting, Replaying, and Caching

We have seen the hot and cold `Observable` in action throughout this book, although most of our examples have been cold Observables (even ones using `Observable.interval()`). As a matter of fact, there are a lot of subtleties in the hotness and coldness of Observables, which we will look at in this chapter. When you have more than one `Observer`, the default behavior is to create a separate stream for each one. This may or may not be desirable, and we need to be aware of when to force an `Observable` to be hot by multicasting using a `ConnectableObservable`. We got a brief introduction to the `ConnectableObservable` in `Chapter 2`, *Observables and Subscribers*, but we will look at it in deeper context within an entire `Observable` chain of operators.

In this chapter, we will learn about multicasting with `ConnectableObservable` in detail and uncover its subtleties. We will also learn about replaying and caching, both of which multicast and leverage the `ConnectableObservable`. Finally, we will learn about Subjects, a utility that can be useful for decoupling while multicasting but should be used conservatively for only certain situations. We will cover the different flavors of subjects as well as when and when not to use them.

Here is a broad outline of what to expect:

- Understanding multicasting
- Automatic connection
- Replaying and caching
- Subjects

Understanding multicasting

We have used the `ConnectableObservable` earlier in Chapter 2, *Observables and Subscribers*. Remember how cold Observables, such as `Observable.range()`, will regenerate emissions for each `Observer`? Let's take a look at the following code:

```
import io.reactivex.Observable;

public class Launcher {
    public static void main(String[] args) {

        Observable<Integer> threeIntegers  = Observable.range(1,
3);

        threeIntegers.subscribe(i -> System.out.println("Observer
One: " + i));
        threeIntegers.subscribe(i -> System.out.println("Observer
Two: " + i));
    }
}
```

The output is as follows:

```
Observer One: 1
Observer One: 2
Observer One: 3
Observer Two: 1
Observer Two: 2
Observer Two: 3
```

Here, `Observer One` received all three emissions and called `onComplete()`. After that, `Observer Two` received the three emissions (which were regenerated again) and called `onComplete()`. These were two separate streams of data generated for two separate subscriptions. If we wanted to consolidate them into a single stream of data that pushes each emission to both Observers simultaneously, we can call `publish()` on `Observable`, which will return a `ConnectableObservable`. We can set up the Observers in advance and then call `connect()` to start firing the emissions so both Observers receive the same emissions simultaneously. This will be indicated by the printing of each `Observer` interleaving here:

```
import io.reactivex.Observable;
import io.reactivex.observables.ConnectableObservable;

public class Launcher {
    public static void main(String[] args) {
```

```
ConnectableObservable<Integer> threeIntegers =
        Observable.range(1, 3).publish();

threeIntegers.subscribe(i -> System.out.println("Observer
One: " + i));
        threeIntegers.subscribe(i -> System.out.println("Observer
Two: " + i));

threeIntegers.connect();
    }
}
```

The output is as follows:

```
Observer One: 1
Observer Two: 1
Observer One: 2
Observer Two: 2
Observer One: 3
Observer Two: 3
```

Using `ConnectableObservable` will force emissions from the source to become hot, pushing a single stream of emissions to all Observers at the same time rather than giving a separate stream to each `Observer`. This idea of stream consolidation is known as multicasting, but there are nuances to it, especially when operators become involved. Even when you call `publish()` and use a `ConnectableObservable`, any operators that follow can create separate streams again. We will take a look at this behavior and how to manage it next.

Multicasting with operators

To see how multicasting works within a chain of operators, we are going to use `Observable.range()` and then map each emission to a random integer. Since these random values will be nondeterministic and different for each subscription, this will provide a good means to see whether our multicasting is working because Observers should receive the same numbers.

Let's start with emitting the numbers 1 through 3 and map each one to a random integer between 0 and 100,000. If we have two Observers, we can expect different integers for each one. Note that your output will be different than mine due to the random number generation and just acknowledge that both Observers are receiving different random integers:

```
import io.reactivex.Observable;
import java.util.concurrent.ThreadLocalRandom;

public class Launcher {
    public static void main(String[] args) {

        Observable<Integer> threeRandoms = Observable.range(1,3)
                    .map(i -> randomInt());

        threeRandoms.subscribe(i -> System.out.println("Observer 1:
" + i));
        threeRandoms.subscribe(i -> System.out.println("Observer 2:
" + i));

    }

    public static int randomInt() {
        return ThreadLocalRandom.current().nextInt(100000);
    }
}
```

The output is as follows:

```
Observer 1: 38895
Observer 1: 36858
Observer 1: 82955
Observer 2: 55957
Observer 2: 47394
Observer 2: 16996
```

What happens here is that the `Observable.range()` source will yield two separate emission generators, and each will coldly emit a separate stream for each `Observer`. Each stream also has its own separate `map()` instance, hence each `Observer` gets different random integers. You can visually see this structure of two separate streams in the following figure:

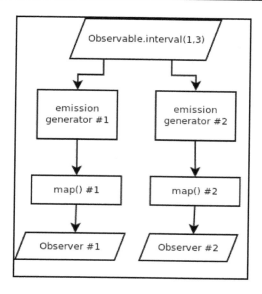

Figure 5.1 - Two separate streams of operations are created for each Observer

Say, you want to emit the same three random integers to both Observers. Your first instinct might be to call `publish()` after `Observable.range()` to yield a `ConnectableObservable`. Then, you may call the `map()` operator on it, followed by the Observers and a `connect()` call. But you will see that this does not achieve our desired result. Each `Observer` still gets three separate random integers:

```
import io.reactivex.Observable;
import io.reactivex.observables.ConnectableObservable;
import java.util.concurrent.ThreadLocalRandom;

public class Launcher {
    public static void main(String[] args) {

        ConnectableObservable<Integer> threeInts =
Observable.range(1,3).publish();

        Observable<Integer> threeRandoms = threeInts.map(i ->
randomInt());

        threeRandoms.subscribe(i -> System.out.println("Observer 1:
" + i));
        threeRandoms.subscribe(i -> System.out.println("Observer 2:
" + i));

        threeInts.connect();
```

```
        }

        public static int randomInt() {
            return ThreadLocalRandom.current().nextInt(100000);
        }
    }
```

The output is as follows:

```
Observer 1: 99350
Observer 2: 96343
Observer 1: 4155
Observer 2: 75273
Observer 1: 14280
Observer 2: 97638
```

This occurred because we multicast *after* Observable.range(), but the multicasting happens before the map() operator. Even though we consolidated to one set of emissions coming from Observable.range(), each Observer is still going to get a separate stream at map(). Everything before publish() was consolidated into a single stream (or more technically, a single proxy Observer). But after publish(), it will fork into separate streams for each Observer again, as shown in the following figure:

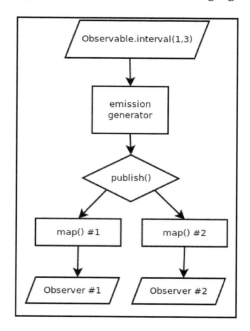

Figure 5.2 - Mulitcasting after Observable.range() will consolidate the interval emissions into a single stream before publish(), but will still fork to two separate streams after publish() for each Observer.

If we want to prevent the `map()` operator from yielding two separate streams for each Observer, we need to call `publish()` after `map()` instead:

```java
import io.reactivex.Observable;
import io.reactivex.observables.ConnectableObservable;
import java.util.concurrent.ThreadLocalRandom;

public class Launcher {
    public static void main(String[] args) {

        ConnectableObservable<Integer> threeRandoms =
Observable.range(1,3)
                .map(i -> randomInt()).publish();

        threeRandoms.subscribe(i -> System.out.println("Observer 1:
" + i));
        threeRandoms.subscribe(i -> System.out.println("Observer 2:
" + i));

        threeRandoms.connect();
    }

    public static int randomInt() {
        return ThreadLocalRandom.current().nextInt(100000);
    }
}
```

The output is as follows:

```
Observer 1: 90125
Observer 2: 90125
Observer 1: 79156
Observer 2: 79156
Observer 1: 76782
Observer 2: 76782
```

That is better! Each `Observer` got the same three random integers, and we have effectively multicast the entire operation right before the two Observers, as shown in the following figure. We now have a single stream instance throughout the entire chain since `map()` is now behind, not in front, of `publish()`:

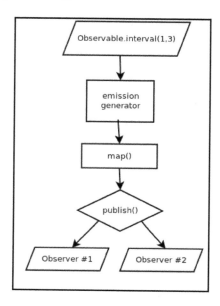

Figure 5.3 - A fully multicast operation that guarantees both Observers get the same emissions since all operators are behind the publish() call

When to multicast

Multicasting is helpful in preventing redundant work being done by multiple Observers and instead makes all Observers subscribe to a single stream, at least to the point where they have operations in common. You may do this to increase performance, reducing memory and CPU usage, or simply because your business logic requires pushing the same emissions to all Observers.

Data-driven cold Observables should only be multicast when you are doing so for performance reasons and have multiple Observers receiving the same data simultaneously. Remember that multicasting creates hot `ConnectableObservables`, and you have to be careful and time the `connect()` call so data is not missed by Observers. Typically in your API, keep your cold Observables cold and call `publish()` when you need to make them hot.

Even if your source `Observable` is hot (such as a UI event in JavaFX or Android), putting operators against that `Observable` can cause redundant work and listeners. It is not necessary to multicast when there is only a single `Observer` (and multicasting can cause unnecessary overhead). But if there are multiple Observers, you need to find the proxy point where you can multicast and consolidate the upstream operations. This point is typically the boundary where Observers have common operations upstream and diverge into different operations downstream.

For instance, you may have one `Observer` that prints the random integers but another one that finds the sum with `reduce()`. At this point, that single stream should, in fact, fork into two separate streams because they are no longer redundant and doing different work, as shown in the following code snippet:

```
import io.reactivex.Observable;
import io.reactivex.observables.ConnectableObservable;
import java.util.concurrent.ThreadLocalRandom;

public class Launcher {
    public static void main(String[] args) {

        ConnectableObservable<Integer> threeRandoms =
Observable.range(1,3)
                .map(i -> randomInt()).publish();

        //Observer 1 - print each random integer
        threeRandoms.subscribe(i -> System.out.println("Observer 1:
" + i));

        //Observer 2 - sum the random integers, then print
        threeRandoms.reduce(0, (total,next) -> total + next)
                .subscribe(i -> System.out.println("Observer 2: " +
i));

        threeRandoms.connect();
    }

    public static int randomInt() {
        return ThreadLocalRandom.current().nextInt(100000);
    }
}
```

The output is as follows:

```
Observer 1: 40021
Observer 1: 78962
Observer 1: 46146
Observer 2: 165129
```

Here is a visual diagram showing the common operations being multicasted:

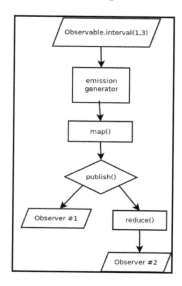

Figure 5.4 - Common operations that are shared between both Observers are put behind publish(), but divergent operations happen after publish()

With a thorough understanding of `ConnectableObservable` and multicasting under our belt, we will move on to some convenience operators that help streamline multicasting.

Automatic connection

There are definitely times you will want to manually call `connect()` on `ConnectableObservable` to precisely control when the emissions start firing. There are convenient operators that automatically call `connect()` for you, but with this convenience, it is important to have awareness of their subscribe timing behaviors. Allowing an `Observable` to dynamically connect can backfire if you are not careful, as emissions can be missed by Observers.

autoConnect()

The autoConnect() operator on ConnectableObservable can be quite handy. For a given ConnectableObservable<T>, calling autoConnect() will return an Observable<T> that will automatically call connect() after a specified number of Observers are subscribed. Since our previous example had two Observers, we can streamline it by calling autoConnect(2) immediately after publish():

```
import io.reactivex.Observable;
import java.util.concurrent.ThreadLocalRandom;

public class Launcher {
    public static void main(String[] args) {

        Observable<Integer> threeRandoms = Observable.range(1,3)
                .map(i -> randomInt())
                .publish()
                .autoConnect(2);

        //Observer 1 - print each random integer
        threeRandoms.subscribe(i -> System.out.println("Observer 1:
" + i));

        //Observer 2 - sum the random integers, then print
        threeRandoms.reduce(0, (total,next) -> total + next)
                .subscribe(i -> System.out.println("Observer 2: " +
i));
    }

    public static int randomInt() {
        return ThreadLocalRandom.current().nextInt(100000);
    }
}
```

The output is as follows:

```
Observer 1: 83428
Observer 1: 77336
Observer 1: 64970
Observer 2: 225734
```

This saved us the trouble of having to save ConnectableObservable and call its connect() method later. Instead, it will start firing when it gets 2 subscriptions, which we have planned and specified as an argument in advance. Obviously, this does not work well when you have an unknown number of Observers and you want all of them to receive all emissions.

Even when all downstream Observers finish or dispose, `autoConnect()` will persist its subscription to the source. If the source is finite and disposes, it will not subscribe to it again when a new `Observer` subscribes downstream. If we add a third `Observer` to our example but keep `autoConnect()` specified at 2 instead of 3, it is likely that the third `Observer` is going to miss the emissions:

```
import io.reactivex.Observable;
import java.util.concurrent.ThreadLocalRandom;

public class Launcher {
    public static void main(String[] args) {

        Observable<Integer> threeRandoms = Observable.range(1,3)
                .map(i -> randomInt()).publish().autoConnect(2);

        //Observer 1 - print each random integer
        threeRandoms.subscribe(i -> System.out.println("Observer 1:
" + i));

        //Observer 2 - sum the random integers, then print
        threeRandoms.reduce(0, (total,next) -> total + next)
                .subscribe(i -> System.out.println("Observer 2: " +
i));

        //Observer 3 - receives nothing
        threeRandoms.subscribe(i -> System.out.println("Observer 3:
" + i);
    }

    public static int randomInt() {
        return ThreadLocalRandom.current().nextInt(100000);
    }
}
```

The output is as follows:

```
Observer 1: 8198
Observer 1: 31718
Observer 1: 97915
Observer 2: 137831
```

Note that if you pass no argument for `numberOfSubscribers`, it will default to 1. This can be helpful if you want it to start firing on the first subscription and do not care about any subsequent Observers missing previous emissions. Here, we `publish` and `autoConnect` the `Observable.interval()`. The first `Observer` starts the firing of emissions, and 3 seconds later, another `Observer` comes in but misses the first few emissions. But it does receive the live emissions from that point on:

```
import io.reactivex.Observable;
import java.util.concurrent.TimeUnit;

public class Launcher {
    public static void main(String[] args) {

        Observable<Long> seconds =
                Observable.interval(1, TimeUnit.SECONDS)
                        .publish()
                        .autoConnect();

        //Observer 1
        seconds.subscribe(i -> System.out.println("Observer 1: " +
i));

        sleep(3000);

        //Observer 2
        seconds.subscribe(i -> System.out.println("Observer 2: " +
i));

        sleep(3000);
    }
    public static void sleep(long millis) {
        try {
            Thread.sleep(millis);
        } catch (InterruptedException e) {
            e.printStackTrace();
        }
    }
}
```

The output is as follows:

```
Observer 1: 0
Observer 1: 1
Observer 1: 2
Observer 1: 3
Observer 2: 3
Observer 1: 4
```

```
Observer 2: 4
Observer 1: 5
Observer 2: 5
```

If you pass 0 to `autoConnect()` for the `numberOfSubscribers` argument, it will start firing immediately and not wait for any `Observers`. This can be handy to start firing emissions immediately without waiting for any Observers.

refCount() and share()

The `refCount()` operator on `ConnectableObservable` is similar to `autoConnect(1)`, which fires after getting one subscription. But there is one important difference; when it has no Observers anymore, it will dispose of itself and start over when a new one comes in. It does not persist the subscription to the source when it has no more Observers, and when another `Observer` follows, it will essentially "start over".

Look at this example: we have `Observable.interval()` emitting every second, and it is multicast with `refCount()`. `Observer` 1 takes five emissions, and `Observer` 2 takes two emissions. We stagger their subscriptions with our `sleep()` function to put three-second gaps between them. Because these two subscriptions are finite due to the `take()` operators, they should be terminated by the time `Observer` 3 comes in, and there should no longer be any previous Observers. Note how `Observer` 3 has started over with a fresh set of intervals starting at 0! Let's take a look at the following code snippet:

```java
import io.reactivex.Observable;
import java.util.concurrent.TimeUnit;

public class Launcher {
    public static void main(String[] args) {

        Observable<Long> seconds =
                Observable.interval(1, TimeUnit.SECONDS)
                        .publish()
                        .refCount();

        //Observer 1
        seconds.take(5)
                .subscribe(l -> System.out.println("Observer 1: " +
l));

        sleep(3000);

        //Observer 2
        seconds.take(2)
```

```
                .subscribe(l -> System.out.println("Observer 2: " +
     l));

          sleep(3000);
          //there should be no more Observers at this point

          //Observer 3
          seconds.subscribe(l -> System.out.println("Observer 3: " +
     l));

          sleep(3000);
       }
     public static void sleep(long millis) {
          try {
              Thread.sleep(millis);
          } catch (InterruptedException e) {
              e.printStackTrace();
          }
       }
     }
```

The output is as follows:

```
     Observer 1: 0
     Observer 1: 1
     Observer 1: 2
     Observer 1: 3
     Observer 2: 3
     Observer 1: 4
     Observer 2: 4
     Observer 3: 0
     Observer 3: 1
     Observer 3: 2
```

Using `refCount()` can be helpful to multicast between multiple Observers but dispose of the upstream connection when no downstream Observers are present anymore. You can also use an alias for `publish().refCount()` using the `share()` operator. This will accomplish the same result:

```
     Observable<Long> seconds =
             Observable.interval(1, TimeUnit.SECONDS).share();
```

Replaying and caching

Multicasting also allows us to cache values that are shared across multiple Observers. This may sound surprising, but when you think about it long enough, you may realize this makes sense. If we are sharing data across multiple Observers, it makes sense that any caching feature would be shared across Observers too. Replaying and caching data is a multicasting activity, and we will explore how to do it safely and efficiently with RxJava.

Replaying

The `replay()` operator is a powerful way to hold onto previous emissions within a certain scope and re-emit them when a new `Observer` comes in. It will return a `ConnectableObservable` that will both multicast emissions as well as emit previous emissions defined in a scope. Previous emissions it caches will fire immediately to a new `Observer` so it is caught up, and then it will fire current emissions from that point forward.

Let's start with a `replay()` with no arguments. This will replay all previous emissions to tardy Observers, and then emit current emissions as soon as the tardy `Observer` is caught up. If we use `Observable.interval()` to emit every second, we can call `replay()` on it to multicast and replay previous integer emissions. Since `replay()` returns `ConnectableObservable`, let's use `autoConnect()` so it starts firing on the first subscription. After 3 seconds, we will bring in a second `Observer`. Look closely at what happens:

```
import io.reactivex.Observable;
import java.util.concurrent.TimeUnit;

public class Launcher {
    public static void main(String[] args) {

        Observable<Long> seconds =
                Observable.interval(1, TimeUnit.SECONDS)
                    .replay()
                    .autoConnect();

        //Observer 1
        seconds.subscribe(l -> System.out.println("Observer 1: " +
l));

        sleep(3000);

        //Observer 2
        seconds.subscribe(l -> System.out.println("Observer 2: " +
```

```
1));

        sleep(3000);
    }
    public static void sleep(long millis) {
        try {
            Thread.sleep(millis);
        } catch (InterruptedException e) {
            e.printStackTrace();
        }
    }
}
```

The output is as follows:

```
Observer 1: 0
Observer 1: 1
Observer 1: 2
Observer 2: 0
Observer 2: 1
Observer 2: 2
Observer 1: 3
Observer 2: 3
Observer 1: 4
Observer 2: 4
Observer 1: 5
Observer 2: 5
```

Did you see that? After 3 seconds, `Observer 2` came in and immediately received the first three emissions it missed: 0, 1, and 2. After that, it receives the same emissions as `Observer 1` going forward. Just note that this can get expensive with memory, as `replay()` will keep caching all emissions it receives. If the source is infinite or you only care about the last previous emissions, you might want to specify a `bufferSize` argument to limit only replaying a certain number of last emissions. If we called `replay(2)` on our second `Observer` to cache the last two emissions, it will not get 0, but it will receive 1 and 2. The 0 fell out of that window and was released from the cache as soon as 2 came in.

The output is as follows:

```
Observer 1: 0
Observer 1: 1
Observer 1: 2
Observer 2: 1
Observer 2: 2
Observer 1: 3
Observer 2: 3
Observer 1: 4
```

```
Observer 2: 4
Observer 1: 5
Observer 2: 5
```

Note that if you always want to persist the cached values in your `replay()` even if there are no subscriptions, use it in conjunction with `autoConnect()`, not `refCount()`. If we emit our `Alpha` through `Epsilon` strings and use `replay(1).autoConnect()` to hold on to the last value, our second `Observer` will only receive the last value, as expected:

```java
import io.reactivex.Observable;

public class Launcher {
    public static void main(String[] args) {

        Observable<String> source =
                Observable.just("Alpha", "Beta", "Gamma",
"Delta", "Epsilon")
                    .replay(1)
                    .autoConnect();

        //Observer 1
        source.subscribe(l -> System.out.println("Observer 1: " +
l));

        //Observer 2
        source.subscribe(l -> System.out.println("Observer 2: " +
l));
    }
}
```

The output is as follows:

```
Observer 1: Alpha
Observer 1: Beta
Observer 1: Gamma
Observer 1: Delta
Observer 1: Epsilon
Observer 2: Epsilon
```

Make a modification here to use `refCount()` instead of `autoConnect()` and see what happens:

```java
Observable<String> source =
        Observable.just("Alpha", "Beta", "Gamma", "Delta",
"Epsilon")
            .replay(1)
            .refCount();
```

The output is as follows:

```
Observer 1: Alpha
Observer 1: Beta
Observer 1: Gamma
Observer 1: Delta
Observer 1: Epsilon
Observer 2: Alpha
Observer 2: Beta
Observer 2: Gamma
Observer 2: Delta
Observer 2: Epsilon
```

What happened here is that `refCount()` causes the cache (and the entire chain) to dispose of and reset the moment `Observer 1` is done, as there are no more Observers. When `Observer 2` came in, it starts all over and emits everything just like it is the first Observer, and another cache is built. This may not be desirable, so you may consider using `autoConnect()` to persist the state of `replay()` and not have it dispose of when no Observers are present.

There are other overloads for `replay()`, particularly a time-based window you can specify. Here, we construct an `Observable.interval()` that emits every 300 milliseconds and subscribe to it. We also map each emitted consecutive integer into the elapsed milliseconds. We will replay only the last 1 second of emissions for each new `Observer`, which we will bring in after 2 seconds:

```java
import io.reactivex.Observable;
import java.util.concurrent.TimeUnit;

public class Launcher {
    public static void main(String[] args) {

        Observable<Long> seconds =
                Observable.interval(300, TimeUnit.MILLISECONDS)
                        .map(l -> (l + 1) * 300) // map to elapsed
milliseconds
                        .replay(1, TimeUnit.SECONDS)
                        .autoConnect();

        //Observer 1
        seconds.subscribe(l -> System.out.println("Observer 1: " +
l));

        sleep(2000);

        //Observer 2
```

```
                 seconds.subscribe(l -> System.out.println("Observer 2: " +
          l));

                 sleep(1000);
            }
        public static void sleep(long millis) {
            try {
                Thread.sleep(millis);
            } catch (InterruptedException e) {
                e.printStackTrace();
            }
        }
    }
```

The output is as follows:

```
Observer 1: 300
Observer 1: 600
Observer 1: 900
Observer 1: 1200
Observer 1: 1500
Observer 1: 1800
Observer 2: 1500
Observer 2: 1800
Observer 1: 2100
Observer 2: 2100
Observer 1: 2400
Observer 2: 2400
Observer 1: 2700
Observer 2: 2700
Observer 1: 3000
Observer 2: 3000
```

Look closely at the output, and you will see that when `Observer 2` comes in, it immediately receives emissions that happened in the last second, which were 1500 and 1800. After these two values are replayed, it receives the same emissions as `Observer 1` from that point on.

You can also specify a `bufferSize` argument on top of a time interval, so only a certain number of last emissions are buffered within that time period. If we modify our example to only replay one emission that occurred within the last second, it should only replay `1800` to `Observer 2`:

```
        Observable<Long> seconds =
                Observable.interval(300, TimeUnit.MILLISECONDS)
                        .map(l -> (l + 1) * 300) // map to elapsed
        milliseconds
```

```
.replay(1, 1, TimeUnit.SECONDS)
.autoConnect();
```

The output is as follows:

```
Observer 1: 300
Observer 1: 600
Observer 1: 900
Observer 1: 1200
Observer 1: 1500
Observer 1: 1800
Observer 2: 1800
Observer 1: 2100
Observer 2: 2100
Observer 1: 2400
Observer 2: 2400
Observer 1: 2700
Observer 2: 2700
Observer 1: 3000
Observer 2: 3000
```

Caching

When you want to cache all emissions indefinitely for the long term and do not need to control the subscription behavior to the source with `ConnectableObservable`, you can use the `cache()` operator. It will subscribe to the source on the first downstream `Observer` that subscribes and hold all values indefinitely. This makes it an unlikely candidate for infinite Observables or large amounts of data that could tax your memory:

```java
import io.reactivex.Observable;

public class Launcher {
    public static void main(String[] args) {

        Observable<Integer> cachedRollingTotals =
                Observable.just(6, 2, 5, 7, 1, 4, 9, 8, 3)
                    .scan(0, (total,next) -> total + next)
                    .cache();

        cachedRollingTotals.subscribe(System.out::println);
    }
}
```

You can also call `cacheWithInitialCapacity()` and specify the number of elements to be expected in the cache. This will optimize the buffer for that size of elements in advance:

```
Observable<Integer> cachedRollingTotals =
        Observable.just(6, 2, 5, 7, 1, 4, 9, 8, 3)
            .scan(0, (total,next) -> total + next)
            .cacheWithInitialCapacity(9);
```

Again, do not use `cache()` unless you really want to hold all elements indefinitely and do not have plans to dispose it at any point. Otherwise, prefer `replay()` so you can more finely control cache sizing and windows as well as disposal policies.

Subjects

Before we discuss Subjects, it would be remiss to not highlight, they have use cases but beginners often use them for the wrong ones, and end up in convoluted situations. As you will learn, they are both an `Observer` and an `Observable`, acting as a proxy mulitcasting device (kind of like an event bus). They do have their place in reactive programming, but you should strive to exhaust your other options before utilizing them. Erik Meijer, the creator of ReactiveX, described them as the *"mutable variables of reactive programming"*. Just like mutable variables are necessary at times even though you should strive for immutability, Subjects are sometimes a necessary tool to reconcile imperative paradigms with reactive ones.

But before we discuss when to and when not to use them, let's take a look at what they exactly do.

PublishSubject

There are a couple implementations of `Subject`, which is an abstract type that implements both `Observable` and `Observer`. This means that you can manually call `onNext()`, `onComplete()`, and `onError()` on a `Subject`, and it will, in turn, pass those events downstream toward its Observers.

The simplest `Subject` type is the `PublishSubject`, which, like all Subjects, hotly broadcasts to its downstream Observers. Other `Subject` types add more behaviors, but `PublishSubject` is the "vanilla" type, if you will.

We can declare a `Subject<String>`, create an `Observer` that maps its lengths and subscribes to it, and then call `onNext()` to pass three strings. We can also call `onComplete()` to communicate that no more events will be passed through this `Subject`:

```
import io.reactivex.subjects.PublishSubject;
import io.reactivex.subjects.Subject;

public class Launcher {
    public static void main(String[] args) {

        Subject<String> subject = PublishSubject.create();

        subject.map(String::length)
                .subscribe(System.out::println);

        subject.onNext("Alpha");
        subject.onNext("Beta");
        subject.onNext("Gamma");
        subject.onComplete();
    }
}
```

The output is as follows:

```
5
4
5
```

This shows Subjects act like magical devices that can bridge imperative programming with reactive programming, and you would be right. Next, let's look at cases of when to and when not to use Subjects.

When to use Subjects

More likely, you will use Subjects to eagerly subscribe to an unknown number of multiple source Observables and consolidate their emissions as a single `Observable`. Since Subjects are an `Observer`, you can pass them to a `subscribe()` method easily. This can be helpful in modularized code bases where decoupling between Observables and Observers takes place and executing `Observable.merge()` is not that easy. Here, I use `Subject` to merge and multicast two `Observable` interval sources:

```
import io.reactivex.Observable;
import io.reactivex.subjects.PublishSubject;
import io.reactivex.subjects.Subject;
import java.util.concurrent.TimeUnit;
```

```
public class Launcher {
    public static void main(String[] args) {

        Observable<String> source1 =
                Observable.interval(1, TimeUnit.SECONDS)
                    .map(l -> (l + 1) + " seconds");

        Observable<String> source2 =
                Observable.interval(300, TimeUnit.MILLISECONDS)
                    .map(l -> ((l + 1) * 300) + " milliseconds");

        Subject<String> subject = PublishSubject.create();

        subject.subscribe(System.out::println);

        source1.subscribe(subject);
        source2.subscribe(subject);

        sleep(3000);
    }

    public static void sleep(long millis) {
        try {
            Thread.sleep(millis);
        } catch (InterruptedException e) {
            e.printStackTrace();
        }
    }
}
```

The output is as follows:

```
300 milliseconds
600 milliseconds
900 milliseconds
1 seconds
1200 milliseconds
1500 milliseconds
1800 milliseconds
2 seconds
2100 milliseconds
2400 milliseconds
2700 milliseconds
3 seconds
3000 milliseconds
```

Of course, I could use `Observable.merge()` to accomplish this (and technically for this case, I should). But when you have modularized code managed through dependency injection or other decoupling mechanisms, you may not have your `Observable` sources prepared in advance to put in `Observable.merge()`. For example, I could have a JavaFX application that has a refresh event coming from a menu bar, button, or a keystroke combination. I can declare these event sources as Observables and subscribe them to a `Subject` in a backing class to consolidate the event streams without any hard coupling.

Another note to make is that the first `Observable` to call `onComplete()` on `Subject` is going to cease other `Observables` from pushing their emissions, and downstream cancellation requests are ignored. This means that you will most likely use Subjects for infinite, event-driven (that is, user action-driven) Observables. That being said, we will next look at cases where Subjects become prone to abuse.

When Subjects go wrong

Hopefully, you will feel that our earlier `Subject` example emitting `Alpha`, `Beta`, and `Gamma` is counterintuitive and backward considering how we have architected our reactive applications so far, and you would be right to think that way. We did not define the source emissions until the end after all the Observers are set up, and the process no longer reads left-to-right, top-to-bottom. Since Subjects are hot, executing the `onNext()` calls before the Observers are set up would result in these emissions being missed with our `Subject`. If you move the `onNext()` calls like this, you will not get any output because the `Observer` will miss these emissions:

```java
import io.reactivex.subjects.PublishSubject;
import io.reactivex.subjects.Subject;

public class Launcher {
    public static void main(String[] args) {

        Subject<String> subject = PublishSubject.create();

        subject.onNext("Alpha");
        subject.onNext("Beta");
        subject.onNext("Gamma");
        subject.onComplete();

        subject.map(String::length)
                .subscribe(System.out::println);
    }
}
```

This shows that Subjects can be somewhat haphazard and dangerous, especially if you expose them to your entire code base and any external code can call onNext() to pass emissions. For instance, say our Subject was exposed to an external API and something can arbitrarily pass the emission Puppy on top of Alpha, Beta, and Gamma. If we want our source to only emit these Greek letters, it is prone to receiving accidental or unwanted emissions. Reactive programming only maintains integrity when source Observables are derived from a well-defined and predictable source. Subjects are not disposable either, as they have no public dispose() method and will not release their sources in the event that dispose() is called downstream.

It is much better to keep data-driven sources like this cold and to multicast using publish() or replay() if you want to make them hot. When you need to use Subject, cast it down to Observable or just do not expose it at all. You can also wrap a Subject inside a class of some sorts and have methods pass the events to it.

Serializing Subjects

A critical *gotcha* to note with Subjects is this: the onSubscribe(), onNext(), onError(), and onComplete() calls are not threadsafe! If you have multiple threads calling these four methods, emissions could start to overlap and break the Observable contract, which demands that emissions happen sequentially. If this happens, a good practice to adopt is to call toSerialized() on Subject to yield a safely serialized Subject implementation (backed by the private SerializedSubject). This will safely sequentialize concurrent event calls so no train wrecks occur downstream:

```
Subject<String> subject =
        PublishSubject.<String>create().toSerialized();
```

Unfortunately, due to limitations with the Java compiler (including Java 8), we have to explicitly declare the type parameter String for our create() factory earlier. The compiler's type inference does not cascade beyond more than one method invocation, so having two invocations as previously demonstrated would have a compilation error without an explicit type declaration.

BehaviorSubject

There are a few other flavors of Subjects. Aside from the commonly used `PublishSubject`, there is also `BehaviorSubject`. It behaves almost the same way as `PublishSubject`, but it will replay the last emitted item to each new `Observer` downstream. This is somewhat like putting `replay(1).autoConnect()` after a `PublishSubject`, but it consolidates these operations into a single optimized `Subject` implementation that subscribes eagerly to the source:

```
import io.reactivex.subjects.BehaviorSubject;
import io.reactivex.subjects.Subject;

public class Launcher {
    public static void main(String[] args) {

        Subject<String> subject =
                BehaviorSubject.create();

        subject.subscribe(s -> System.out.println("Observer 1: " +
s));

        subject.onNext("Alpha");
        subject.onNext("Beta");
        subject.onNext("Gamma");

        subject.subscribe(s -> System.out.println("Observer 2: " +
s));
    }
}
```

The output is as follows:

```
Observer 1: Alpha
Observer 1: Beta
Observer 1: Gamma
Observer 2: Gamma
```

Here, you can see that `Observer 2` received the last emission `Gamma` even though it missed the three emissions that `Observer 1` received. If you find yourself needing a `Subject` and want to cache the last emission for new Observers, you will want to use a `BehaviorSubject`.

ReplaySubject

ReplaySubject is similar to PublishSubject followed by a cache() operator. It immediately captures emissions regardless of the presence of downstream Observers and optimizes the caching to occur inside the Subject itself:

```java
import io.reactivex.subjects.ReplaySubject;
import io.reactivex.subjects.Subject;

public class Launcher {
    public static void main(String[] args) {

        Subject<String> subject =
                ReplaySubject.create();

        subject.subscribe(s -> System.out.println("Observer 1: " +
s));

        subject.onNext("Alpha");
        subject.onNext("Beta");
        subject.onNext("Gamma");
        subject.onComplete();

        subject.subscribe(s -> System.out.println("Observer 2: " +
s));
    }
}
```

The output is as follows:

```
Observer 1: Alpha
Observer 1: Beta
Observer 1: Gamma
Observer 2: Alpha
Observer 2: Beta
Observer 2: Gamma
```

Obviously, just like using a parameterless replay() or a cache() operator, you need to be wary of using this with a large volume of emissions or infinite sources because it will cache them all and take up memory.

AsyncSubject

`AsyncSubject` has a highly tailored, finite-specific behavior: it will only push the last value it receives, followed by an `onComplete()` event:

```java
import io.reactivex.subjects.AsyncSubject;
import io.reactivex.subjects.Subject;

public class Launcher {
    public static void main(String[] args) {

        Subject<String> subject =
                AsyncSubject.create();

        subject.subscribe(s ->
        System.out.println("Observer 1: " + s),
                Throwable::printStackTrace,
                () -> System.out.println("Observer 1 done!")
        );

        subject.onNext("Alpha");
        subject.onNext("Beta");
        subject.onNext("Gamma");
        subject.onComplete();

        subject.subscribe(s ->
        System.out.println("Observer 2: " + s),
                Throwable::printStackTrace,
                () -> System.out.println("Observer 2 done!")
        );
    }
}
```

The output is as follows:

```
Observer 1: Gamma
Observer 1 done!
Observer 2: Gamma
Observer 2 done!
```

As you can tell from the preceding command, the last value to be pushed to `AsyncSubject` was `Gamma` before `onComplete()` was called. Therefore, it only emitted `Gamma` to all Observers. This is a `Subject` you do not want to use with infinite sources since it only emits when `onComplete()` is called.

AsyncSubject resembles CompletableFuture from Java 8 as it will do a computation that you can choose to observe for completion and get the value. You can also imitate AsyncSubject using takeLast(1).replay(1) on an Observable. Try to use this approach first before resorting to AsyncSubject.

UnicastSubject

An interesting and possibly helpful kind of Subject is UnicastSubject. A UnicastSubject, like all Subjects, will be used to observe and subscribe to the sources. But it will buffer all the emissions it receives until an Observer subscribes to it, and then it will release all these emissions to the Observer and clear its cache:

```java
import io.reactivex.Observable;
import io.reactivex.subjects.ReplaySubject;
import io.reactivex.subjects.Subject;
import io.reactivex.subjects.UnicastSubject;
import java.util.concurrent.TimeUnit;

public class Launcher {
    public static void main(String[] args) {

        Subject<String> subject =
                UnicastSubject.create();

        Observable.interval(300, TimeUnit.MILLISECONDS)
                .map(l -> ((l + 1) * 300) + " milliseconds")
                .subscribe(subject);

        sleep(2000);

        subject.subscribe(s -> System.out.println("Observer 1: " +
s));

        sleep(2000);

    }
    public static void sleep(long millis) {
        try {
            Thread.sleep(millis);
        } catch (InterruptedException e) {
            e.printStackTrace();
        }
    }
}
```

The output is as follows:

```
Observer 1: 300 milliseconds
Observer 1: 600 milliseconds
Observer 1: 900 milliseconds
Observer 1: 1200 milliseconds
Observer 1: 1500 milliseconds
Observer 1: 1800 milliseconds
Observer 1: 2100 milliseconds
Observer 1: 2400 milliseconds
Observer 1: 2700 milliseconds
Observer 1: 3000 milliseconds
Observer 1: 3300 milliseconds
Observer 1: 3600 milliseconds
Observer 1: 3900 milliseconds
```

When you run this code, you will see that after 2 seconds, the first six emissions are released immediately to the `Observer` when it subscribes. Then, it will receive live emissions from that point on. But there is one important property of `UnicastSubject`; it will only work with one `Observer` and will throw an error for any subsequent ones. Logically, this makes sense because it is designed to release buffered emissions from its internal queue once it gets an `Observer`. But when these cached emissions are released, they cannot be released again to a second `Observer` since they are already gone. If you want a second `Observer` to receive missed emissions, you might as well use `ReplaySubject`. The benefit of `UnicastSubject` is that it clears its buffer, and consequently frees the memory used for that buffer, once it gets an `Observer`.

If you want to support more than one `Observer` and just let subsequent Observers receive the live emissions without receiving the missed emissions, you can trick it by calling `publish()` to create a single `Observer` proxy that multicasts to more than one `Observer` as shown in the following code snippet:

```java
import io.reactivex.Observable;
import io.reactivex.subjects.Subject;
import io.reactivex.subjects.UnicastSubject;
import java.util.concurrent.TimeUnit;

public class Launcher {
    public static void main(String[] args) {

        Subject<String> subject =
                UnicastSubject.create();

        Observable.interval(300, TimeUnit.MILLISECONDS)
                .map(l -> ((l + 1) * 300) + " milliseconds")
                .subscribe(subject);
```

```
            sleep(2000);

            //multicast to support multiple Observers
            Observable<String> multicast =
    subject.publish().autoConnect();

            //bring in first Observer
            multicast.subscribe(s -> System.out.println("Observer 1: "
    + s));
            sleep(2000);

            //bring in second Observer
            multicast.subscribe(s -> System.out.println("Observer 2: "
    + s));
            sleep(1000);
        }
        public static void sleep(long millis) {
            try {
                Thread.sleep(millis);
            } catch (InterruptedException e) {
                e.printStackTrace();
            }
        }
    }
```

The output is as follows:

```
Observer 1: 300 milliseconds
Observer 1: 600 milliseconds
Observer 1: 900 milliseconds
Observer 1: 1200 milliseconds
...
Observer 1: 3900 milliseconds
Observer 1: 4200 milliseconds
Observer 2: 4200 milliseconds
Observer 1: 4500 milliseconds
Observer 2: 4500 milliseconds
```

Summary

In this chapter, we covered multicasting using `ConnectableObservable` and `Subject`. The biggest takeaway is that `Observable` operators result in separate streams of events for each `Observer` that subscribes. If you want to consolidate these multiple streams into a single stream to prevent redundant work, the best way is to call `publish()` on an `Observable` to yield `ConnectableObservable`. You can then manually call `connect()` to fire emissions once your Observers are set up or automatically trigger a connection using `autoConnect()` or `refCount()`.

Mutlicasting also enables replaying and caching, so tardy Observers can receive missed emissions. Subjects provide a means to multicast and cache emissions as well, but you should only utilize them if existing operators cannot achieve what you want.

In the next chapter, we will start working with concurrency. This is where RxJava truly shines and is often the selling point of reactive programming.

6
Concurrency and Parallelization

The need for concurrency has grown rapidly in the past 10 years and has become a necessity for every professional Java programmer. Concurrency (also called **multithreading**) is essentially multitasking, where you have several processes executing at the same time. If you want to fully utilize your hardware's computing power (whether it is a phone, server, laptop, or desktop computer), you need to learn how to multithread and leverage concurrency. Thankfully, RxJava makes concurrency much easier and safer to achieve.

In this chapter, we will cover the following:

- An overview of concurrency and its necessity
- subscribeOn()
- observeOn()
- Parallelization
- unsubscribeOn()

Why concurrency is necessary

In simpler times, computers had only one CPU and this marginalized the need for concurrency. Hardware manufacturers successfully found ways to make CPUs faster, and this made single-threaded programs faster. But eventually, this had a diminishing return, and manufacturers found they could increase computational power by putting multiple CPUs in a device. From desktops and laptops to servers and smartphones, most hardware nowadays sports multiple CPUs, or cores.

For developers, this is a major disruption in building software and how coding is done. Single-threaded software is easier to code and works fine on a single-core device. But a single-threaded program on a multi-core device will only use one core, leaving the others not utilized. If you want your program to scale, it needs to be coded in a way that utilizes all cores available in a processor.

However, concurrency is traditionally not easy to implement. If you have several independent processes that do not interact with each other, it is easier to accomplish. But when resources, especially mutable objects, are shared across different threads and processes, chaos can ensue if locking and synchronization are not carefully implemented. Not only can threads race each other chaotically to read and change an object's properties, but a thread may simply not see a value changed by another thread! This is why you should strive to make your objects immutable and make as many properties and variables `final` as possible. This ensures that properties and variables are thread-safe and anything that is mutable should be synchronized or at least utilize the `volatile` keyword.

Thankfully, RxJava makes concurrency and multithreading much easier and safer. There are ways you can undermine the safety it provides, but generally, RxJava handles concurrency safely for you mainly using two operators: `subscribeOn()` and `observeOn()`. As we will find out in this chapter, other operators such as `flatMap()` can be combined with these two operators to create powerful concurrency dataflows.

 While RxJava can help you make safe and powerful concurrent applications with little effort, it can be helpful to be aware of the traps and pitfalls in multithreading. Joshua Bloch's famous book *Effective Java* is an excellent resource that every Java developer should have, and it succinctly covers best practices for concurrent applications. If you want deep knowledge in Java concurrency, ensure that you read Brian Goetz' *Java Concurrency in Practice* as well.

Concurrency in a nutshell

Concurrency, also called **multithreading,** can be applied in a variety of ways. Usually, the motivation behind concurrency is to run more than one task simultaneously in order to get work done faster. As we discussed in the beginning of this book, concurrency can also help our code resemble the real world more, where multiple activities occur at the same time.

First, let's cover some fundamental concepts behind concurrency.

One common application of concurrency is to run different tasks simultaneously. Imagine that you have three yard chores: mow the lawn, trim the trees, and pull the weeds. If you do these three chores by yourself, you can only do one chore at a time. You cannot mow the lawn and trim the trees simultaneously. You have to sequentially mow the lawn first, then trim the trees, then pull the weeds. But if you have a friend to help you, one of you can mow the lawn while the other trims the trees. The first one of you to get done can then move on to the third task: pulling the weeds. This way, these three tasks get done much more quickly.

Metaphorically, you and your friend are **threads**. You do work together. Collectively, you both are a **thread pool** ready to execute tasks. The chores are tasks that are queued for the thread pool, which you can execute two at a time. If you have more threads, your thread pool will have more bandwidth to take on more tasks concurrently. However, depending on how many cores your computer has (as well as the nature of the tasks), you can only have so many threads. Threads are expensive to create, maintain, and destroy, and there is a diminishing return in performance as you create them excessively. That is why it is better to have a thread pool to *reuse* threads and have them work a queue of tasks.

Understanding parallelization

Parallelization (also called parallelism) is a broad term that could encompass the preceding scenario. In effect, you and your friend are executing two tasks at the same time and are thus processing in parallel. But let's apply parallelization to processing multiple identical tasks at the same time. Take, for example, a grocery store that has 10 customers waiting in a line for checkout. These 10 customers represent 10 tasks that are identical. They each need to check out their groceries. If a cashier represents a thread, we can have multiple cashiers to process these customers more quickly. But like threads, cashiers are expensive. We do not want to create a cashier for each customer, but rather pool a fixed number of cashiers and reuse them. If we have five cashiers, we can process five customers at a time while the rest wait in the queue. The moment a cashier finishes a customer, they can process the next one.

This is essentially what parallelization achieves. If you have 1000 objects and you need to perform an expensive calculation on each one, you can use five threads to process five objects at a time and potentially finish this process five times more quickly. It is critical to pool these threads and reuse them because creating 1000 threads to process these 1000 objects could overwhelm your memory and crash your program.

With a conceptual understanding of concurrency, we will move on to discussing how it is achieved in RxJava.

Introducing RxJava concurrency

Concurrency in RxJava is simple to execute, but somewhat abstract to understand. By default, Observables execute work on the immediate thread, which is the thread that declared the `Observer` and subscribed it. In many of our earlier examples, this was the main thread that kicked off our `main()` method.

But as hinted in a few other examples, not all Observables will fire on the immediate thread. Remember those times we used `Observable.interval()`, as shown in the following code? Let's take a look:

```
import io.reactivex.Observable;
import java.util.concurrent.TimeUnit;

public class Launcher {

    public static void main(String[] args) {

        Observable.interval(1, TimeUnit.SECONDS)
                .map(i -> i + " Mississippi")
                .subscribe(System.out::println);

        sleep(5000);
    }
    public static void sleep(long millis) {
        try {
            Thread.sleep(millis);
        } catch (InterruptedException e) {
            e.printStackTrace();
        }
    }
}
```

The output is as follows:

```
0 Mississippi
1 Mississippi
2 Mississippi
3 Mississippi
4 Mississippi
```

This `Observable` will actually fire on a thread other than the main one. Effectively, the main thread will kick-off `Observable.interval()`, but not wait for it to complete because it is operating on its own separate thread now. This, in fact, makes it a concurrent application because it is leveraging two threads now. If we do not call a `sleep()` method to pause the main thread, it will charge to the end of the `main()` method and quit the application before the intervals have a chance to fire.

Usually, concurrency is useful only when you have long-running or calculation-intensive processes. To help us learn concurrency without creating noisy examples, we will create a helper method called `intenseCalculation()` to emulate a long-running process. It will simply accept any value and then sleep for 0-3 seconds and then return the same value. Sleeping a thread, or pausing it, is a great way to simulate a busy thread doing work:

```
public static <T> T intenseCalculation(T value) {
    sleep(ThreadLocalRandom.current().nextInt(3000));
    return value;
}
public static void sleep(long millis) {
    try {
        Thread.sleep(millis);
    } catch (InterruptedException e) {
        e.printStackTrace();
    }
}
```

Let's create two Observables with two Observers subscribing to them. In each operation. map each emission to the `intenseCalculation()` method in order to slow them down:

```
import rx.Observable;
import java.util.concurrent.ThreadLocalRandom;
import io.reactivex.Observable;

public class Launcher {

    public static void main(String[] args) {

        Observable.just("Alpha", "Beta", "Gamma", "Delta",
"Epsilon")
                .map(s -> intenseCalculation((s)))
                .subscribe(System.out::println);

        Observable.range(1,6)
                .map(s -> intenseCalculation((s)))
                .subscribe(System.out::println);
    }
```

```
public static <T> T intenseCalculation(T value) {
    sleep(ThreadLocalRandom.current().nextInt(3000));
    return value;
}
public static void sleep(long millis) {
    try {
        Thread.sleep(millis);
    } catch (InterruptedException e) {
        e.printStackTrace();
    }
}
}
```

The output is as follows:

```
Alpha
Beta
Gamma
Delta
Epsilon
1
2
3
4
5
6
```

Note how both Observables fire emissions slowly as each one is slowed by 0-3 seconds in the map() operation. More importantly, note how the first Observable firing Alpha, Beta, Gamma must finish first and call onComplete() before firing the second Observable emitting the numbers 1 through 6. If we fire both Observables at the same time rather than waiting for one to complete before starting the other, we could get this operation done much more quickly.

We can achieve this using the subscribeOn() operator, which suggests to the source to fire emissions on a specified Scheduler. In this case, let us use Schedulers.computation(), which pools a fixed number of threads appropriate for computation operations. It will provide a thread to push emissions for each Observer. When onComplete() is called, the thread will be given back to Scheduler so it can be reused elsewhere:

```
import io.reactivex.Observable;
import io.reactivex.schedulers.Schedulers;
import java.util.concurrent.ThreadLocalRandom;

public class Launcher {
```

```
public static void main(String[] args) {

    Observable.just("Alpha", "Beta", "Gamma", "Delta",
"Epsilon")
            .subscribeOn(Schedulers.computation())
            .map(s -> intenseCalculation((s)))
            .subscribe(System.out::println);

    Observable.range(1,6)
            .subscribeOn(Schedulers.computation())
            .map(s -> intenseCalculation((s)))
            .subscribe(System.out::println);

    sleep(20000);
}

public static <T> T intenseCalculation(T value) {
    sleep(ThreadLocalRandom.current().nextInt(3000));
    return value;
}
public static void sleep(long millis) {
    try {
        Thread.sleep(millis);
    } catch (InterruptedException e) {
        e.printStackTrace();
    }
}
}
```

The output is as follows (yours may be different):

```
1
2
Alpha
3
4
Beta
5
Gamma
Delta
6
Epsilon
```

Your output will likely be different from mine due to the random sleeping times. But note how both operations are firing simultaneously now, allowing the program to finish much more quickly. Rather than the main thread becoming occupied, executing emissions for the first `Observable` before moving onto the second, it will fire-off both Observables immediately and move on. It will not wait for either `Observable` to complete.

Having multiple processes occurring at the same time is what makes an application concurrent. It can result in much greater efficiency as it will utilize more cores and finish work more quickly. Concurrency also makes code models more powerful and more representative of how our world works, where multiple activities occur simultaneously.

Something else that is exciting about RxJava is its operators (at least the official ones and the custom ones built properly). They can work with Observables on different threads safely. Even operators and factories that combine multiple Observables, such as `merge()` and `zip()`, will safely combine emissions pushed by different threads. For instance, we can use `zip()` on our two Observables in the preceding example even if they are emitting on two separate computation threads:

```java
import io.reactivex.Observable;
import io.reactivex.schedulers.Schedulers;
import java.util.concurrent.ThreadLocalRandom;

public class Launcher {

    public static void main(String[] args) {

        Observable<String> source1 =
                Observable.just("Alpha", "Beta", "Gamma", "Delta",
"Epsilon")
                    .subscribeOn(Schedulers.computation())
                    .map(s -> intenseCalculation((s)));

        Observable<Integer> source2 =
                Observable.range(1,6)
                    .subscribeOn(Schedulers.computation())
                    .map(s -> intenseCalculation((s)));

        Observable.zip(source1, source2, (s,i) -> s + "-" + i)
                .subscribe(System.out::println);

        sleep(20000);
    }

    public static <T> T intenseCalculation(T value) {
        sleep(ThreadLocalRandom.current().nextInt(3000));
        return value;
```

```
        }
        public static void sleep(long millis) {
            try {
                Thread.sleep(millis);
            } catch (InterruptedException e) {
                e.printStackTrace();
            }
        }
    }
```

The output is as follows:

```
Alpha-1
Beta-2
Gamma-3
Delta-4
Epsilon-5
```

Being able to split and combine Observables happening on different threads is powerful and eliminates the pain points of callbacks. Observables are agnostic to whatever thread they work on, making concurrency easy to implement, configure, and evolve at any time.

 When you start making reactive applications concurrent, a subtle complication can creep in. By default, a non-concurrent application will have one thread doing all the work from the source to the final `Observer`. But having multiple threads can cause emissions to be produced faster than an `Observer` can consume them (for instance, the `zip()` operator may have one source producing emissions faster than the other). This can overwhelm the program and memory can run out as backlogged emissions are cached by certain operators. When you are working with a high volume of emissions (more than 10,000) and leveraging concurrency, you will likely want to use Flowables instead of Observables, which we will cover in `Chapter 8`, *Flowables and Backpressure*.

Keeping an application alive

Up until this point, we have used a `sleep()` method to keep concurrent reactive applications from quitting prematurely, just long enough for the Observables to fire. If you are using Android, JavaFX, or other frameworks that manage their own non-daemon threads, this is not a concern as the application will be kept alive for you. But if you are simply firing off a program with a `main()` method and you want to kick off long-running or infinite Observables, you may have to keep the main thread alive for a period longer than 5-20 seconds. Sometimes, you may want to keep it alive indefinitely.

One way to keep an application alive indefinitely is to simply pass `Long.MAX_VALUE` to the `Thread.sleep()` method, as shown in the following code, where we have `Observable.interval()` firing emissions forever:

```java
import io.reactivex.Observable;
import java.util.concurrent.ThreadLocalRandom;
import java.util.concurrent.TimeUnit;

public class Launcher {

    public static void main(String[] args) {

        Observable.interval(1, TimeUnit.SECONDS)
                .map(l -> intenseCalculation((l)))
                .subscribe(System.out::println);

        sleep(Long.MAX_VALUE);
    }

    public static <T> T intenseCalculation(T value) {
        sleep(ThreadLocalRandom.current().nextInt(3000));
        return value;
    }
    public static void sleep(long millis) {
        try {
            Thread.sleep(millis);
        } catch (InterruptedException e) {
            e.printStackTrace();
        }
    }
}
```

Okay, sleeping your main thread for 9,223,372,036,854,775,807 milliseconds is not forever, but that is the equivalent to 292,471,208.7 years. For the purposes of sleeping a thread, that might as well be forever!

There are ways to keep an application alive only long enough for a subscription to finish. With classical concurrency tools discussed in Brian Goetz' book *Java Concurrency in Practice*, you can keep an application alive using `CountDownLatch` to wait for two subscriptions to finish. But an easier way is to use blocking operators in RxJava.

You can use blocking operators to stop the declaring thread and wait for emissions. Usually, blocking operators are used for unit testing (as we will discuss in Chapter 10, *Testing and Debugging*), and they can attract antipatterns if used improperly in production. However, keeping an application alive based on the life cycle of a finite Observable subscription is a valid case to use a blocking operator. As shown here, blockingSubscribe() can be used in place of subscribe() to stop and wait for onComplete() to be called before the main thread is allowed to proceed and exit the application:

```
import io.reactivex.schedulers.Schedulers;
import io.reactivex.Observable;
import java.util.concurrent.ThreadLocalRandom;

public class Launcher {

    public static void main(String[] args) {

        Observable.just("Alpha", "Beta", "Gamma", "Delta",
"Epsilon")
                .subscribeOn(Schedulers.computation())
                .map(Launcher::intenseCalculation)
                .blockingSubscribe(System.out::println,
                        Throwable::printStackTrace,
                        () -> System.out.println("Done!"));
    }

    public static <T> T intenseCalculation(T value) {
        sleep(ThreadLocalRandom.current().nextInt(3000));
        return value;
    }
    public static void sleep(int millis) {
        try {
            Thread.sleep(millis);
        } catch (InterruptedException e) {
            e.printStackTrace();
        }
    }
}
```

The output is as follows:

```
Alpha
Beta
Gamma
Delta
Epsilon
Done!
```

We will discuss blocking operators in further detail in Chapter 10, *Testing and Debugging*. For the remainder of this chapter, we will explore concurrency in detail using the subscribeOn() and observeOn() operators. But first, we will cover the different Scheduler types available in RxJava.

Understanding Schedulers

As discussed earlier, thread pools are a collection of threads. Depending on the policy of that thread pool, threads may be persisted and maintained so they can be reused. A queue of tasks is then executed by that thread pool.

Some thread pools hold a fixed number of threads (such as the computation() one we used earlier), while others dynamically create and destroy threads as needed. Typically in Java, you use an ExecutorService as your thread pool. However, RxJava implements its own concurrency abstraction called Scheduler. It define methods and rules that an actual concurrency provider such as an ExecutorService or actor system must obey. The construct flexibly makes RxJava non-opinionated on the source of concurrency.

Many of the default Scheduler implementations can be found in the Schedulers static factory class. For a given Observer, a Scheduler will provide a thread from its pool that will push the emissions. When onComplete() is called, the operation will be disposed of and the thread will be given back to the pool, where it may be persisted and reused by another Observer.

> To keep this book practical, we will only look at Schedulers in their natural environment: being used with subscribeOn() and observeOn(). If you want to learn more about Schedulers and how they work in isolation, refer to Appendix X to learn more.

Here are a few Scheduler types in RxJava. There are also some common third-party ones available in other libraries such as RxAndroid (covered in Chapter 11, *RxJava for Android*) and RxJavaFX (covered later in this chapter).

Computation

We already saw the computation `Scheduler`, which you can get the global instance of by calling `Schedulers.computation()`. This will maintain a fixed number of threads based on the processor count available to your Java session, making it appropriate for computational tasks. Computational tasks (such as math, algorithms, and complex logic) may utilize cores to their fullest extent. Therefore, there is no benefit in having more worker threads than available cores to perform such work, and the computational `Scheduler` will ensure that:

```
Observable.just("Alpha", "Beta", "Gamma", "Delta", "Epsilon")
    .subscribeOn(Schedulers.computation());
```

When you are unsure how many tasks will be executed concurrently or are simply unsure which `Scheduler` is the right one to use, prefer the computation one by default.

 A number of operators and factories will use the computation `Scheduler` by default unless you specify a different one as an argument. These include one or more overloads for `interval()`, `delay()`, `timer()`, `timeout()`, `buffer()`, `take()`, `skip()`, `takeWhile()`, `skipWhile()`, `window()`, and a few others.

IO

IO tasks such as reading and writing databases, web requests, and disk storage are less expensive on the CPU and often have idle time waiting for the data to be sent or come back. This means you can create threads more liberally, and `Schedulers.io()` is appropriate for this. It will maintain as many threads as there are tasks and will dynamically grow, cache, and reduce the number of threads as needed. For instance, you may use `Schedulers.io()` to perform SQL operations using RxJava-JDBC (`https://github.com/davidmoten/rxjava-jdbc`):

```
Database db = Database.from(conn);

Observable<String> customerNames =
    db.select("SELECT NAME FROM CUSTOMER")
        .getAs(String.class)
        .subscribeOn(Schedulers.io());
```

But you have to be careful! As a rule of thumb, assume that each subscription will result in a new thread.

New thread

The `Schedulers.newThread()` factory will return a `Scheduler` that does not pool threads at all. It will create a new thread for each `Observer` and then destroy the thread when it is done. This is different than `Schedulers.io()` because it does not attempt to persist and cache threads for reuse:

```
Observable.just("Alpha", "Beta", "Gamma", "Delta", "Epsilon")
    .subscribeOn(Schedulers.newThread());
```

This may be helpful in cases where you want to create, use, and then destroy a thread immediately so it does not take up memory. But for complex applications generally, you will want to use `Schedulers.io()` so there is some attempt to reuse threads if possible. You also have to be careful as `Schedulers.newThread()` can run amok in complex applications (as can `Schedulers.io()`) and create a high volume of threads, which could crash your application.

Single

When you want to run tasks sequentially on a single thread, you can invoke `Schedulers.single()`. This is backed by a single-threaded implementation appropriate for event looping. It can also be helpful to isolate fragile, non-threadsafe operations to a single thread:

```
Observable.just("Alpha", "Beta", "Gamma", "Delta", "Epsilon")
    .subscribeOn(Schedulers.single());
```

Trampoline

`Schedulers.trampoline()` is an interesting `Scheduler`. In practicality, you will not invoke it often as it is used primarily in RxJava's internal implementation. Its pattern is also borrowed for UI Schedulers such as RxJavaFX and RxAndroid. It is just like default scheduling on the immediate thread, but it prevents cases of recursive scheduling where a task schedules a task while on the same thread. Instead of causing a stack overflow error, it will allow the current task to finish and *then* execute that new scheduled task afterward.

ExecutorService

You can build a Scheduler off a standard Java `ExecutorService`. You may choose to do this in order to have more custom and fine-tuned control over your thread management policies. For example, say, we want to create a Scheduler that uses 20 threads. We can create a new fixed `ExecutorService` specified with this number of threads. Then, you can wrap it inside a `Scheduler` implementation by calling `Schedulers.from()`:

```java
import io.reactivex.Observable;
import io.reactivex.Scheduler;
import io.reactivex.schedulers.Schedulers;
import java.util.concurrent.ExecutorService;
import java.util.concurrent.Executors;

public class Launcher {

    public static void main(String[] args) {

        int numberOfThreads = 20;

        ExecutorService executor =
                Executors.newFixedThreadPool(numberOfThreads);

        Scheduler scheduler = Schedulers.from(executor);

        Observable.just("Alpha", "Beta", "Gamma", "Delta",
"Epsilon")
                .subscribeOn(scheduler)
                .doFinally(executor::shutdown)
                .subscribe(System.out::println);
    }
}
```

`ExecutorService` will likely keep your program alive indefinitely, so you have to manage its disposal if its life is supposed to be finite. If I only wanted to support the life cycle of one `Observable` subscription, I need to call its `shutdown()` method. That is why I called its `shutdown()` method after the operation terminates or disposes via the `doFinally()` operator.

Starting and shutting down Schedulers

Each default `Scheduler` is lazily instantiated when you first invoke its usage. You can dispose the `computation()`, `io()`, `newThread()`, `single()`, and `trampoline()` Schedulers at any time by calling their `shutdown()` method or all of them by calling `Schedulers.shutdown()`. This will stop all their threads and forbid new tasks from coming in and will throw an error if you try otherwise. You can also call their `start()` method, or `Schedulersers.start()`, to reinitialize the Schedulers so they can accept tasks again.

In desktop and mobile app environments, you should not run into many cases where you have to start and stop the Schedulers. On the server side, however, J2EE-based applications (for example, Servlets) may get unloaded and reloaded and use a different classloader, causing the old Schedulers instances to leak. To prevent this from occurring, the Servlet should shut down the `Schedulers` manually in its `destroy()` method.

Only manage the life cycle of your Schedulers if you absolutely have to. It is better to let the Schedulers dynamically manage their usage of resources and keep them initialized and available so tasks can quickly be executed at a moment's notice. Note carefully that it is better to ensure that all outstanding tasks are completed or disposed of before you shut down the Schedulers, or else you may leave the sequences in an inconsistent state.

Understanding subscribeOn()

We kind of touched on using `subscribeOn()` already, but in this section, we will explore it in more detail and look at how it works.

The `subscribeOn()` operator will suggest to the source `Observable` upstream which `Scheduler` to use and how to execute operations on one of its threads. If that source is not already tied to a particular `Scheduler`, it will use the `Scheduler` you specify. It will then push emissions *all the way* to the final `Observer` using that thread (unless you add `observeOn()` calls, which we will cover later). You can put `subscribeOn()` anywhere in the `Observable` chain, and it will suggest to the upstream all the way to the origin `Observable` which thread to execute emissions with.

In the following example, it makes no difference whether you put this `subscribeOn()` right after `Observable.just()` or after one of the operators. The `subscribeOn()` will communicate upstream to the `Observable.just()` which `Scheduler` to use no matter where you put it. For clarity, though, you should place it as close to the source as possible:

```
//All three accomplish the same effect with subscribeOn()

Observable.just("Alpha", "Beta", "Gamma", "Delta", "Epsilon")
        .subscribeOn(Schedulers.computation()) //preferred
        .map(String::length)
        .filter(i -> i > 5)
        .subscribe(System.out::println);

Observable.just("Alpha", "Beta", "Gamma", "Delta", "Epsilon")
        .map(String::length)
        .subscribeOn(Schedulers.computation())
        .filter(i -> i > 5)
        .subscribe(System.out::println);

Observable.just("Alpha", "Beta", "Gamma", "Delta", "Epsilon")
        .map(String::length)
        .filter(i -> i > 5)
        .subscribeOn(Schedulers.computation())
        .subscribe(System.out::println);
```

Having multiple Observers to the same `Observable` with `subscribeOn()` will result in each one getting its own thread (or have them waiting for an available thread if none are available). In the `Observer`, you can print the executing thread's name by calling `Thread.currentThread().getName()`. We will print that with each emission to see that two threads, in fact, are being used for both Observers:

```
import io.reactivex.Observable;
import io.reactivex.schedulers.Schedulers;
import java.util.concurrent.ThreadLocalRandom;

public class Launcher {

    public static void main(String[] args) {

        Observable<Integer> lengths =
                Observable.just("Alpha", "Beta", "Gamma", "Delta",
"Epsilon")
                    .subscribeOn(Schedulers.computation())
                    .map(Launcher::intenseCalculation)
                    .map(String::length);
```

```
                lengths.subscribe(i ->
        System.out.println("Received " + i + " on thread " +
                            Thread.currentThread().getName()));

                lengths.subscribe(i ->
        System.out.println("Received " + i + " on thread " +
                            Thread.currentThread().getName()));

            sleep(10000);

        }
        public static <T> T intenseCalculation(T value) {
            sleep(ThreadLocalRandom.current().nextInt(3000));
            return value;
        }
        public static void sleep(int millis) {
            try {
                Thread.sleep(millis);
            } catch (InterruptedException e) {
                e.printStackTrace();
            }
        }
    }
}
```

The output is as follows:

```
        Received 5 on thread RxComputationThreadPool-2
        Received 4 on thread RxComputationThreadPool-2
        Received 5 on thread RxComputationThreadPool-2
        Received 5 on thread RxComputationThreadPool-2
        Received 5 on thread RxComputationThreadPool-1
        Received 7 on thread RxComputationThreadPool-2
        Received 4 on thread RxComputationThreadPool-1
        Received 5 on thread RxComputationThreadPool-1
        Received 5 on thread RxComputationThreadPool-1
```

Note how one Observer is using a thread named RxComputationThreadPool-2, while the other is using RxComputationThreadPool-1. These names indicate which Scheduler they came from (which is the Computation one) and what their index is. As shown here, if we want only one thread to serve both Observers, we can multicast this operation. Just make sure subscribeOn() is before the multicast operators:

```
        import io.reactivex.Observable;
        import io.reactivex.schedulers.Schedulers;
        import java.util.concurrent.ThreadLocalRandom;

        public class Launcher {
```

```
public static void main(String[] args) {

    Observable<Integer> lengths =
            Observable.just("Alpha", "Beta", "Gamma", "Delta",
"Epsilon")
            .subscribeOn(Schedulers.computation())
            .map(Launcher::intenseCalculation)
            .map(String::length)
            .publish()
            .autoConnect(2);

    lengths.subscribe(i ->
System.out.println("Received " + i + " on thread " +
                    Thread.currentThread().getName()));

    lengths.subscribe(i ->
System.out.println("Received " + i + " on thread " +
                    Thread.currentThread().getName()));

    sleep(10000);

}
public static <T> T intenseCalculation(T value) {
    sleep(ThreadLocalRandom.current().nextInt(3000));
    return value;
}
public static void sleep(int millis) {
    try {
        Thread.sleep(millis);
    } catch (InterruptedException e) {
        e.printStackTrace();
    }
}
}
}
```

The output is as follows:

```
Received 5 on thread RxComputationThreadPool-1
Received 5 on thread RxComputationThreadPool-1
Received 4 on thread RxComputationThreadPool-1
Received 4 on thread RxComputationThreadPool-1
Received 5 on thread RxComputationThreadPool-1
Received 5 on thread RxComputationThreadPool-1
Received 5 on thread RxComputationThreadPool-1
```

Most `Observable` factories, such as `Observable.fromIterable()` and `Observable.just()`, will emit items on the `Scheduler` specified by `subscribeOn()`. For factories such as `Observable.fromCallable()` and `Observable.defer()`, the initialization of these sources will also run on the specified `Scheduler` when using `subscribeOn()`. For instance, if you use `Observable.fromCallable()` to wait on a URL response, you can actually do that work on the IO Scheduler so the main thread is not blocking and waiting for it:

```java
import io.reactivex.Observable;
import io.reactivex.schedulers.Schedulers;
import java.net.URL;
import java.util.Scanner;

public class Launcher {

    public static void main(String[] args) {

        Observable.fromCallable(() ->
getResponse("https://api.github.com/users/thomasnield/starred")
        ).subscribeOn(Schedulers.io())
            .subscribe(System.out::println);

        sleep(10000);
    }
    private static String getResponse(String path) {
        try {
            return new Scanner(new URL(path).openStream(),
"UTF-8").useDelimiter("\\A").next();
        } catch (Exception e) {
            return e.getMessage();
        }
    }
    public static void sleep(int millis) {
        try {
            Thread.sleep(millis);
        } catch (InterruptedException e) {
            e.printStackTrace();
        }
    }
}
```

The output is as follows:

```
[{"id":23095928,"name":"RxScala","full_name":"ReactiveX/RxScala","o
....
```

Nuances of subscribeOn()

It is important to note that `subscribeOn()` will have no practical effect with certain sources (and will keep a worker thread unnecessarily on standby until that operation terminates). This might be because these Observables already use a specific `Scheduler`, and if you want to change it, you can provide a `Scheduler` as an argument. For example, `Observable.interval()` will use `Schedulers.computation()` and will ignore any `subscribeOn()` you specify otherwise. But you can provide a third argument to specify a different `Scheduler` to use. Here, I specify `Observable.interval()` to use `Schedulers.newThread()`, as shown here:

```java
import io.reactivex.Observable;
import io.reactivex.schedulers.Schedulers;
import java.util.concurrent.TimeUnit;

public class Launcher {

    public static void main(String[] args) {

        Observable.interval(1, TimeUnit.SECONDS,
Schedulers.newThread())
                .subscribe(i -> System.out.println("Received " + i +
                        " on thread " +
Thread.currentThread().getName()));

        sleep(5000);
    }

    public static void sleep(int millis) {
        try {
            Thread.sleep(millis);
        } catch (InterruptedException e) {
            e.printStackTrace();
        }
    }
}
```

The output is as follows:

```
Received 0 on thread RxNewThreadScheduler-1
Received 1 on thread RxNewThreadScheduler-1
Received 2 on thread RxNewThreadScheduler-1
Received 3 on thread RxNewThreadScheduler-1
Received 4 on thread RxNewThreadScheduler-1
```

This also brings up another point: if you have multiple `subscribeOn()` calls on a given `Observable` chain, the top-most one, or the one closest to the source, will win and cause any subsequent ones to have no practical effect (other than unnecessary resource usage). If I call `subscribeOn()` with `Schedulers.computation()` and then call `subscribeOn()` for `Schedulers.io()`, `Schedulers.computation()` is the one that will be used:

```
import io.reactivex.Observable;
import io.reactivex.schedulers.Schedulers;

public class Launcher {

    public static void main(String[] args) {

        Observable.just("Alpha", "Beta", "Gamma", "Delta",
"Epsilon")
                .subscribeOn(Schedulers.computation())
                .filter(s -> s.length() == 5)
                .subscribeOn(Schedulers.io())
                .subscribe(i -> System.out.println("Received " + i
+
                    " on thread " +
Thread.currentThread().getName()));

        sleep(5000);
    }
    public static void sleep(int millis) {
        try {
            Thread.sleep(millis);
        } catch (InterruptedException e) {
            e.printStackTrace();
        }
    }
}
```

The output is as follows:

```
Received Alpha on thread RxComputationThreadPool-1
Received Gamma on thread RxComputationThreadPool-1
Received Delta on thread RxComputationThreadPool-1
```

This can happen when an API returns an `Observable` already preapplied with a `Scheduler` via `subscribeOn()`, although the consumer of the API wants a different `Scheduler`. API designers are, therefore, encouraged to provide methods or overloads that allow parameterizing which `Scheduler` to use, just like RxJava's Scheduler-dependent operators (for example, `Observable.interval()`).

In summary, `subscribeOn()` specifies which `Scheduler` the source `Observable` should use, and it will use a worker from this `Scheduler` to push emissions all the way to the final `Observer`. Next, we will learn about `observeOn()`, which switches to a different `Scheduler` at that point in the `Observable` chain.

Understanding observeOn()

The `subscribeOn()` operator instructs the source `Observable` which `Scheduler` to emit emissions on. If `subscribeOn()` is the only concurrent operation in an `Observable` chain, the thread from that `Scheduler` will work the entire `Observable` chain, pushing emissions from the source all the way to the final `Observer`. The `observeOn()` operator, however, will intercept emissions at that point in the `Observable` chain and switch them to a different `Scheduler` going forward.

Unlike `subscribeOn()`, the placement of `observeOn()` matters. It will leave all operations upstream on the default or `subscribeOn()`-defined `Scheduler`, but will switch to a different `Scheduler` downstream. Here, I can have an `Observable` emit a series of strings that are /-separated values and break them up on an IO `Scheduler`. But after that, I can switch to a computation `Scheduler` to filter only numbers and calculate their sum, as shown in the following code snippet:

```java
import io.reactivex.Observable;
import io.reactivex.schedulers.Schedulers;

public class Launcher {

    public static void main(String[] args) {

        //Happens on IO Scheduler
        Observable.just("WHISKEY/27653/TANGO", "6555/BRAVO",
"232352/5675675/FOXTROT")
                .subscribeOn(Schedulers.io())
                .flatMap(s -> Observable.fromArray(s.split("/")))

                //Happens on Computation Scheduler
                .observeOn(Schedulers.computation())
                .filter(s -> s.matches("[0-9]+"))
                .map(Integer::valueOf)
                .reduce((total, next) -> total + next)
                .subscribe(i -> System.out.println("Received " + i
+ " on thread "
                        + Thread.currentThread().getName()));
```

```
            sleep(1000);
        }

    public static void sleep(int millis) {
        try {
            Thread.sleep(millis);
        } catch (InterruptedException e) {
            e.printStackTrace();
        }
    }
}
```

The output is as follows:

```
Received 5942235 on thread RxComputationThreadPool-1
```

Of course, this example is not computationally intensive, and in real life, it should be done on a single thread. The overhead of concurrency that we introduced is not warranted, but let's pretend it is a long-running process.

Again, use `observeOn()` to intercept each emission and push them forward on a different `Scheduler`. In the preceding example, operators before `observeOn()` are executed on `Scheduler.io()`, but the ones after it are executed by `Schedulers.computation()`. Upstream operators before `observeOn()` are not impacted, but downstream ones are.

You might use `observeOn()` for a situation like the one emulated earlier. If you want to read one or more data sources and wait for the response to come back, you will want to do that part on `Schedulers.io()` and will likely leverage `subscribeOn()` since that is the initial operation. But once you have that data, you may want to do intensive computations with it, and `Scheduler.io()` may no longer be appropriate. You will want to constrain these operations to a few threads that will fully utilize the CPU. Therefore, you use `observeOn()` to redirect data to `Schedulers.computation()`.

You can actually use multiple `observeOn()` operators to switch `Schedulers` more than once. Continuing with our earlier example, let's say we want to write our computed sum to a disk and write it in a file. Let's pretend this was a lot of data rather than a single number and we want to get this disk-writing operation off the computation `Scheduler` and put it back in the IO `Scheduler`. We can achieve this by introducing a second `observeOn()`. Let's also add some `doOnNext()` and `doOnSuccess()` (due to the `Maybe`) operators to peek at which thread each operation is using:

```
import io.reactivex.Observable;
import io.reactivex.schedulers.Schedulers;
import java.io.BufferedWriter;
import java.io.File;
```

```
import java.io.FileWriter;

public class Launcher {

    public static void main(String[] args) {

        //Happens on IO Scheduler
        Observable.just("WHISKEY/27653/TANGO", "6555/BRAVO",
"232352/5675675/FOXTROT")
                .subscribeOn(Schedulers.io())
                .flatMap(s -> Observable.fromArray(s.split("/")))
                .doOnNext(s -> System.out.println("Split out " + s
+ " on thread "
                        + Thread.currentThread().getName()))

                //Happens on Computation Scheduler
                .observeOn(Schedulers.computation())
                .filter(s -> s.matches("[0-9]+"))
                .map(Integer::valueOf)
                .reduce((total, next) -> total + next)
                .doOnSuccess(i -> System.out.println("Calculated
sum " + i + " on thread "
                        + Thread.currentThread().getName()))

                //Switch back to IO Scheduler
                .observeOn(Schedulers.io())
                .map(i -> i.toString())
                .doOnSuccess(s -> System.out.println("Writing " + s
+ " to file on thread "
                        + Thread.currentThread().getName()))
                .subscribe(s ->
write(s,"/home/thomas/Desktop/output.txt"));

        sleep(1000);
    }
    public static void write(String text, String path) {
        BufferedWriter writer = null;
        try {
            //create a temporary file
            File file = new File(path);
            writer = new BufferedWriter(new FileWriter(file));
            writer.append(text);
        } catch (Exception e) {
            e.printStackTrace();
        } finally {
            try {
                writer.close();
            } catch (Exception e) {
```

```
            }
        }
    }

    public static void sleep(int millis) {
        try {
            Thread.sleep(millis);
        } catch (InterruptedException e) {
            e.printStackTrace();
        }
    }
}
```

The output is as follows:

```
Split out WHISKEY on thread RxCachedThreadScheduler-1
Split out 27653 on thread RxCachedThreadScheduler-1
Split out TANGO on thread RxCachedThreadScheduler-1
Split out 6555 on thread RxCachedThreadScheduler-1
Split out BRAVO on thread RxCachedThreadScheduler-1
Split out 232352 on thread RxCachedThreadScheduler-1
Split out 5675675 on thread RxCachedThreadScheduler-1
Split out FOXTROT on thread RxCachedThreadScheduler-1
Calculated sum 5942235 on thread RxComputationThreadPool-1
Writing 5942235 to file on thread RxCachedThreadSchedule
```

If you look closely at the output, you will see that the String emissions were initially pushed and split on the IO Scheduler via the thread RxCachedThreadScheduler-1. After that, each emission was switched to the computation Scheduler and pushed into a sum calculation, which was all done on the thread RxComputationThreadPool-1. That sum was then switched to the IO scheduler to be written to a text file (which I specified to output on my Linux Mint desktop), and that work was done on RxCachedThreadScheduler-1 (which happened to be the thread that pushed the initial emissions and was reused!).

Using observeOn() for UI event threads

When it comes to building mobile apps, desktop applications, and other user experiences, users have little patience for interfaces that hang up or freeze while work is being done. The visual updating of user interfaces is often done by a single dedicated UI thread, and changes to the user interface must be done on that thread. User input events are typically fired on the UI thread as well. If a user input triggers work, and that work is not moved to another thread, that UI thread will become busy. This is what makes the user interface unresponsive, and today's users expect better than this. They want to still interact with the application while work is happening in the background, so concurrency is a must-have.

Thankfully, RxJava can come to the rescue! You can use `observeOn()` to move UI events to a computation or IO `Scheduler` to do the work, and when the result is ready, move it back to the UI thread with another `observeOn()`. This second usage of `observeOn()` will put emissions on a UI thread using a custom `Scheduler` that wraps around the UI thread. RxJava extension libraries such as RxAndroid (`https://github.com/ReactiveX/RxAndroid`), RxJavaFX (`https://github.com/ReactiveX/RxJavaFX`), and RxSwing (`https://github.com/ReactiveX/RxSwing`) come with these custom `Scheduler` implementations.

For instance, say we have a simple JavaFX application that displays a `ListView<String>` of the 50 U.S. states every time a button is clicked on. We can create `Observable<ActionEvent>` off the button and then switch to an IO `Scheduler` with `observeOn()` (`subscribeOn()` will have no effect against UI event sources). We can load the 50 states from a text web response while on the IO `Scheduler`. Once the states are returned, we can use another `observeOn()` to put them back on `JavaFxScheduler`, and safely populate them into `ListView<String>` on the JavaFX UI thread:

```
import javafx.application.Application;
import javafx.scene.Scene;
import javafx.scene.control.Button;
import javafx.scene.control.ListView;
import javafx.scene.layout.VBox;
import javafx.stage.Stage;
import io.reactivex.Observable;
import io.reactivex.rxjavafx.observables.JavaFxObservable;
import io.reactivex.rxjavafx.schedulers.JavaFxScheduler;
import io.reactivex.schedulers.Schedulers;
public final class JavaFxApp extends Application {

    @Override
    public void start(Stage stage) throws Exception {

        VBox root = new VBox();
```

```
            ListView<String> listView = new ListView<>();
            Button refreshButton = new Button("REFRESH");

            JavaFxObservable.actionEventsOf(refreshButton)
                    .observeOn(Schedulers.io())
                    .flatMapSingle(a ->
              Observable.fromArray(getResponse("https://goo.gl/S0xuOi")
              .split("\\r?\\n")
              ).toList()
                    ).observeOn(JavaFxScheduler.platform())
                    .subscribe(list ->
      listView.getItems().setAll(list));

            root.getChildren().addAll(listView, refreshButton);
            stage.setScene(new Scene(root));
            stage.show();
        }

    private static String getResponse(String path) {
        try {
            return new Scanner(new URL(path).openStream(),
"UTF-8").useDelimiter("\\A").next();
        } catch (Exception e) {
            return e.getMessage();
        }
    }
}
```

The code should run the JavaFX application shown as follows:

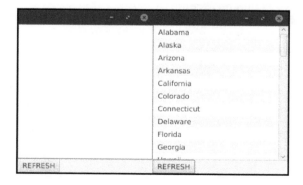

The preceding screenshot demonstrates that hitting the **REFRESH** button will emit an event but switch it to an IO `Scheduler` where the work is done to retrieve the U.S. states. When the response is ready, it will emit a `List<String>` and put it back on the JavaFX `Scheduler` to be displayed in a `ListView`.

These concepts apply to Android development as well, and you put all operations affecting the app user interface on `AndroidSchedulers.mainThread()` rather than `JavaFxScheduler.platform()`. We will cover Android development in `Chapter 11`, *RxJava for Android*.

Nuances of observeOn()

`observeOn()` comes with nuances to be aware of, especially when it comes to performance implications due to lack of backpressure, which we will cover in `Chapter 8`, *Flowables and Backpressure*.

Say, you have an `Observable` chain with two sets of operations, Operation A and Operation B. Let's not worry what operators each one is using. If you do not have any `observeOn()` between them, the operation will pass emissions strictly one at a time from the source to Operation A, then Operation B, and finally to the `Observer`. Even with a `subscribeOn()`, the source will not pass the next emission down the chain until the current one is passed all the way to the `Observer`.

This changes when you introduce an `observeOn()` and say we put it between Operation A and Operation B. What happens is after Operation A hands an emission to the `observeOn()`, it will immediately start the next emission and not wait for the downstream to finish the current one, including Operation B and the `Observer`. This means that the source and Operation A can *produce* emissions faster than Operation B and the `Observer` can *consume* them. This is a classic producer/consumer scenario where the producer is producing emissions faster than the consumer can consume them. If this is the case, unprocessed emissions will be queued in `observeOn()` until the downstream is able to process them. But if you have a lot of emissions, you can potentially run into memory issues.

This is why when you have a flow of 10,000 emissions or more, you will definitely want to use a `Flowable` (which supports backpressure) instead of an `Observable`. Backpressure communicates upstream all the way to the source to slow down and only produce so many emissions at a time. It restores *pull-based* requesting of emissions even when complex concurrency operations are introduced. We will cover this in `Chapter 8`, *Flowables and Backpressure*.

Parallelization

Parallelization, also called **parallelism** or **parallel computing**, is a broad term that can be used for any concurrent activity (including what we covered). But for the purposes of RxJava, let's define it as processing multiple emissions at a time for a given `Observable`. If we have 1000 emissions to process in a given `Observable` chain, we might be able to get work done faster if we process eight emissions at a time instead of one. If you recall, the `Observable` contract dictates that emissions must be pushed *serially* down an `Observable` chain and never race each other due to concurrency. As a matter of fact, pushing eight emissions down an `Observable` chain at a time would be downright catastrophic and wreak havoc.

This seems to put us at odds with what we want to accomplish, but thankfully, RxJava gives you enough operators and tools to be clever. While you cannot push items concurrently on the same `Observable`, you are allowed to have multiple Observables running at once, each having its own single thread pushing items through. As we have done throughout this chapter, we created several Observables running on different threads/schedulers and *even combined them*. You actually have the tools already, and the secret to achieving parallelization is in the `flatMap()` operator, which is, in fact, a powerful concurrency operator.

Here, we have an `Observable` emitting 10 integers, and we are performing `intenseCalculation()` on each one. This process can take a while due to the artificial processing we emulated with `sleep()`. Let's print each one with the time in the `Observer` so we can measure the performance, as shown in the following code:

```
import io.reactivex.Observable;
import java.time.LocalTime;
import java.util.concurrent.ThreadLocalRandom;

public class Launcher {
    public static void main(String[] args) {

        Observable.range(1,10)
                .map(i -> intenseCalculation(i))
                .subscribe(i -> System.out.println("Received " + i +
" "
                        + LocalTime.now()));
    }

    public static <T> T intenseCalculation(T value) {
        sleep(ThreadLocalRandom.current().nextInt(3000));
        return value;
    }
```

```
public static void sleep(long millis) {
    try {
        Thread.sleep(millis);
    } catch (InterruptedException e) {
        e.printStackTrace();
    }
}
```

The output is as follows (yours will be different):

```
Received 1 19:11:41.812
Received 2 19:11:44.174
Received 3 19:11:45.588
Received 4 19:11:46.034
Received 5 19:11:47.059
Received 6 19:11:49.569
Received 7 19:11:51.259
Received 8 19:11:54.192
Received 9 19:11:56.196
Received 10 19:11:58.926
```

The randomness causes some variability, of course, but in this instance, it took roughly 17 seconds to complete (although your time will likely vary). We will probably get better performance if we process emissions in parallel, so how do we do that?

Remember, serialization (emitting items one at a time) only needs to happen on the same `Observable`. The `flatMap()` operator will merge multiple Observables derived off each emission even if they are *concurrent*. If a light bulb has not gone off yet, read on. In `flatMap()`, let's wrap each emission into `Observable.just()`, use `subscribeOn()` to emit it on `Schedulers.computation()`, and then map it to the `intenseCalculation()`. For good measure, let's print the current thread in the `Observer` as well, as shown in the following code:

```
import io.reactivex.Observable;
import io.reactivex.schedulers.Schedulers;
import java.time.LocalTime;
import java.util.concurrent.ThreadLocalRandom;

public class Launcher {
    public static void main(String[] args) {

        Observable.range(1,10)
            .flatMap(i -> Observable.just(i)
                    .subscribeOn(Schedulers.computation())
                    .map(i2 -> intenseCalculation(i2))
            )
```

```
                              .subscribe(i -> System.out.println("Received " + i +
   " "
                            + LocalTime.now() + " on thread "
                            + Thread.currentThread().getName()));

        sleep(20000);
    }

    public static <T> T intenseCalculation(T value) {
        sleep(ThreadLocalRandom.current().nextInt(3000));
        return value;
    }
    public static void sleep(long millis) {
        try {
            Thread.sleep(millis);
        } catch (InterruptedException e) {
            e.printStackTrace();
        }
    }
}
}
```

The output is as follows (yours will be different):

```
Received 1 19:28:11.163 on thread RxComputationThreadPool-1
Received 7 19:28:11.381 on thread RxComputationThreadPool-7
Received 9 19:28:11.534 on thread RxComputationThreadPool-1
Received 6 19:28:11.603 on thread RxComputationThreadPool-6
Received 8 19:28:11.629 on thread RxComputationThreadPool-8
Received 3 19:28:12.214 on thread RxComputationThreadPool-3
Received 4 19:28:12.961 on thread RxComputationThreadPool-4
Received 5 19:28:13.274 on thread RxComputationThreadPool-5
Received 2 19:28:13.374 on thread RxComputationThreadPool-2
Received 10 19:28:14.335 on thread RxComputationThreadPool-2
```

This took three seconds to complete, and you will find that this processes items much faster. Of course, my computer has eight cores and that is why my output likely indicates that there are eight threads in use. If you have a computer with less cores, this process will take longer and use fewer threads. But it will likely still be faster than the single-threaded implementation we ran earlier.

What we did is we created a Observable off each emission, used subscribeOn() to emit it on the computation Scheduler, and then performed the intenseCalculation(), which will occur on one of the computation threads. Each instance will request its own thread from the computation Scheduler, and flatMap() will merge all of them safely back into a serialized stream.

The `flatMap()` will only let one thread out of it at a time to push emissions downstream, which maintains that the `Observable` contract demanding emissions stays serialized. A neat little behavior with `flatMap()` is that it will not use excessive synchronization or blocking to accomplish this. If a thread is already pushing an emission out of `flatMap()` downstream toward `Observer`, any threads also waiting to push emissions will simply leave their emissions for that occupying thread to take ownership of.

The example here is not necessarily optimal, however. Creating an `Observable` for each emission might create some unwanted overhead. There is a leaner way to achieve parallelization, although it has a few more moving parts. If we want to avoid creating excessive `Observable` instances, maybe we should split the source `Observable` into a fixed number of Observables where emissions are evenly divided and distributed through each one. Then, we can parallelize and merge them with `flatMap()`. Even better, since I have eight cores on my computer, maybe it would be ideal that I have eight Observables for eight streams of calculations.

We can achieve this using a `groupBy()` trick. If I have eight cores, I want to key each emission to a number in the range 0 through 7. This will yield me eight `GroupedObservables` that cleanly divide the emissions into eight streams. More specifically, I want to cycle through these eight numbers and assign them as a key to each emission. `GroupedObservables` are not necessarily impacted by `subscribeOn()` (it will emit on the source's thread with the exception of the cached emissions), so I will need to use `observeOn()` to parallelize them instead. I can also use an `io()` or `newThread()` scheduler since I have already constrained the number of workers to the number of cores, simply by constraining the number of `GroupedObservables`.

Here is how I do this, but instead of hardcoding for eight cores, I dynamically query the number of cores available:

```
import io.reactivex.Observable;
import io.reactivex.schedulers.Schedulers;
import java.time.LocalTime;
import java.util.concurrent.ThreadLocalRandom;
import java.util.concurrent.atomic.AtomicInteger;

public class Launcher {
    public static void main(String[] args) {

        int coreCount = Runtime.getRuntime().availableProcessors();
        AtomicInteger assigner = new AtomicInteger(0);
        Observable.range(1,10)
```

```
                   .groupBy(i -> assigner.incrementAndGet() %
coreCount)
                   .flatMap(grp -> grp.observeOn(Schedulers.io())
                       .map(i2 -> intenseCalculation(i2))
                   )
                   .subscribe(i -> System.out.println("Received " + i +
" "
                       + LocalTime.now() + " on thread "
                       + Thread.currentThread().getName()));

          sleep(20000);
      }

    public static <T> T intenseCalculation(T value) {
        sleep(ThreadLocalRandom.current().nextInt(3000));
        return value;
    }
    public static void sleep(long millis) {
        try {
            Thread.sleep(millis);
        } catch (InterruptedException e) {
            e.printStackTrace();
        }
    }
}
```

Here is the output (yours will be different):

```
Received 8 20:27:03.291 on thread RxCachedThreadScheduler-8
Received 6 20:27:03.446 on thread RxCachedThreadScheduler-6
Received 5 20:27:03.495 on thread RxCachedThreadScheduler-5
Received 4 20:27:03.681 on thread RxCachedThreadScheduler-4
Received 7 20:27:03.989 on thread RxCachedThreadScheduler-7
Received 2 20:27:04.797 on thread RxCachedThreadScheduler-2
Received 1 20:27:05.172 on thread RxCachedThreadScheduler-1
Received 9 20:27:05.327 on thread RxCachedThreadScheduler-1
Received 10 20:27:05.913 on thread RxCachedThreadScheduler-2
Received 3 20:27:05.957 on thread RxCachedThreadScheduler-3
```

For each emission, I will need to increment the number it groups on, and after it reaches 7, it will start over at 0. This ensures that the emissions are distributed as evenly as possible. We achieve this using AtomicInteger with a modulus operation. If we keep incrementing AtomicInteger for each emission, we can divide that result by the numbers of cores, but return the remainder, which will always be a number between 0 and 7.

AtomicInteger is just an integer protected inside a threadsafe container and has convenient threadsafe methods, such as incrementAndGet(). Typically, when you have an object or state existing outside an Observable chain but is modified by the Observable chain's operations (this is known as creating side effects), that object should be made threadsafe, especially when concurrency is involved. You can learn more about AtomicInteger and other utilities in Brian Goetz's *Java Concurrency in Practice*.

You do not have to use the processor count to control how many GroupedObservables are created. You can specify any number if you, for some reason, deem that more workers would result in better performance. If your concurrent operations are a mix between IO and computation, and you find that there is more IO, you might benefit from increasing the number of threads/GroupedObservables allowed.

unsubscribeOn()

One last concurrency operator that we need to cover is unsubscribeOn(). When you dispose an Observable, sometimes, that can be an expensive operation depending on the nature of the source. For instance, if your Observable is emitting the results of a database query using RxJava-JDBC, (https://github.com/davidmoten/rxjava-jdbc) it can be expensive to stop and dispose that Observable because it needs to shut down the JDBC resources it is using.

This can cause the thread that calls dispose() to become busy, as it will be doing all the work stopping an Observable subscription and disposing it. If this is a UI thread in JavaFX or Android (for instance, because a **CANCEL PROCESSING** button was clicked), this can cause undesirable UI freezing because the UI thread is working to stop and dispose the Observable operation.

Here is a simple Observable that is emitting every one second. We stop the main thread for three seconds, and then it will call dispose() to shut the operation down. Let's use doOnDispose() (which will be executed by the disposing thread) to see that the main thread is indeed disposing of the operation:

```
import io.reactivex.Observable;
import io.reactivex.disposables.Disposable;
import java.util.concurrent.TimeUnit;

public class Launcher {
    public static void main(String[] args) {
```

```
                Disposable d = Observable.interval(1, TimeUnit.SECONDS)
                        .doOnDispose(() -> System.out.println("Disposing on
        thread "
                            + Thread.currentThread().getName()))
                        .subscribe(i -> System.out.println("Received " +
        i));

            sleep(3000);
            d.dispose();
            sleep(3000);
        }

        public static void sleep(long millis) {
            try {
                Thread.sleep(millis);
            } catch (InterruptedException e) {
                e.printStackTrace();
            }
        }
    }
}
```

The output is as follows:

```
        Received 0
        Received 1
        Received 2
        Disposing on thread main
```

Let's add `unsubscribeOn()` and specify to unsubscribe on `Schedulers.io()`. You should put `unsubscribeOn()` wherever you want all operations upstream to be affected:

```
        import io.reactivex.Observable;
        import io.reactivex.disposables.Disposable;
        import io.reactivex.schedulers.Schedulers;
        import java.util.concurrent.TimeUnit;

        public class Launcher {
            public static void main(String[] args) {

                Disposable d = Observable.interval(1, TimeUnit.SECONDS)
                        .doOnDispose(() -> System.out.println("Disposing on
        thread "
                            + Thread.currentThread().getName()))
                        .unsubscribeOn(Schedulers.io())
                        .subscribe(i -> System.out.println("Received " +
        i));

                sleep(3000);
```

```
            d.dispose();
            sleep(3000);
        }

        public static void sleep(long millis) {
            try {
                Thread.sleep(millis);
            } catch (InterruptedException e) {
                e.printStackTrace();
            }
        }
    }
```

The output is as follows:

```
Received 0
Received 1
Received 2
Disposing on thread RxCachedThreadScheduler-1
```

Now you will see that disposal is being done by the IO `Scheduler`, whose thread is identified by the name `RxCachedThreadScheduler-1`. This allows the main thread to kick off disposal and continue without waiting for it to complete.

Like any concurrency operators, you really should not need to use `unsubscribeOn()` for lightweight operations such as this example, as it adds unnecessary overhead. But if you have `Observable` operations that are heavy with resources which are slow to dispose of, `unsubscribeOn()` can be a crucial tool if threads calling `dispose()` are sensitive to high workloads.

 You can use multiple `unsubscribeOn()` calls if you want to target specific parts of the `Observable` chain to be disposed of with different Schedulers. Everything upstream to an `unsubscribeOn()` will be disposed of with that `Scheduler` until another `unsubscribeOn()` is encountered, which will own the next upstream segment.

Summary

This was probably our most intense chapter yet, but it provides a turning point in your proficiency as an RxJava developer as well as a master of concurrency! We covered the different Schedulers available in RxJava as well as ones available in other libraries such as RxJavaFX and RxAndroid. The `subscribeOn()` operator is used to suggest to the upstream in an `Observable` chain which `Scheduler` to push emissions on. The `observeOn()` will switch emissions to a different `Scheduler` *at that point* in the `Observable` chain and use that `Scheduler` downstream. You can use these two operators in conjunction with `flatMap()` to create powerful parallelization patterns so you can fully utilize your multi-CPU power. We finally covered `unsubscribeOn()`, which helps us specify a different `Scheduler` to dispose operations on, preventing subtle hang-ups on threads we want to keep free and available even if they call the `dispose()` method.

It is important to note that when you start playing with concurrency, you need to become wary of how much data you are juggling between threads now. A lot of data can queue up in your `Observable` chain, and some threads will produce work faster than other threads can consume them. When you are dealing with 10,000+ elements, you will want to use Flowables to prevent memory issues, and we will cover this in Chapter 8, *Flowables and Backpressure*.

The next chapter will look into this topic of dealing with Observables that produce emissions too quickly, and there are some operators that can help with this without backpressure. We will hit that next.

7
Switching, Throttling, Windowing, and Buffering

It is not uncommon to run into situations where an `Observable` is producing emissions faster than an `Observer` can consume them. This happens particularly when you introduce concurrency, and the `Observable` chain has different operators running on different Schedulers. Whether it is one operator struggling to keep up with a preceding one, or the final `Observer` struggling to keep up with emissions from the upstream, bottlenecks can occur where emissions start to queue up behind slow operations.

Of course, the ideal way to handle bottlenecks is to leverage backpressure using Flowable instead of `Observable`. The `Flowable` is not much different than the `Observable` other than that it tells the source to slow down by having the `Observer` request emissions at its own pace, as we will learn about it in Chapter 8, *Flowables and Backpressure*. But not every source of emissions can be backpressured. You cannot instruct `Observable.interval()` (or even `Flowable.interval()`) to slow down because the emissions are logically time-sensitive. Asking it to slow down would make those time-based emissions inaccurate. User input events, such as button clicks, logically cannot be backpressured either because you cannot programmatically control the user.

Thankfully, there are some operators that help cope with rapidly firing sources without using backpressure and are especially appropriate for situations where backpressure cannot be utilized. Some of these operators batch up emissions into chunks that are more easily consumed downstream. Others simply sample emissions while ignoring the rest. There is even a powerful `switchMap()` operator that functions similarly to `flatMap()` but will only subscribe to the `Observable` derived from the latest emission and dispose of any previous ones.

We will cover all of these topics in this chapter:

- Buffering
- Windowing
- Throttling
- Switching

We will also end the chapter with an exercise that groups up keystrokes to emit strings of user inputs.

Buffering

The `buffer()` operator will gather emissions within a certain scope and emit each batch as a list or another collection type. The scope can be defined by a fixed buffer sizing or a timing window that cuts off at intervals or even slices by the emissions of another `Observable`.

Fixed-size buffering

The simplest overload for `buffer()` accepts a `count` argument that batches emissions in that fixed size. If we wanted to batch up emissions into lists of eight elements, we can do that as follows:

```
import io.reactivex.Observable;

public class Launcher {
public static void main(String[] args) {
    Observable.range(1,50)
            .buffer(8)
            .subscribe(System.out::println);
    }
}
```

The output is as follows:

```
[1, 2, 3, 4, 5, 6, 7, 8]
[9, 10, 11, 12, 13, 14, 15, 16]
[17, 18, 19, 20, 21, 22, 23, 24]
[25, 26, 27, 28, 29, 30, 31, 32]
[33, 34, 35, 36, 37, 38, 39, 40]
[41, 42, 43, 44, 45, 46, 47, 48]
[49, 50]
```

Of course, if the number of emissions does not cleanly divide, the remaining elements will be emitted in a final list even if it is less than the specified count. This is why the last emission in the preceding code has a list of two elements (not eight), containing only 49 and 50.

You can also supply a second `bufferSupplier` lambda argument to put items in another collection besides a list, such as `HashSet`, as demonstrated here (this should yield the same output):

```
import io.reactivex.Observable;
import java.util.HashSet;
public class Launcher {
    public static void main(String[] args) {
        Observable.range(1,50)
                .buffer(8, HashSet::new)
                .subscribe(System.out::println);
    }
}
```

To make things more interesting, you can also provide a `skip` argument that specifies how many items should be skipped before starting a new buffer. If `skip` is equal to `count`, the `skip` has no effect. But if they are different, you can get some interesting behaviors. For instance, you can buffer 2 emissions but skip 3 before the next buffer starts, as shown here. This will essentially cause every third element to not be buffered:

```
import io.reactivex.Observable;
public class Launcher {
    public static void main(String[] args) {
        Observable.range(1,10)
                .buffer(2, 3)
                .subscribe(System.out::println);
    }
}
```

The output is as follows:

```
[1, 2]
[4, 5]
[7, 8]
[10]
```

If you make `skip` less than `count`, you can get some interesting rolling buffers. If you buffer items into a size of 3 but have `skip` of 1, you will get rolling buffers. In the following code, for instance, we emit the numbers 1 through 10 but create buffers `[1, 2, 3]`, then `[2, 3, 4]`, then `[3, 4, 5]`, and so on:

```java
import io.reactivex.Observable;
public class Launcher {
    public static void main(String[] args) {
        Observable.range(1,10)
                .buffer(3, 1)
                .subscribe(System.out::println);
    }
}
```

The output is as follows:

```
[1, 2, 3]
[2, 3, 4]
[3, 4, 5]
[4, 5, 6]
[5, 6, 7]
[6, 7, 8]
[7, 8, 9]
[8, 9, 10]
[9, 10]
[10]
```

Definitely play with the `skip` argument for `buffer()`, and you may find surprising use cases for it. For example, I sometimes use `buffer(2,1)` to emit the "previous" emission and the next emission together, as shown here. I also use `filter()` to omit the last list, which only contains `10`:

```java
import io.reactivex.Observable;
public class Launcher {
    public static void main(String[] args) {
        Observable.range(1,10)
                .buffer(2, 1)
                .filter(c -> c.size() == 2)
```

```
                    .subscribe(System.out::println);
        }
    }
```

The output is as follows:

```
[1,  2]
[2,  3]
[3,  4]
[4,  5]
[5,  6]
[6,  7]
[7,  8]
[8,  9]
[9, 10]
```

Time-based buffering

You can use `buffer()` at fixed time intervals by providing a long and `TimeUnit`. To buffer emissions into a list at 1-second intervals, you can run the following code. Note that we are making the source emit every 300 milliseconds, and each resulting buffered list will likely contain three or four emissions due to the one-second interval cut-offs:

```
import io.reactivex.Observable;
import java.util.concurrent.TimeUnit;
public class Launcher {
    public static void main(String[] args) {
        Observable.interval(300, TimeUnit.MILLISECONDS)
                .map(i -> (i + 1) * 300) // map to elapsed time
                .buffer(1, TimeUnit.SECONDS)
                .subscribe(System.out::println);
        sleep(4000);
    }
    public static void sleep(int millis) {
        try {
            Thread.sleep(millis);
        }
        catch (InterruptedException e) {
            e.printStackTrace();
        }
    }
}
```

The output is as follows:

```
[300, 600, 900]
[1200, 1500, 1800]
[2100, 2400, 2700]
[3000, 3300, 3600, 3900]
```

There is an option to also specify a `timeskip` argument, which is the timer-based counterpart to `skip`. It controls the timing of when each buffer starts.

You can also leverage a third `count` argument to provide a maximum buffer size. This will result in a buffer emission at each time interval or when `count` is reached, whichever happens first. If the `count` is reached right before the time window closes, it will result in an empty buffer being emitted.

Here, we buffer emissions every 1 second, but we limit the buffer size to 2:

```java
import io.reactivex.Observable;
import java.util.concurrent.TimeUnit;
public class Launcher {
    public static void main(String[] args) {
        Observable.interval(300, TimeUnit.MILLISECONDS)
                .map(i -> (i + 1) * 300) // map to elapsed time
                .buffer(1, TimeUnit.SECONDS, 2)
                .subscribe(System.out::println);
        sleep(5000);
    }
    public static void sleep(int millis) {
        try {
            Thread.sleep(millis);
        } catch (InterruptedException e) {
            e.printStackTrace();
        }
    }
}
```

The output is as follows:

```
[300, 600]
[900]
[1200, 1500]
[1800]
[2100, 2400]
[2700]
[3000, 3300]
[3600, 3900]
[]
```

```
[4200, 4500]
[4800]
```

Note that time-based `buffer()` operators will operate on the computation `Scheduler`. This makes sense since a separate thread needs to run on a timer to execute the cutoffs.

Boundary-based buffering

The most powerful variance of `buffer()` is accepting another `Observable` as a `boundary` argument. It does not matter what type this other `Observable` emits. All that matters is every time it emits something, it will use the timing of that emission as the buffer cut-off. In other words, the arbitrary occurrence of emissions of another `Observable` will determine when to "slice" each buffer.

For example, we can perform our previous example with 300-millisecond emissions buffered every 1-second using this technique. We can have `Observable.interval()` of 1 second serve as the boundary for our `Observable.interval()` emitting every 300 milliseconds:

```java
import io.reactivex.Observable;
import java.util.concurrent.TimeUnit;
public class Launcher {
    public static void main(String[] args) {
        Observable<Long> cutOffs =
                Observable.interval(1, TimeUnit.SECONDS);
        Observable.interval(300, TimeUnit.MILLISECONDS)
            .map(i -> (i + 1) * 300) // map to elapsed time
            .buffer(cutOffs)
            .subscribe(System.out::println);
        sleep(5000);
    }
    public static void sleep(int millis) {
        try {
            Thread.sleep(millis);
        } catch (InterruptedException e) {
            e.printStackTrace();
        }
    }
}
```

The output is as follows:

```
[300, 600, 900]
[1200, 1500, 1800]
[2100, 2400, 2700]
[3000, 3300, 3600, 3900]
[4200, 4500, 4800]
```

This is probably the most flexible way to buffer items based on highly variable events. While the timing of each slicing is consistent in the preceding example (which is every 1 second), the `boundary` can be any `Observable` representing any kind of event happening at any time. This idea of an `Observable` serving as a cut-off for another `Observable` is a powerful pattern we will see throughout this chapter.

Windowing

The `window()` operators are almost identical to `buffer()`, except that they buffer into other Observables rather than collections. This results in an `Observable<Observable<T>>` that emits Observables. Each `Observable` emission will cache emissions for each scope and then flush them once subscribed (much like the `GroupedObservable` from `groupBy()`, which we worked with in `Chapter 4`, *Combining Observables*). This allows emissions to be worked with immediately as they become available rather than waiting for each list or collection to be finalized and emitted. The `window()` operator is also convenient to work with if you want to use operators to transform each batch.

Just like `buffer()`, you can cut-off each batch using fixed sizing, a time interval, or a boundary from another `Observable`.

Fixed-size windowing

Let's modify our earlier example, where we buffered 50 integers into lists of size 8, but we will use `window()` to buffer them as Observables instead. We can reactively transform each batch into something else besides a collection, such as concatenating emissions into strings with pipe "|" separators:

```
import io.reactivex.Observable;
public class Launcher {
    public static void main(String[] args) {
        Observable.range(1,50)
                .window(8)
```

```
                              .flatMapSingle(obs -> obs.reduce("", (total,
    next) -> total
                                  + (total.equals("") ? "" : "|") + next))
                              .subscribe(System.out::println);
            }
        }
```

The output is as follows:

```
1|2|3|4|5|6|7|8
9|10|11|12|13|14|15|16
17|18|19|20|21|22|23|24
25|26|27|28|29|30|31|32
33|34|35|36|37|38|39|40
41|42|43|44|45|46|47|48
49|50
```

Just like `buffer()`, you can also provide a `skip` argument. This is how many emissions need to be skipped before starting a new window. Here, our window size is 2, but we skip three items. We then take each windowed `Observable` and reduce it to a `String` concatenation:

```
import io.reactivex.Observable;
public class Launcher {
    public static void main(String[] args) {
        Observable.range(1,50)
                .window(2, 3)
                .flatMapSingle(obs -> obs.reduce("", (total,
    next) -> total
                        + (total.equals("") ? "" : "|") + next))
                .subscribe(System.out::println);
            }
        }
```

The output is as follows:

```
1|2
4|5
7|8
10|11
13|14
16|17
19|20
22|23
25|26
28|29
31|32
34|35
```

```
37|38
40|41
43|44
46|47
49|50
```

Time-based windowing

As you might be able to guess, you can cut-off windowed Observables at time intervals just like `buffer()`. Here, we have an `Observable` emitting every 300 milliseconds like earlier, and we are slicing it into separate Observables every 1 second. We will then use `flatMapSingle()` on each `Observable` to a `String` concatenation of the emissions:

```java
import io.reactivex.Observable;
import java.util.concurrent.TimeUnit;
public class Launcher {
    public static void main(String[] args) {
        Observable.interval(300, TimeUnit.MILLISECONDS)
                .map(i -> (i + 1) * 300) // map to elapsed time
                .window(1, TimeUnit.SECONDS)
                .flatMapSingle(obs -> obs.reduce("", (total,
next) -> total
                        + (total.equals("") ? "" : "|") + next))
                .subscribe(System.out::println);
        sleep(5000);
    }
    public static void sleep(int millis) {
        try {
            Thread.sleep(millis);
        } catch (InterruptedException e) {
            e.printStackTrace();
        }
    }
}
```

The output is as follows:

```
300|600|900
1200|1500|1800
2100|2400|2700
3000|3300|3600|3900
4200|4500|4800
```

Of course, you can use these yielded Observables for other transformations besides `String` concatenations. You can use all the operators we learned up to this point to perform different operations on each windowed `Observable`, and you will likely do that work in `flatMap()`, `concatMap()`, or `switchMap()`.

With time-based `window()` operators, you can also specify `count` or `timeshift` arguments, just like its `buffer()` counterpart.

Boundary-based windowing

It probably is no surprise that since `window()` is similar to `buffer()` (other than that it emits Observables instead of connections), you can also use another `Observable` as `boundary`.

Here, we use an `Observable.interval()` emitting every 1 second to serve as the `boundary` on an `Observable` emitting every 300 milliseconds. We leverage each emitted `Observable` to concatenate emissions into concatenated strings:

```java
import io.reactivex.Observable;
import java.util.concurrent.TimeUnit;
public class Launcher {
    public static void main(String[] args) {
        Observable<Long> cutOffs =
                Observable.interval(1, TimeUnit.SECONDS);
        Observable.interval(300, TimeUnit.MILLISECONDS)
            .map(i -> (i + 1) * 300) // map to elapsed time
            .window(cutOffs)
            .flatMapSingle(obs -> obs.reduce("", (total, next) ->
total
                + (total.equals("") ? "" : "|") + next))
            .subscribe(System.out::println);
        sleep(5000);
    }
    public static void sleep(int millis) {
        try {
            Thread.sleep(millis);
        } catch (InterruptedException e) {
            e.printStackTrace();
        }
    }
}
```

The output is as follows:

```
300|600|900
1200|1500|1800
2100|2400|2700
3000|3300|3600|3900
4200|4500|4800
```

Again, the benefit of using another `Observable` as a `boundary` is that it allows you to use the arbitrary timing of emissions from any `Observable` to cut-off each window, whether it is a button click, a web request, or any other event. This makes it the most flexible way to slice `window()` or `buffer()` operations when variability is involved.

Throttling

The `buffer()` and `window()` operators batch up emissions into collections or Observables based on a defined scope, which regularly consolidates rather than omits emissions.The `throttle()` operator, however, omits emissions when they occur rapidly. This is helpful when rapid emissions are assumed to be redundant or unwanted, such as a user clicking on a button repeatedly. For these situations, you can use the `throttleLast()`, `throttleFirst()`, and `throttleWithTimeout()` operators to only let the first or last element in a rapid sequence of emissions through. How you choose one of the many rapid emissions is determined by your choice of operator, parameters, and arguments.

For the examples in this section, we are going to work with this case: we have three `Observable.interval()` sources, the first emitting every 100 milliseconds, the second every 300 milliseconds, and the third every 2000 milliseconds. We only take 10 emissions from the first source, three from the second, and two from the third. As you can see here, we will use `Observable.concat()` on them together in order to create a rapid sequence that changes pace at three different intervals:

```
import io.reactivex.Observable;
import java.util.concurrent.TimeUnit;
public class Launcher {
    public static void main(String[] args) {
        Observable<String> source1 = Observable.interval(100,
TimeUnit.MILLISECONDS)
                .map(i -> (i + 1) * 100) // map to elapsed time
                .map(i -> "SOURCE 1: " + i)
                .take(10);
        Observable<String> source2 = Observable.interval(300,
TimeUnit.MILLISECONDS)
```

```
                          .map(i -> (i + 1) * 300) // map to elapsed time
                          .map(i -> "SOURCE 2: " + i)
                          .take(3);
                Observable<String> source3 = Observable.interval(2000,
        TimeUnit.MILLISECONDS)
                          .map(i -> (i + 1) * 2000) // map to elapsed time
                          .map(i -> "SOURCE 3: " + i)
                          .take(2);
                Observable.concat(source1, source2, source3)
                          .subscribe(System.out::println);
                sleep(6000);
        }
        public static void sleep(int millis) {
            try {
                Thread.sleep(millis);
            } catch (InterruptedException e) {
                e.printStackTrace();
            }
        }
    }
```

The output is as follows:

```
    SOURCE 1: 100
    SOURCE 1: 200
    SOURCE 1: 300
    SOURCE 1: 400
    SOURCE 1: 500
    SOURCE 1: 600
    SOURCE 1: 700
    SOURCE 1: 800
    SOURCE 1: 900
    SOURCE 1: 1000
    SOURCE 2: 300
    SOURCE 2: 600
    SOURCE 2: 900
    SOURCE 3: 2000
    SOURCE 3: 4000
```

The first source rapidly pushes 10 emissions within a second, the second pushes three within a second, and the third pushes two within four seconds. Let's use some `throttle()` operators to only choose a few of these emissions and ignore the rest.

throttleLast() / sample()

The `throttleLast()` operator (which is aliased as `sample()`) will only emit the last item at a fixed time interval. Modify your earlier example to use `throttleLast()` at 1-second intervals, as shown here:

```
Observable.concat(source1, source2, source3)
        .throttleLast(1, TimeUnit.SECONDS)
        .subscribe(System.out::println);
```

The output is as follows:

```
SOURCE 1: 900
SOURCE 2: 900
SOURCE 3: 2000
```

If you study the output, you can see that the last emission at every 1-second interval was all that got through. This effectively samples emissions by dipping into the stream on a timer and pulling out the latest one.

If you want to throttle more liberally at larger time intervals, you will get fewer emissions as this effectively reduces the sample frequency. Here, we use `throttleLast()` every two seconds:

```
Observable.concat(source1, source2, source3)
        .throttleLast(2, TimeUnit.SECONDS)
        .subscribe(System.out::println);
```

The output is as follows:

```
SOURCE 2: 900
SOURCE 3: 2000
```

If you want to throttle more aggressively at shorter time intervals, you will get more emissions, as this increases the sample frequency. Here, we use `throttleLast()` every 500 milliseconds:

```
Observable.concat(source1, source2, source3)
        .throttleLast(500, TimeUnit.MILLISECONDS)
        .subscribe(System.out::println);
```

The output is as follows:

```
SOURCE 1: 400
SOURCE 1: 900
SOURCE 2: 300
SOURCE 2: 900
SOURCE 3: 2000
```

Again, `throttleLast()` will push the last emission at every fixed time interval. Next, we will cover `throttleFirst()`, which emits the first item instead.

throttleFirst()

The `throttleFirst()` operates almost identically to `throttleLast()`, but it will emit the *first* item that occurs at every fixed time interval. If we modify our example to `throttleFirst()` every 1 second, we should get an output like this:

```
Observable.concat(source1, source2, source3)
        .throttleFirst(1, TimeUnit.SECONDS)
        .subscribe(System.out::println);
```

The output is as follows:

```
SOURCE 1: 100
SOURCE 2: 300
SOURCE 3: 2000
SOURCE 3: 4000
```

Effectively, the first emission found after each interval starts is the emission that gets pushed through. The 100 from `source1` was the first emission found on the first interval. On the next interval, 300 from `source2` was emitted, then 2000, followed by 4000. The 4000 was emitted right on the cusp of the application quitting, hence we got four emissions from `throttleFirst()` as opposed to three from `throttleLast()`.

Besides the first item being emitted rather than the last at each interval, all the behaviors from `throttleLast()` also apply to `throttleFirst()`. Specifying shorter intervals will yield more emissions, whereas longer intervals will yield less.

Both `throttleFirst()` and `throttleLast()` emit on the computation `Scheduler`, but you can specify your own `Scheduler` as a third argument.

throttleWithTimeout() / debounce()

If you play with `throttleFirst()` and `throttleLast()`, you might be dissatisfied with one aspect of their behavior. They are agnostic to the variability of emission frequency, and they simply "dip in" at fixed intervals and pull the first or last emission they find. There is no notion of waiting for a "period of silence" where emissions stop for a moment, and that might be an opportune time to push the last emission that occurred forward.

Think of Hollywood action movies where a protagonist is under heavy gunfire. While bullets are flying, he/she has to take cover and is unable to act. But the moment their attackers stop to reload, there is a period of silence where they have time to react. This is essentially what `throttleWithTimout()` does. While emissions are firing rapidly, it will not emit anything until there is a "period of silence", and then it will push the last emission forward.

`throttleWithTimout()` (also called `debounce()`) accepts time interval arguments that specify how long a period of inactivity (which means no emissions are coming from the source) must be before the last emission can be pushed forward. In our earlier example, our three concatenated `Observable.interval()` sources are rapidly firing at 100 milliseconds and then 300-millisecond spurts for approximately 2 seconds. But after that, intervals slow down to every 2 seconds. If we wanted to only emit after 1 second of silence, we are not going to emit anything until we hit that third `Observable.interval()`, emitting every 2 seconds, as shown here:

```
import io.reactivex.Observable;
import java.util.concurrent.TimeUnit;
public class Launcher {
    public static void main(String[] args) {
        Observable<String> source1 = Observable.interval(100,
TimeUnit.MILLISECONDS)
                .map(i -> (i + 1) * 100) // map to elapsed time
                .map(i -> "SOURCE 1: " + i)
                .take(10);
        Observable<String> source2 = Observable.interval(300,
TimeUnit.MILLISECONDS)
                .map(i -> (i + 1) * 300) // map to elapsed time
                .map(i -> "SOURCE 2: " + i)
                .take(3);
        Observable<String> source3 = Observable.interval(2000,
TimeUnit.MILLISECONDS)
                .map(i -> (i + 1) * 2000) // map to elapsed time
                .map(i -> "SOURCE 3: " + i)
                .take(2);
        Observable.concat(source1, source2, source3)
                .throttleWithTimeout(1, TimeUnit.SECONDS)
```

```
                .subscribe(System.out::println);
            sleep(6000);
        }
        public static void sleep(int millis) {
            try {
                Thread.sleep(millis);
            } catch (InterruptedException e) {
                e.printStackTrace();
            }
        }
    }
```

The output is as follows:

```
SOURCE 2: 900
SOURCE 3: 2000
SOURCE 3: 4000
```

The 900 emission from `source2` was the last emission as soon as `source3` started, since `source3` will not push its first emission for 2 seconds, which gave more than the needed 1-second period of silence for the 900 emission to be fired. The 2000 emission then emitted next and 1 second later no further emissions occurred, so it was pushed forward by `throttleWithTimeout()`. Another second later, the 4000 emission was pushed and the 2-second silence (before the program exited) allowed it to fire as well.

The `throttleWithTimeout()` is an effective way to handle excessive inputs (such as a user clicking on a button rapidly) and other noisy, redundant events that sporadically speed up, slow down, or cease. The only disadvantage of `throttleWithTimeout()` is that it will delay each winning emission. If an emission does make it through `throttleWithTimeout()`, it will be delayed by the specified time interval in order to ensure no more emissions are coming. Especially for user experiences, this artificial delay may be unwelcome. For these situations, which are sensitive to delays, a better option might be to leverage `switchMap()`, which we will cover next.

Switching

In RxJava, there is a powerful operator called `switchMap()`. Its usage feels like `flatMap()`, but it has one important behavioral difference: it will emit from the latest `Observable` derived from the latest emission and dispose of any previous Observables that were processing. In other words, it allows you to cancel an emitting `Observable` and switch to a new one, preventing stale or redundant processing.

Say we have a process that emits nine strings, and it delays each string emission randomly from 0 to 2000 milliseconds. This is to emulate an intense calculation done to each one, as demonstrated here:

```
import io.reactivex.Observable;
import java.util.concurrent.ThreadLocalRandom;
import java.util.concurrent.TimeUnit;
public class Launcher {
    public static void main(String[] args) {
        Observable<String> items = Observable.just("Alpha", "Beta",
"Gamma", "Delta", "Epsilon",
                        "Zeta", "Eta", "Theta", "Iota");
        //delay each String to emulate an intense calculation
        Observable<String> processStrings = items.concatMap(s ->
                Observable.just(s)
                        .delay(randomSleepTime(),
TimeUnit.MILLISECONDS)
        );
        processStrings.subscribe(System.out::println);
        //keep application alive for 20 seconds
        sleep(20000);
    }
    public static int randomSleepTime() {
        //returns random sleep time between 0 to 2000 milliseconds
        return ThreadLocalRandom.current().nextInt(2000);
    }
    public static void sleep(int millis) {
        try {
            Thread.sleep(millis);
        } catch (InterruptedException e) {
            e.printStackTrace();
        }
    }
}
```

The output is as follows:

```
Alpha
Beta
Gamma
Delta
Epsilon
Zeta
Eta
Theta
Iota
```

As you can tell, each emission takes between 0-2 seconds to be emitted, and processing all the strings can take up to 20 seconds.

Say we want to run this process every 5 seconds, but we want to cancel (or more technically, `dispose()`) previous instances of the process and only run the latest one. This is easy to do with `switchMap()`. Here, we create another `Observable.interval()`, emitting every 5 seconds and then we use `switchMap()` on it to the `Observable` we want to process (which in this case is `processStrings`). Every 5 seconds, the emission going into `switchMap()` will promptly dispose of the currently processing `Observable` (if there are any) and then emit from the new `Observable` it maps to. To prove that `dispose()` is being called, we will put `doOnDispose()` on the `Observable` inside `switchMap()` to display a message:

```
import io.reactivex.Observable;
import java.util.concurrent.ThreadLocalRandom;
import java.util.concurrent.TimeUnit;
public class Launcher {
    public static void main(String[] args) {
        Observable<String> items = Observable.just("Alpha", "Beta",
"Gamma", "Delta", "Epsilon",
                "Zeta", "Eta", "Theta", "Iota");
        //delay each String to emulate an intense calculation
        Observable<String> processStrings = items.concatMap(s ->
                Observable.just(s)
                        .delay(randomSleepTime(),
TimeUnit.MILLISECONDS)
        );
        //run processStrings every 5 seconds, and kill each
previous instance to start next
        Observable.interval(5, TimeUnit.SECONDS)
                .switchMap(i ->
                        processStrings
                                .doOnDispose(() ->
System.out.println("Disposing! Starting next"))
                ).subscribe(System.out::println);
        //keep application alive for 20 seconds
        sleep(20000);
    }
    public static int randomSleepTime() {
        //returns random sleep time between 0 to 2000 milliseconds
        return ThreadLocalRandom.current().nextInt(2000);
    }
    public static void sleep(int millis) {
        try {
            Thread.sleep(millis);
        } catch (InterruptedException e) {
```

```
                    e.printStackTrace();
            }
        }
    }
```

The output is as follows (yours will be different):

```
Alpha
Beta
Gamma
Delta
Epsilon
Zeta
Eta
Disposing! Starting next
Alpha
Beta
Gamma
Delta
Disposing! Starting next
Alpha
Beta
Gamma
Delta
Disposing! Starting next
```

Again, switchMap() is just like flatMap() except that it will cancel any previous Observables that were processing and only chase after the latest one. This can be helpful in many situations to prevent redundant or stale work and is especially effective in user interfaces where rapid user inputs create stale requests. You can use it to cancel database queries, web requests, and other expensive tasks and replace it with a new task.

For switchMap() to work effectively, the thread pushing emissions into switchMap() cannot be occupied doing the work inside switchMap(). This means that you may have to use observeOn() or subscribeOn() inside switchMap() to do work on a different thread. If the operations inside switchMap() are expensive to stop (for instance, a database query using RxJava-JDBC), you might want to use unsubscribeOn() as well to keep the triggering thread from becoming occupied with disposal.

A neat trick you can do to cancel work within switchMap() (without providing new work immediately) is to conditionally yield Observable.empty(). This can be helpful to cancel a long-running or infinite process. For example, if you bring in RxJavaFX (https://github .com/ReactiveX/RxJavaFX) as a dependency, we can quickly create a stop watch application using switchMap(), as shown in the following code snippet:

```
import io.reactivex.Observable;
```

```
import io.reactivex.rxjavafx.observables.JavaFxObservable;
import io.reactivex.rxjavafx.schedulers.JavaFxScheduler;
import javafx.application.Application;
import javafx.scene.Scene;
import javafx.scene.control.Label;
import javafx.scene.control.ToggleButton;
import javafx.scene.layout.VBox;
import javafx.stage.Stage;
import java.util.concurrent.TimeUnit;
public final class JavaFxApp extends Application {
    @Override
    public void start(Stage stage) throws Exception {
        VBox root = new VBox();
        Label counterLabel = new Label("");
        ToggleButton startStopButton = new ToggleButton();
    // Multicast the ToggleButton's true/false selected state
        Observable<Boolean> selectedStates =
JavaFxObservable.valuesOf(startStopButton.selectedProperty())
                        .publish()
                        .autoConnect(2);
        // Using switchMap() with ToggleButton's selected state will
drive
        // whether to kick off an Observable.interval(),
        // or dispose() it by switching to empty Observable
        selectedStates.switchMap(selected -> {
                    if (selected)
                        return Observable.interval(1,
TimeUnit.MILLISECONDS);
                    else
                        return Observable.empty();
                }).observeOn(JavaFxScheduler.platform()) // Observe
on JavaFX UI thread
                .map(Object::toString)
                .subscribe(counterLabel::setText);
        // Change ToggleButton's text depending on its state
        selectedStates.subscribe(selected ->
                startStopButton.setText(selected ? "STOP" :
"START")
        );
        root.getChildren().addAll(counterLabel, startStopButton);
        stage.setScene(new Scene(root));
        stage.show();
    }
}
```

The code preceding yields a stopwatch application that uses `switchMap()` , as shown below in Figure 7.1:

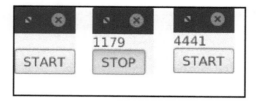

Figure 7.1 - A stopwatch application that uses switchMap()

Pressing the `ToggleButton` will start and stop the stopwatch, which displays in milliseconds. Note that the `ToggleButton` will emit a Boolean `True/False` value through an `Observable` called `selectedStates`. We multicast it to prevent duplicate listeners on JavaFX, and we have two Observers. The first will use `switchMap()` on each Boolean value, where `true` will emit from an `Observable.interval()` every millisecond, and `false` will cancel it by replacing it with an `Observable.empty()`. Since `Observable.interval()` will emit on a `Scheduler` computation, we will use `observeOn()` to put it back on the JavaFX `Scheduler` provided by RxJavaFX. The other `Observer` will change the text of the `ToggleButton` to STOP or START depending on its state.

Grouping keystrokes

We will wrap up this chapter by integrating most of what we learned and achieve a complex task: grouping keystrokes that happen in rapid succession to form strings without any delay! It can be helpful in user interfaces to immediately "jump" to items in a list based on what is being typed or perform auto-completion in some way. This can be a challenging task, but as we will see, it is not that difficult with RxJava.

This exercise will use JavaFX again with RxJavaFX. Our user interface will simply have a `Label` that receives rolling concatenations of keys we are typing. But after 300 milliseconds, it will reset and receive an empty `""` to clear it. Here is the code that achieves this as well as some screenshots with the console output when I type "`Hello`" and then type "`World`" a moment later:

```
import io.reactivex.Observable;
import io.reactivex.rxjavafx.observables.JavaFxObservable;
import io.reactivex.rxjavafx.schedulers.JavaFxScheduler;
import javafx.application.Application;
```

```
import javafx.scene.Scene;
import javafx.scene.control.Label;
import javafx.scene.input.KeyEvent;
import javafx.scene.layout.VBox;
import javafx.stage.Stage;
import java.util.concurrent.TimeUnit;
public final class JavaFxApp extends Application {
    @Override
    public void start(Stage stage) throws Exception {
        VBox root = new VBox();
        root.setMinSize(200, 100);
        Label typedTextLabel = new Label("");
        root.getChildren().addAll(typedTextLabel);
        Scene scene = new Scene(root);
        // Multicast typed keys
        Observable<String> typedLetters =
                JavaFxObservable.eventsOf(scene,
KeyEvent.KEY_TYPED)
                    .map(KeyEvent::getCharacter)
                    .share();
        // Signal 300 milliseconds of inactivity
        Observable<String> restSignal =
                typedLetters
                        .throttleWithTimeout(500,
TimeUnit.MILLISECONDS)
                        .startWith(""); //trigger initial
        // switchMap() each period of inactivity to
        // an infinite scan() concatenating typed letters
        restSignal.switchMap(s ->
                typedLetters.scan("", (rolling, next) -> rolling +
next)
        ).observeOn(JavaFxScheduler.platform())
         .subscribe(s -> {
            typedTextLabel.setText(s);
            System.out.println(s);
         });
        stage.setScene(scene);
        stage.show();
    }
}
```

The output is as follows:

```
H
He
Hel
Hell
Hello
W
Wo
Wor
Worl
World
```

This is the rendered UI:

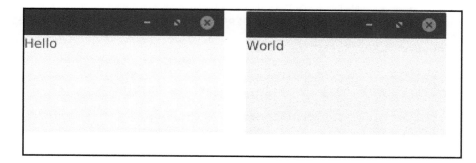

When you type keys, the `Label` will display a rolling `String` concatenation of their characters in live time on both the UI as well as the console. Note that after 500 milliseconds of no activity, it resets and emits a new `scan()` operation and disposes of the old one, starting with an empty `""` string. This can be enormously helpful to instantly send search requests or autocomplete suggestions while the user is typing.

The way it works is that we have an `Observable` emitting the characters that were pressed on the keyboard, but it is multicast with `share()` and used for two purposes. It is first used to create another `Observable` that signals the last character typed after 500 milliseconds of inactivity. But we do not care about the character as much as the emission's timing, which signals 500 milliseconds of inactivity has occurred. We then use `switchMap()` on it to the `Observable` emitting the characters again, and we infinitely concatenate each typed character in succession and emit each resulting string. However, this `scan()` operation in `switchMap()` will be disposed of when 500 milliseconds of inactivity occurs and start over with a new `scan()` instance.

If you find this example dizzying, take your time and keep studying it. It will click ultimately and once it does, you will have truly mastered the ideas in this chapter!

Summary

In this chapter, you learned how to leverage buffering, windowing, throttling, and switching to cope with rapidly emitting Observables. Ideally, we should leverage Flowables and backpressure when we see that Observables are emitting faster than the Observers can keep up with, which we will learn about in the next chapter. But for situations where backpressure cannot work, such as user inputs or timer events, you can leverage these three categories of operations to limit how many emissions are passed downstream.

In the next chapter, we will learn about backpressuring with Flowables, which provides more proactive ways to cope with common cases of rapid emissions overwhelming Observers.

8
Flowables and Backpressure

In the previous chapter, we learned about different operators that intercept rapidly firing emissions and either consolidate or omit them to decrease the emissions passed downstream. But for most cases where a source is producing emissions faster than the downstream can process them, it is better to proactively make the source slow down in the first place and emit at a pace that agrees with the downstream operations. This is known as backpressure or flow control, and it can be enabled by using a `Flowable` instead of an `Observable`. This will be the core type that we work with in this chapter, and we will learn about the right times to leverage it in our applications. We will cover the following topics in this chapter:

- Understanding backpressure
- `Flowable` and `Subscriber`
- Using `Flowable.create()`
- Interoperating Observables and Flowables
- Backpressure operators
- Using `Flowable.generate()`

Understanding backpressure

Throughout this book, I emphasized the "push-based" nature of Observables. Pushing items synchronously and one at a time from the source all the way to the `Observer` is indeed how `Observable` chains work by default without any concurrency.

For instance, the following is an `Observable` that will emit the numbers 1 through 999,999,999. It will map each integer to a `MyItem` instance, which simply holds it as a property. But let's slow down the processing of each emission by 50 milliseconds in the `Observer`. This shows that even if the downstream is slowly processing each emission, the upstream synchronously keeps pace with it. This is because one thread is doing all the work:

```java
import io.reactivex.Observable;

public class Launcher {

    public static void main(String[] args) {

        Observable.range(1, 999_999_999)
                .map(MyItem::new)
                .subscribe(myItem -> {
                    sleep(50);
                    System.out.println("Received MyItem " +
myItem.id);
                });
    }

    static void sleep(long milliseconds) {
        try {
            Thread.sleep(milliseconds);
        } catch (InterruptedException e) {
            e.printStackTrace();
        }
    }

    static final class MyItem {

        final int id;

        MyItem(int id) {
            this.id = id;
            System.out.println("Constructing MyItem " + id);
        }
    }
}
```

The output is as follows:

```
Constructing MyItem 1
Received MyItem 1
Constructing MyItem 2
Received MyItem 2
```

```
Constructing MyItem 3
Received MyItem 3
Constructing MyItem 4
Received MyItem 4
Constructing MyItem 5
Received MyItem 5
Constructing MyItem 6
Received MyItem 6
Constructing MyItem 7
Received MyItem 7
...
```

The outputted alternation between `Constructing MyItem` and `Received MyItem` shows that each emission is bring processed one at a time from the source all the way to the terminal `Observer`. This is because one thread is doing all the work for this entire operation, making everything synchronous. The consumers and producers are passing emissions in a serialized, consistent flow.

An example that needs backpressure

When you add concurrency operations to an `Observable` chain (particularly `observeOn()`, parallelization, and operators such as `delay()`), the operation become *asynchronous*. This means hat multiple parts of the `Observable` chain can be processing emissions at a given time, and producers can outpace consumers as they are now operating on different threads. An emission is no longer strictly being handed downstream one at a time from the source all the way to the `Observer` before starting the next one. This is because once an emission hits a different `Scheduler` through `observeOn()` (or other concurrent operators), the source is no longer in charge of pushing that emission to the `Observer`. Therefore, the source will start pushing the next emission even though the previous emission may not have reached the Observer yet.

If we take our previous example and add `observeOn(Shedulers.io())` right before `subscribe()` (as shown in the following code), you will notice something very blatant:

```
import io.reactivex.Observable;
import io.reactivex.schedulers.Schedulers;

public class Launcher {

    public static void main(String[] args) {

        Observable.range(1, 999_999_999)
```

```
                        .map(MyItem::new)
                        .observeOn(Schedulers.io())
                        .subscribe(myItem -> {
                            sleep(50);
                            System.out.println("Received MyItem " +
myItem.id);
                        });

            sleep(Long.MAX_VALUE);
        }

        static void sleep(long milliseconds) {
            try {
                Thread.sleep(milliseconds);
            } catch (InterruptedException e) {
                e.printStackTrace();
            }
        }

        static final class MyItem {

            final int id;

            MyItem(int id) {
                this.id = id;
                System.out.println("Constructing MyItem " + id);
            }
        }
    }
}
```

The output is as follows:

```
...
Constructing MyItem 1001899
Constructing MyItem 1001900
Constructing MyItem 1001901
Constructing MyItem 1001902
Received MyItem 38
Constructing MyItem 1001903
Constructing MyItem 1001904
Constructing MyItem 1001905
Constructing MyItem 1001906
Constructing MyItem 1001907
..
```

This is just a section of my console output. Note that when `MyItem 1001902` is created, the `Observer` is still only processing `MyItem 38`. The emissions are being pushed much faster than the `Observer` can process them, and because backlogged emissions get queued by `observeOn()` in an unbounded manner, this could lead to many problems, including `OutOfMemoryError` exceptions.

Introducing the Flowable

So how do we mitigate this? You could get hacky and try to use native Java concurrency tools such as semaphores. But thankfully, RxJava has a streamlined solution to this problem: the `Flowable`. The `Flowable` is a backpressured variant of the `Observable` that tells the source to emit at a pace specified by the downstream operations.

In the following code, replace `Observable.range()` with `Flowable.range()`, and this will make this entire chain work with Flowables instead of Observables. Run the code and you will see a very different behavior with the output:

```
import io.reactivex.Observable;
import io.reactivex.schedulers.Schedulers;
import io.reactivex.Flowable;

public class Launcher {

    public static void main(String[] args) {

        Flowable.range(1, 999_999_999)
                .map(MyItem::new)
                .observeOn(Schedulers.io())
                .subscribe(myItem -> {
                    sleep(50);
                    System.out.println("Received MyItem " +
myItem.id);
                });

        sleep(Long.MAX_VALUE);
    }

    static void sleep(long milliseconds) {
        try {
            Thread.sleep(milliseconds);
        } catch (InterruptedException e) {
            e.printStackTrace();
        }
    }
}
```

```
static final class MyItem {

    final int id;

    MyItem(int id) {
        this.id = id;
        System.out.println("Constructing MyItem " + id);
    }
}
}
```

The output is as follows:

```
Constructing MyItem 1
Constructing MyItem 2
Constructing MyItem 3
. . .
Constructing MyItem 127
Constructing MyItem 128
Received MyItem 1
Received MyItem 2
Received MyItem 3
. . .
Received MyItem 95
Received MyItem 96
Constructing MyItem 129
Constructing MyItem 130
Constructing MyItem 131
. . .
Constructing MyItem 223
Constructing MyItem 224
Received MyItem 97
Received MyItem 98
Received MyItem 99
. . .
```

Note that Flowables do not subscribe with Observers but rather Subscribers, which we will dive into later.

You will notice something very different with the output when using `Flowable`. I omitted parts of the preceding output using . . . to highlight some key events. 128 emissions were immediately pushed from `Flowable.range()`, which constructed 128 `MyItem` instances. After that, `observeOn()` pushed 96 of them downstream to `Subscriber`. After these 96 emissions were processed by `Subscriber`, another 96 were pushed from the source. Then another 96 were passed to `Subscriber`.

Do you see a pattern yet? The source started by pushing 128 emissions, and after that, a steady flow of 96 emissions at a time was processed by the `Flowable` chain. It is almost like the entire `Flowable` chain strives to have no more than 96 emissions in its pipeline at any given time. Effectively, that is exactly what is happening! This is what we call **backpressure**, and it effectively introduces a pull dynamic to the push-based operation to limit how frequently the source emits.

But why did `Flowable.range()` start with 128 emissions, and why did `observeOn()` only send 96 downstream before requesting another 96, leaving 32 unprocessed emissions? The initial batch of emissions is a bit larger so some extra work is queued if there is any idle time. If (in theory) our `Flowable` operation started by requesting 96 emissions and continued to emit steadily at 96 emissions at a time, there would be moments where operations might wait idly for the next 96. Therefore, an extra rolling cache of 32 emissions is maintained to provide work during these idle moments, which can provide greater throughput. This is much like a warehouse holding a little extra inventory to supply orders while it waits for more from the factory.

What is great about Flowables and their operators is that they usually do all the work for you. You do not have to specify any backpressure policies or parameters unless you need to create your own Flowables from scratch or deal with sources (such as Observables) that do not implement backpressure. We will cover these cases in the rest of the chapter, and hopefully, you will not run into them often.

Otherwise, Flowable is just like an `Observable` with nearly all the operators we learned so far. You can convert from an `Observable` into a `Flowable` and vice-versa, which we will cover later. But first, let's cover when we should use Flowables instead of Observables.

When to use Flowables and backpressure

It is critical to know when to use `Flowable` versus `Observable`. Overall, the benefits offered from the `Flowable` are leaner usage of memory (preventing `OutOfMemoryError` exceptions) as well as prevention of `MissingBackpressureException`. The latter can occur if operations backpressure against a source but the source has no backpressure protocol in its implementation. However, the disadvantage of Flowable is that it adds overhead and may not perform as quickly as an `Observable`.

Here are a few guidelines to help you choose between an `Observable` versus a `Flowable`.

Use an Observable If...

- You expect few emissions over the life of the `Observable` subscription (less than 1000) or the emissions are intermittent and far apart. If you expect only a trickle of emissions coming from a source, an `Observable` will do the job just fine and have less overhead. But when you are dealing with large amounts of data and performing complex operations on them, you will likely want to use a `Flowable`.
- Your operation is strictly synchronous and has limited usage of concurrency. This includes simple usage of `subscribeOn()` at the start of an `Observable` chain because the process is still operating on a single thread and emitting items synchronously downstream. However, when you start zipping and combining different streams on different threads, parallelize, or use operators such as `observeOn()`, `interval()`, and `delay()`, your application is no longer synchronous and you might be better-off using a `Flowable`.
- You want to emit user interface events such as button clicks, `ListView` selections, or other user inputs on Android, JavaFX, or Swing. Since users cannot programmatically be told to slow down, there is rarely any opportunity using a `Flowable`. To cope with rapid user inputs, you are likely better-off using the operators discussed in `Chapter 7`, *Switching, Throttling, Windowing, and Buffering*.

Use a Flowable If...

- You are dealing with over 10,000 elements and there is opportunity for the source to generate emissions in a regulated manner. This is especially true when the source is asynchronous and pushes large amounts of data.
- You want to emit from IO operations that support blocking while returning results, which is how many IO sources work. Data sources that iterate records, such as lines from files or a `ResultSet` in JDBC, are especially easy to control because iteration can pause and resume as needed. Network and Streaming APIs that can request a certain amount of returned results can easily be backpressured as well.

Note in RxJava 1.0, the `Observable` was backpressured and was essentially what the `Flowable` is in RxJava 2.0. The reason the `Flowable` and `Observable` became separate types is due to the merits of both for different situations, as described precedingly.

You will find that you can easily interoperate Observables and Flowables together. But you need to be careful and aware of the context they are being used in and where undesired bottlenecks can occur.

Understanding the Flowable and Subscriber

Pretty much all the `Observable` factories and operators you learned up to this point also apply to Flowable. On the factory side, there is `Flowable.range()`, `Flowable.just()`, `Flowable.fromIterable()`, and `Flowable.interval()`. Most of these implement backpressure for you, and usage is generally the same as the `Observable` equivalent.

However, consider `Flowable.interval()`, which pushes time-based emissions at fixed time intervals. Can this be backpressured logically? Contemplate the fact that each emission is sensitively tied to the time it emits. If we slowed down `Flowable.interval()`, our emissions would no longer reflect time intervals and become misleading. Therefore, `Flowable.interval()` is one of those few cases in the standard API that can throw `MissingBackpressureException` the moment downstream requests backpressure. Here, if we emit every millisecond against a slow `intenseCalculation()` that occurs after `observeOn()`, we will get this error:

```java
import io.reactivex.Flowable;
import io.reactivex.schedulers.Schedulers;
import java.util.concurrent.ThreadLocalRandom;
import java.util.concurrent.TimeUnit;
public class Launcher {
    public static void main(String[] args) {
        Flowable.interval(1, TimeUnit.MILLISECONDS)
                .observeOn(Schedulers.io())
                .map(i -> intenseCalculation(i))
                .subscribe(System.out::println,
Throwable::printStackTrace);
        sleep(Long.MAX_VALUE);
    }
    public static <T> T intenseCalculation(T value) {
        sleep(ThreadLocalRandom.current().nextInt(3000));
        return value;
    }
    public static void sleep(long millis) {
        try {          `
            Thread.sleep(millis);
        } catch (InterruptedException e) {
            e.printStackTrace();
        }
    }
}
```

The output is as follows:

```
0
io.reactivex.exceptions.MissingBackpressureException: Cant deliver
value 128 due to lack of requests
    at io.reactivex.internal.operators.flowable.FlowableInterval
...
```

To overcome this issue, you can use operators such as `onBackpresureDrop()` or `onBackPressureBuffer()`, which we will learn about later in this chapter. `Flowable.interval()` is one of those factories that logically cannot be backpressured at the source, so you can use operators after it to handle backpressure for you. Otherwise, most of the other `Flowable` factories you work with support backpressure. Later, we need to call out how to create our own `Flowable` sources that conform to backpressure, and we will discuss this shortly. But first, we will explore the Subscriber a bit more.

The Subscriber

Instead of an `Observer`, the `Flowable` uses a `Subscriber` to consume emissions and events at the end of a `Flowable` chain. If you pass only lambda event arguments (and not an entire `Subscriber` object), `subscribe()` does not return a `Disposable` but rather a `Subscription`, which can be disposed of by calling `cancel()` instead of `dispose()`. The `Subscription` can also serve another purpose; it communicates upstream how many items are wanted using its `request()` method. `Subscription` can also be leveraged in the `onSubscribe()` method of `Subscriber` to `request()` elements the moment it is ready to receive emissions.

Just like an `Observer`, the quickest way to create a `Subscriber` is to pass lambda arguments to `subscribe()`, as we have been doing earlier (and shown again in the following code). This default implementation of `Subscriber` will request an unbounded number of emissions upstream, but any operators preceding it will still automatically handle backpressure:

```
import io.reactivex.Flowable;
import io.reactivex.schedulers.Schedulers;
import java.util.concurrent.ThreadLocalRandom;
public class Launcher {
    public static void main(String[] args) {
        Flowable.range(1,1000)
                .doOnNext(s -> System.out.println("Source pushed "
+ s))
                .observeOn(Schedulers.io())
                .map(i -> intenseCalculation(i))
```

```
                    .subscribe(s -> System.out.println("Subscriber
          received " + s),
                              Throwable::printStackTrace,
                              () -> System.out.println("Done!")
                    );
              sleep(20000);
          }
          public static <T> T intenseCalculation(T value) {
              //sleep up to 200 milliseconds
              sleep(ThreadLocalRandom.current().nextInt(200));
              return value;
          }
          public static void sleep(long millis) {
              try {
                  Thread.sleep(millis);
              } catch (InterruptedException e) {
                  e.printStackTrace();
              }
          }
      }
```

Of course, you can implement your own `Subscriber` as well, which, of course, has
the `onNext()`, `onError()`, and `onComplete()` methods as well as `onSubscribe()`. This
is not as straightforward as implementing an `Observer` because you need to call
`request()` on `Subscription` to request emissions at the right moments.

The quickest and easiest way to implement a `Subscriber` is to have the `onSubscribe()`
method call `request(Long.MAX_VALUE)` on `Subscription`, which essentially tells the
upstream "give me everything now". Even though the operators preceding `Subscriber`
will request emissions at their own backpressured pace, no backpressure will exist between
the last operator and the `Subscriber`. This is usually fine since the upstream operators will
constrain the flow anyway.

Here, we reimplement our previous example but implement our own `Subscriber`:

```
import io.reactivex.Flowable;
import io.reactivex.schedulers.Schedulers;
import org.reactivestreams.Subscriber;
import org.reactivestreams.Subscription;
import java.util.concurrent.ThreadLocalRandom;
public class Launcher {
    public static void main(String[] args) {
        Flowable.range(1,1000)
                .doOnNext(s -> System.out.println("Source pushed "
+ s))
                .observeOn(Schedulers.io())
```

```
                    .map(i -> intenseCalculation(i))
                    .subscribe(new Subscriber<Integer>() {
                        @Override
                        public void onSubscribe(Subscription
subscription) {
                            subscription.request(Long.MAX_VALUE);
                        }
                        @Override
                        public void onNext(Integer s) {
                            sleep(50);
                            System.out.println("Subscriber received " +
s);

                        }
                        @Override
                        public void onError(Throwable e) {
                            e.printStackTrace();
                        }
                        @Override
                        public void onComplete() {
                            System.out.println("Done!");
                        }
                    });
            sleep(20000);
        }
        public static <T> T intenseCalculation(T value) {
            //sleep up to 200 milliseconds
            sleep(ThreadLocalRandom.current().nextInt(200));
            return value;
        }
        public static void sleep(long millis) {
            try {
                Thread.sleep(millis);
            } catch (InterruptedException e) {
                e.printStackTrace();
            }
        }
    }
}
```

If you want your `Subscriber` to establish an explicit backpressured relationship with the operator preceding it, you will need to micromanage the `request()` calls. Say, for some extreme situation, you decide that you want `Subscriber` to request 40 emissions initially and then 20 emissions at a time after that. This is what you would need to do:

```
import io.reactivex.Flowable;
import io.reactivex.schedulers.Schedulers;
import org.reactivestreams.Subscriber;
import org.reactivestreams.Subscription;
import java.util.concurrent.ThreadLocalRandom;
```

```
import java.util.concurrent.atomic.AtomicInteger;
public class Launcher {
    public static void main(String[] args) {
        Flowable.range(1,1000)
                .doOnNext(s -> System.out.println("Source pushed "
+ s))
                .observeOn(Schedulers.io())
                .map(i -> intenseCalculation(i))
                .subscribe(new Subscriber<Integer>() {
                    Subscription subscription;
                     AtomicInteger count = new AtomicInteger(0);
                    @Override
                     public void onSubscribe(Subscription
subscription) {
                         this.subscription = subscription;
                         System.out.println("Requesting 40 items!");
                         subscription.request(40);
                    }
                    @Override
                     public void onNext(Integer s) {
                         sleep(50);
                         System.out.println("Subscriber received " +
s);

                         if (count.incrementAndGet() % 20 == 0 &&
count.get() >= 40)

                             System.out.println("Requesting 20
more!");

                             subscription.request(20);
                    }
                    @Override
                     public void onError(Throwable e) {
                         e.printStackTrace();
                    }
                    @Override
                     public void onComplete() {
                         System.out.println("Done!");
                    }
                });
        sleep(20000);
    }
    public static <T> T intenseCalculation(T value) {
        //sleep up to 200 milliseconds
        sleep(ThreadLocalRandom.current().nextInt(200));
        return value;
    }
    public static void sleep(long millis) {
        try {
            Thread.sleep(millis);
```

```
            } catch (InterruptedException e) {
                e.printStackTrace();
            }
        }
    }
```

The output is as follows:

```
Requesting 40 items!
Source pushed 1
Source pushed 2
...
Source pushed 127
Source pushed 128
Subscriber received 1
Subscriber received 2
...
Subscriber received 39
Subscriber received 40
Requesting 20 more!
Subscriber received 41
Subscriber received 42
...
Subscriber received 59
Subscriber received 60
Requesting 20 more!
Subscriber received 61
Subscriber received 62
...
Subscriber received 79
Subscriber received 80
Requesting 20 more!
Subscriber received 81
Subscriber received 82
...
```

Note that the source is still emitting 128 emissions initially and then still pushes 96 emissions at a time. But our Subscriber received only 40 emissions, as specified, and then consistently calls for 20 more. The request() calls in our Subscriber only communicate to the immediate operator upstream to it, which is map(). The map() operator likely relays that request to observeOn(), which is caching items and only flushing out 40 and then 20, as requested by the Subscriber. When its cache gets low or clears out, it will request another 96 from the upstream.

This is a warning: you should not rely on these exact numbers of requested emissions, such as 128 and 96. These are an internal implementation we happen to observe, and these numbers may be changed to aid further implementation optimizations in the future.

This custom implementation may actually be reducing our throughput, but it demonstrates how to manage custom backpressure with your own `Subscriber` implementation. Just keep in mind that the `request()` calls do not go all the way upstream. They only go to the preceding operator, which decides how to relay that request upstream.

Creating a Flowable

Earlier in this book, we used `Observable.create()` a handful of times to create our own `Observable` from scratch, which describes how to emit items when it is subscribed to, as shown in the following code snippet:

```
import io.reactivex.Observable;
import io.reactivex.schedulers.Schedulers;
public class Launcher {
    public static void main(String[] args) {
        Observable<Integer> source = Observable.create(emitter -> {
            for (int i=0; i<=1000; i++) {
                if (emitter.isDisposed())
                    return;
                emitter.onNext(i);
            }
            emitter.onComplete();
        });
        source.observeOn(Schedulers.io())
                .subscribe(System.out::println);
        sleep(1000);
    }
}
```

The output is as follows:

```
0
1
2
3
4
...
```

This `Observable.create()` will emit the integers 0 to 1000 and then call `onComplete()`. It can be stopped abruptly if `dispose()` is called on the `Disposable` returned from `subscribe()`, and the for-loop will check for this.

However, think for a moment how something like this can be backpressured if we execute `Flowable.create()`, the `Flowable` equivalent of `Observable.create()`. Using a simple for-loop like the preceding one, there is no notion of emissions *stopping* and *resuming* based on the requests of a downstream `Subscriber`. Doing backpressure properly is going to add some complexity. There are simpler ways to support backpressure, but they often involve compromised strategies such as buffering and dropping, which we will cover first. There are also a few utilities to implement backpressure at the source, which we will cover afterward.

Using Flowable.create() and BackpressureStrategy

Leveraging `Flowable.create()` to create a `Flowable` feels much like `Observable.create()`, but there is one critical difference; you must specify a `BackpressureStrategy` as a second argument. This enumerable type does not by any means provide magic implementations of backpressure support. As a matter of fact, this simply supports backpressure by caching or dropping emissions or not implementing backpressure at all.

Here, we use `Flowable.create()` to create a `Flowable`, but we provide a second `BackpressureStrategy.BUFFER` argument to buffer the emissions before they are backpressured:

```java
import io.reactivex.BackpressureStrategy;
import io.reactivex.Flowable;
import io.reactivex.schedulers.Schedulers;
public class Launcher {
    public static void main(String[] args) {
        Flowable<Integer> source = Flowable.create(emitter -> {
            for (int i=0; i<=1000; i++) {
                if (emitter.isCancelled())
                    return;
                emitter.onNext(i);
            }
            emitter.onComplete();
        }, BackpressureStrategy.BUFFER);
        source.observeOn(Schedulers.io())
            .subscribe(System.out::println);
```

```
            sleep(1000);
        }
    public static void sleep(long millis) {
        try {
            Thread.sleep(millis);
        } catch (InterruptedException e) {
            e.printStackTrace();
        }
    }
}
```

The output is as follows:

```
0
1
2
3
4
. . .
```

This is not optimal because the emissions will be held in an unbounded queue, and it is possible that when `Flowable.create()` pushes too many emissions, you will get an `OutOfMemoryError`. But at least it prevents `MissingBackpressureException` and can make your custom `Flowable` workable to a small degree. We will learn about a more robust way to implement backpressure later in this chapter using `Flowable.generate()`.

There are currently five `BackpressureStrategy` options you can choose from.

BackpressureStrategy	Description
MISSING	Essentially results in no backpressure implementation at all. The downstream must deal with backpressure overflow, which can be helpful when used with `onBackpressureXXX()` operators, which we will cover later in this chapter.
ERROR	Signals a `MissingBackpressureException` the moment the downstream cannot keep up with the source.
BUFFER	Queues up emissions in an unbounded queue until the downstream is able to consume them, but can cause an `OutOfMemoryError` if the queue gets too large.
DROP	If the downstream cannot keep up, this will ignore upstream emissions and not queue anything while the downstream is busy.
LATEST	This will keep only the latest emission until the downstream is ready to receive it.

Next, we will see some of these strategies used as operators, particularly converting Observables into Flowables.

Turning an Observable into a Flowable (and vice-versa)

There is another way that you can implement BackpressureStrategy against a source that has no notion of backpressure. You can turn an Observable into Flowable easily by calling its toFlowable() operator, which accepts a BackpressureStrategy as an argument. In the following code, we turn Observable.range() into Flowable using BackpressureStrategy.BUFFER. The Observable has no notion of backpressure, so it is going to push items as quickly as it can regardless if the downstream can keep up. But toFlowable(), with a buffering strategy, will act as a proxy to backlog the emissions when the downstream cannot keep up:

```
import io.reactivex.BackpressureStrategy;
import io.reactivex.Observable;
import io.reactivex.schedulers.Schedulers;
public class Launcher {
    public static void main(String[] args) {
        Observable<Integer> source = Observable.range(1,1000);
        source.toFlowable(BackpressureStrategy.BUFFER)
                .observeOn(Schedulers.io())
                .subscribe(System.out::println);
        sleep(10000);
    }
    public static void sleep(long millis) {
        try {
            Thread.sleep(millis);
        } catch (InterruptedException e) {
            e.printStackTrace();
        }
    }
}
```

 Again, note that toFlowable(), with a buffering strategy, is going to have an unbounded queue, which can cause an OutOfMemoryError. In the real world, it would be better to use Flowable.range() in the first place, but sometimes, you may only be provided with an Observable.

The `Flowable` also has a `toObservable()` operator, which will turn a `Flowable<T>` into an `Observable<T>`. This can be helpful in making a `Flowable` usable in an `Observable` chain, especially with operators such as `flatMap()`, as shown in the following code:

```java
import io.reactivex.Flowable;
import io.reactivex.Observable;
import io.reactivex.schedulers.Schedulers;
public class Launcher {
    public static void main(String[] args) {
        Flowable<Integer> integers =
                Flowable.range(1, 1000)
                        .subscribeOn(Schedulers.computation());
        Observable.just("Alpha","Beta","Gamma","Delta","Epsilon")
                .flatMap(s -> integers.map(i -> i + "-" +
s).toObservable())
                .subscribe(System.out::println);
        sleep(5000);
    }
    public static void sleep(long millis) {
        try {
            Thread.sleep(millis);
        } catch (InterruptedException e) {
            e.printStackTrace();
        }
    }
}
```

If `Observable<String>` had much more than five emissions (such as 1,000 or 10,000), then it would probably be better to turn that into a `Flowable` instead of turning the flat-mapped `Flowable` into an `Observable`.

Even if you call `toObservable()`, the `Flowable` will still leverage backpressure upstream. But at the point it becomes an `Observable`, the downstream will no longer be backpressured and will request a `Long.MAX_VALUE` number of emissions. This may be fine as long as no more intensive operations or concurrency changes happen downstream and the `Flowable` operations upstream constrains the number of emissions.

But typically, when you commit to using a `Flowable`, you should strive to make your operations remain `Flowable`.

Using onBackpressureXXX() operators

If you are provided a `Flowable` that has no backpressure implementation (including ones derived from `Observable`), you can apply `BackpressureStrategy` using `onBackpressureXXX()` operators. These also provide a few additional configuration options. This can be helpful if, for example, you have a `Flowable.interval()` that emits faster than consumers can keep up. `Flowable.interval()` cannot be slowed down at the source because it is time-driven, but we can use an `onBackpressureXXX()` operator to proxy between it and the downstream. We will use `Flowable.interval()` for these examples, but this can apply to any `Flowable` that does not have backpressure implemented.

Sometimes, `Flowable` may simply be configured with `BackpressureStrategy.MISSING` so these `onBackpressureXXX()` operators can specify the strategy later.

onBackPressureBuffer()

The `onBackPressureBuffer()` will take an existing `Flowable` that is assumed to not have backpressure implemented and then essentially apply `BackpressureStrategy.BUFFER` at that point to the downstream. Since `Flowable.interval()` cannot be backpressured at the source, putting `onBackPressureBuffer()` after it will proxy a backpressured queue to the downstream:

```
import io.reactivex.Flowable;
 import io.reactivex.schedulers.Schedulers;
 import java.util.concurrent.TimeUnit;
public class Launcher {
    public static void main(String[] args) {
        Flowable.interval(1, TimeUnit.MILLISECONDS)
                .onBackpressureBuffer()
                .observeOn(Schedulers.io())
                .subscribe(i -> {
                    sleep(5);
                    System.out.println(i);
                });
        sleep(5000);
    }
    public static void sleep(long millis) {
        try {
            Thread.sleep(millis);
        } catch (InterruptedException e) {
```

```
                        e.printStackTrace();
                }
        }
}
```

The output is as follows:

```
0
1
2
3
4
5
6
7
. . .
```

There are a number of overload arguments that you can provide as well. We will not get into all of them, and you can refer to the JavaDocs for more information, but we will highlight the common ones. The capacity argument will create a maximum threshold for the buffer rather than allowing it to be unbounded. An onOverflow Action lambda can be specified to fire an action when an overflow exceeds the capacity. You can also specify a BackpressureOverflowStrategy enum to instruct how to handle an overflow that exceeds the capacity.

Here are the three BackpressureOverflowStrategy enum items that you can choose from:

BackpressureOverflowStrategy	Description
ERROR	Simply throws an error the moment capacity is exceeded
DROP_OLDEST	Drops the oldest value from the buffer to make way for a new one
DROP_LATEST	Drops the latest value from the buffer to prioritize older, unconsumed values

In the following code, we hold a maximum capacity of 10 and specify to use BackpressureOverflowStrategy.DROP_LATEST in the event of an overflow. We also will print a notification in the event of an overflow:

```
import io.reactivex.BackpressureOverflowStrategy;
import io.reactivex.Flowable;
import io.reactivex.schedulers.Schedulers;
import java.util.concurrent.TimeUnit;
public class Launcher {
```

```
public static void main(String[] args) {
    Flowable.interval(1, TimeUnit.MILLISECONDS)
            .onBackpressureBuffer(10,
                    () -> System.out.println("overflow!"),
                    BackpressureOverflowStrategy.DROP_LATEST)
            .observeOn(Schedulers.io())
            .subscribe(i -> {
                sleep(5);
                System.out.println(i);
            });
    sleep(5000);
}
public static void sleep(long millis) {
    try {
        Thread.sleep(millis);
    } catch (InterruptedException e) {
        e.printStackTrace();
    }
}
}
```

The output is as follows:

```
...
overflow!
overflow!
135
overflow!
overflow!
overflow!
overflow!
overflow!
136
overflow!
overflow!
overflow!
overflow!
overflow!
492
overflow!
overflow!
overflow!
...
```

Note that in this part of my noisy output, there was a large range of numbers skipped between 136 and 492. This is because these emissions were dropped from the queue due to BackpressureOverflowStrategy.DROP_LATEST. The queue was already filled with emissions waiting to be consumed, so the new emissions were ignored.

onBackPressureLatest()

A slight variant of onBackpressureBuffer() is onBackPressureLatest(). This will retain the latest value from the source while the downstream is busy, and once the downstream is free to process more, it will provide the latest value. Any previous values emitted during this busy period will be lost:

```java
import io.reactivex.Flowable;
 import io.reactivex.schedulers.Schedulers;
import java.util.concurrent.TimeUnit;
public class Launcher {
    public static void main(String[] args) {
        Flowable.interval(1, TimeUnit.MILLISECONDS)
                .onBackpressureLatest()
                .observeOn(Schedulers.io())
                .subscribe(i -> {
                    sleep(5);
                    System.out.println(i);
                });
        sleep(5000);
    }
    public static void sleep(long millis) {
        try {
            Thread.sleep(millis);
        } catch (InterruptedException e) {
            e.printStackTrace();
        }
    }
}
```

The output is as follows:

```
...
122
123
124
125
126
127
494
495
496
497
...
```

If you study my output, you will notice that there is a jump between 127 and 494. This is because all numbers in between were ultimately beaten by 494 being the latest value, and at that time, the downstream was ready to process more emissions. It started by consuming the cached 494 and the others before it was dropped.

onBackPressureDrop()

The onBackpressureDrop() will simply discard emissions if the downstream is too busy to process them. This is helpful when emissions are considered redundant if the downstream is already occupied (such as a "RUN" request being sent repeatedly, although the resulting process is already running). You can optionally provide an onDrop lambda argument specifying what to do with each dropped item, which we will simply print, as shown in the following code:

```
import io.reactivex.Flowable;
import io.reactivex.schedulers.Schedulers;
import java.util.concurrent.TimeUnit;
public class Launcher {
    public static void main(String[] args) {
        Flowable.interval(1, TimeUnit.MILLISECONDS)
                .onBackpressureDrop(i ->
System.out.println("Dropping " + i))
                .observeOn(Schedulers.io())
                .subscribe(i -> {
                    sleep(5);
                    System.out.println(i);
                });
        sleep(5000);
    }
    public static void sleep(long millis) {
        try {
            Thread.sleep(millis);
        } catch (InterruptedException e) {
            e.printStackTrace();
        }
    }
}
```

The output is as follows:

```
. . .
Dropping 653
Dropping 654
Dropping 655
Dropping 656
```

```
127
Dropping 657
Dropping 658
Dropping 659
Dropping 660
Dropping 661
493
Dropping 662
Dropping 663
Dropping 664
...
```

In my output, note that there is a large jump between `127` and `493`. The numbers between them were dropped because the downstream was already busy when they were ready to be processed, so they were discarded rather than queued.

Using Flowable.generate()

A lot of the content we covered so far in this chapter did not show the optimal approaches to backpressure a source. Yes, using a `Flowable` and most of the standard factories and operators will automatically handle backpressure for you. However, if you are creating your own custom sources, `Flowable.create()` or the `onBackPressureXXX()` operators are somewhat compromised in how they handle backpressure requests. While quick and effective for some cases, caching emissions or simply dropping them is not always desirable. It would be better to make the source backpressured in the first place.

Thankfully, `Flowable.generate()` exists to help create backpressure, respecting sources at a nicely abstracted level. It will accept a `Consumer<Emitter<T>>` much like `Flowable.create()`, but it will use a lambda to specify what `onNext()`, `onComplete()`, and `onError()` events to pass each time an item is requested from the upstream.

Before you use `Flowable.generate()`, consider making your source `Iterable<T>` instead and passing it to `Flowable.fromIterable()`. The `Flowable.fromIterable()` will respect backpressure and might be easier to use for many cases. Otherwise, `Flowable.generate()` is your next best option if you need something more specific.

The simplest overload for `Flowable.generate()` accepts just
`Consumer<Emitter<T>>` and assumes that there is no state maintained between emissions.
This can be helpful in creating a backpressure-aware random integer generator, as
displayed here. Note that 128 emissions are immediately emitted, but after that, 96 are
pushed downstream before another 96 are sent from the source:

```java
import io.reactivex.Flowable;
 import io.reactivex.schedulers.Schedulers;
 import java.util.concurrent.ThreadLocalRandom;
public class Launcher {
    public static void main(String[] args) {
        randomGenerator(1,10000)
                .subscribeOn(Schedulers.computation())
                .doOnNext(i -> System.out.println("Emitting " +
i))
                .observeOn(Schedulers.io())
                .subscribe(i -> {
                    sleep(50);
                    System.out.println("Received " + i);
                });
        sleep(10000);
    }
    static Flowable<Integer> randomGenerator(int min, int max) {
        return Flowable.generate(emitter ->

emitter.onNext(ThreadLocalRandom.current().nextInt(min, max))
        );
    }
    public static void sleep(long millis) {
        try {
            Thread.sleep(millis);
        } catch (InterruptedException e) {
            e.printStackTrace();
        }
    }
}
```

The output is as follows:

```
...
Emitting 8014
Emitting 3112
Emitting 5958
Emitting 4834 //128th emission
Received 9563
Received 4359
Received 9362
```

```
. . .
Received 4880
Received 3192
Received 979 //96th emission
Emitting 8268
Emitting 3889
Emitting 2595
. . .
```

With `Flowable.generate()`, invoking multiple `onNext()` operators within `Consumer<Emitter<T>>` will result in `IllegalStateException`. The downstream needs it only to invoke `onNext()` once, so it can make the repeated calls, as required, to maintain flow. It will also emit `onError()` for you in the event that an exception occurs.

You can also provide a state that can act somewhat like a "seed" similar to `reduce()` and maintain a state that is passed from one emission to the next. Suppose we want to create something similar to `Flowable.range()` but instead, we want to emit the integers in reverse between `upperBound` and `lowerBound`. Using `AtomicInteger` as our state, we can decrement it and pass its value to the emitter's `onNext()` operator until `lowerBound` is encountered. This is demonstrated as follows:

```java
import io.reactivex.Flowable;
 import io.reactivex.schedulers.Schedulers;
 import java.util.concurrent.atomic.AtomicInteger;
public class Launcher {
    public static void main(String[] args) {
        rangeReverse(100,-100)
                .subscribeOn(Schedulers.computation())
                .doOnNext(i -> System.out.println("Emitting " +
i))
                .observeOn(Schedulers.io())
                .subscribe(i -> {
                    sleep(50);
                    System.out.println("Received " + i);
                });
        sleep(50000);
    }
    static Flowable<Integer> rangeReverse(int upperBound, int
lowerBound) {
        return Flowable.generate(() -> new
AtomicInteger(upperBound + 1),
                (state, emitter) -> {
                    int current = state.decrementAndGet();
                    emitter.onNext(current);
                    if (current == lowerBound)
                        emitter.onComplete();
```

```
                    }
              );
        }
        public static void sleep(long millis) {
            try {
                Thread.sleep(millis);
            } catch (InterruptedException e) {
                e.printStackTrace();
            }
        }
    }
}
```

The output is as follows:

```
Emitting 100
Emitting 99
...
Emitting -25
Emitting -26
Emitting -27 //128th emission
Received 100
Received 99
Received 98
...
Received 7
Received 6
Received 5 // 96th emission
Emitting -28
Emitting -29
Emitting -30
```

`Flowable.generator()` provides a nicely abstracted mechanism to create a source that respects backpressure. For this reason, you might want to prefer this over `Flowable.create()` if you do not want to mess with caching or dropping emissions.

With `Flowable.generate()`, you can also provide a third `Consumer<? super S>` `disposeState` argument to do any disposal operations on termination, which can be helpful for IO sources.

Summary

In this chapter, you learned about `Flowable` and backpressure and which situations it should be preferred over an `Observable`. Flowables are especially preferable when concurrency enters your application and a lot of data can flow through it, as it regulates how much data comes from the source at a given time. Some Flowables, such as `Flowable.interval()` or those derived from an `Observable`, do not have backpressure implemented. In these situations, you can use `onBackpressureXXX()` operators to queue or drop emissions for the downstream. If you are creating your own `Flowable` source from scratch, prefer to use the existing `Flowable` factories, and if that fails, prefer `Flowable.generate()` instead of `Flowable.create()`.

If you got to this point and understand most of the content in this book so far, congrats! You have all the core concepts of RxJava in your toolkit, and the rest of the book is all a walk in the park from here. The next chapter will cover how to create your own operators, which can be a somewhat advanced task. At a minimum, you should know how to compose existing operators to create new operators, which will be one of the next topics.

9
Transformers and Custom Operators

In RxJava, there are ways to implement your own custom operators using the `compose()` and `lift()` methods, which exist on both `Observable` and `Flowable`. Most of the time, you will likely want to compose existing RxJava operators to create a new operator. But on occasion, you may find yourself needing an operator that must be built from scratch. The latter is a lot more work, but we will cover how to do both of these tasks.

In this chapter, we will cover the following topics:

- Composing new operators with existing operators using `compose()` and Transformers
- The `to()` operator
- Implementing operators from scratch with `lift()`
- RxJava2-Extras and RxJava2Extensions

Transformers

When working with RxJava, you may find yourself wanting to reuse pieces of an `Observable` or `Flowable` chain and somehow consolidate these operators into a new operator. Good developers find opportunities to reuse code, and RxJava provides this ability using `ObservableTransformer` and `FlowableTransformer`, which you can pass to the `compose()` operator.

ObservableTransformer

Bring back *Google Guava* as a dependency. In Chapter 3, *Basic Operators,* we covered the `collect()` operator and used it to turn `Observable<T>` into a `Single<ImmutableList<T>>`. Effectively, we want to collect `T` emissions into a Google Guava `ImmutableList<T>`. Suppose we do this operation enough times until it starts to feel redundant. Here, we use this `ImmutableList` operation for two different `Observable` subscriptions:

```java
import com.google.common.collect.ImmutableList;
import io.reactivex.Observable;

public class Launcher {

    public static void main(String[] args) {

        Observable.just("Alpha", "Beta", "Gamma", "Delta",
"Epsilon")
                .collect(ImmutableList::builder,
ImmutableList.Builder::add)
                .map(ImmutableList.Builder::build)
                .subscribe(System.out::println);

        Observable.range(1,15)
                .collect(ImmutableList::builder,
ImmutableList.Builder::add)
                .map(ImmutableList.Builder::build)
                .subscribe(System.out::println);
    }
}
```

The output is as follows:

```
[Alpha, Beta, Gamma, Delta, Epsilon]
 [1, 2, 3, 4, 5, 6, 7, 8, 9, 10]
```

Take a look at this part of the Observable chain used in two places above:

```java
collect(ImmutableList::builder, ImmutableList.Builder::add)
    .map(ImmutableList.Builder::build)
```

This is a bit redundant to invoke twice, so is it possible that we can compose these operators into a single operator that collects emissions into an `ImmutableList`? As a matter of fact, yes! To target an `Observable<T>`, you can implement `ObservableTransformer<T, R>`. This type has an `apply()` method that accepts an `Observable<T>` upstream and returns an `Observable<R>` downstream. In your implementation, you can return an `Observable` chain that adds on any operators to the upstream, and after those transformations, it returns an `Observable<R>`.

For our example, we will target any generic type `T` for a given `Observable<T>`, and `R` will be an `ImmutableList<T>` emitted through an `Observable<ImmutableList<T>>`. We will package all of this up in an `ObservableTransformer<T, ImmutableList<T>>` implementation, as shown in the following code snippet:

```
public static <T> ObservableTransformer<T, ImmutableList<T>>
toImmutableList() {

    return new ObservableTransformer<T, ImmutableList<T>>() {
        @Override
        public ObservableSource<ImmutableList<T>>
apply(Observable<T> upstream) {
            return upstream.collect(ImmutableList::<T>builder,
ImmutableList.Builder::add)
                    .map(ImmutableList.Builder::build)
                    .toObservable(); // must turn Single into
Observable
        }
    };
}
```

Since `collect()` returns a `Single`, we will invoke `toObservable()` on it since `ObservableTransformer` expects an `Observable`, not `Single`, to be returned. It is not uncommon for Transformers to be delivered through static factory methods, so that is what we did here.

Since there is only one single abstract method in `ObservableTransformer`, we can streamline this more using a lambda instead. This reads a bit easier, as it reads left-to-right/top-to-bottom and expresses *for a given upstream Observable, return it with these operators added to the downstream*:

```
public static <T> ObservableTransformer<T, ImmutableList<T>>
toImmutableList() {

    return  upstream ->
upstream.collect(ImmutableList::<T>builder,
ImmutableList.Builder::add)
```

```
                              .map(ImmutableList.Builder::build)
                              .toObservable(); // must turn Single into
Observable
      }
```

To invoke a Transformer into an `Observable` chain, you pass it to the `compose()` operator. When called on an `Observable<T>`, the `compose()` operator accepts an `ObservableTransformer<T, R>` and returns the transformed `Observable<R>`. This allows you to reuse Rx logic and invoke it in multiple places, and now we can call `compose(toImmutableList())` on both of our `Observable` operations:

```java
import com.google.common.collect.ImmutableList;
import io.reactivex.Observable;
import io.reactivex.ObservableTransformer;

public class Launcher {

    public static void main(String[] args) {

        Observable.just("Alpha", "Beta", "Gamma", "Delta",
"Epsilon")
                    .compose(toImmutableList())
                    .subscribe(System.out::println);

        Observable.range(1,10)
                    .compose(toImmutableList())
                    .subscribe(System.out::println);
    }


    public static <T> ObservableTransformer<T, ImmutableList<T>>
toImmutableList() {

        return  upstream ->
upstream.collect(ImmutableList::<T>builder,
ImmutableList.Builder::add)
                         .map(ImmutableList.Builder::build)
                         .toObservable(); // must turn Single into
Observable
      }
   }
```

The output is as follows:

```
[Alpha, Beta, Gamma, Delta, Epsilon]
[1, 2, 3, 4, 5, 6, 7, 8, 9, 10]
```

It is common for APIs to organize Transformers in a static factory class. In a real-world application, you may store your `toImmutableList()` Transformer inside a `GuavaTransformers` class. Then, you can invoke it by calling `compose(GuavaTransformers.toImmutableList())` in your `Observable` operation.

Note for this example, we could actually make the `toImmutableList()` a reusable singleton since it does not take any parameters.

You can also create Transformers that target specific emission types and accept arguments. For example, you can create a `joinToString()` Transformer that accepts a separator argument and concatenates `String` emissions with that separator. Usage of this `ObservableTransformer` will only compile when invoked on an `Observable<String>`:

```
import io.reactivex.Observable;
import io.reactivex.ObservableTransformer;

public class Launcher {

    public static void main(String[] args) {

        Observable.just("Alpha", "Beta", "Gamma", "Delta",
"Epsilon")
                .compose(joinToString("/"))
                .subscribe(System.out::println);
    }

    public static ObservableTransformer<String, String>
joinToString(String separator) {
        return  upstream -> upstream
                .collect(StringBuilder::new, (b,s) ->  {
                    if (b.length() == 0)
                        b.append(s);
                    else
                        b.append(separator).append(s);
                })
                .map(StringBuilder::toString)
                .toObservable();
    }
}
```

The output is as follows:

```
Alpha/Beta/Gamma/Delta/Epsilon
```

Transformers are a great way to reuse a series of operators that perform a common task, and leveraging them can greatly increase your Rx code reusability. Usually, you will get the most flexibility and speed by implementing them through static factory methods, but you can also extend `ObservableTransformer` onto your own class implementation.

As we will learn in Chapter 12, *Using RxJava with Kotlin*, the Kotlin language enables powerful language features that streamline RxJava even more. Instead of using Transformers, you can leverage extension functions to add operators to the `Observable` and `Flowable` types without inheritance. We will learn more about this later.

FlowableTransformer

When you implement your own `ObservableTransformer`, you might want to create a `FlowableTransformer` counterpart as well. This way, you can use your operator on both Observables and Flowables.

The `FlowableTransformer` is not much different from `ObservableTransformer`. Of course, it will support backpressure since it is composed with Flowables. Otherwise, it is pretty much the same in its usage except that you obviously pass it to `compose()` on a `Flowable`, not `Observable`.

Here, we take our `toImmutableList()` method returning an `ObservableTransformer` and implement it as `FlowableTransformer` instead:

```
import com.google.common.collect.ImmutableList;
import io.reactivex.Flowable;
import io.reactivex.FlowableTransformer;

public class Launcher {

    public static void main(String[] args) {

        Flowable.just("Alpha", "Beta", "Gamma", "Delta",
"Epsilon")
                .compose(toImmutableList())
                .subscribe(System.out::println);

        Flowable.range(1,10)
                .compose(toImmutableList())
                .subscribe(System.out::println);
    }


    public static <T> FlowableTransformer<T, ImmutableList<T>>
```

```
toImmutableList() {

            return    upstream ->
upstream.collect(ImmutableList::<T>builder,
ImmutableList.Builder::add)
               .map(ImmutableList.Builder::build)
               .toFlowable(); // must turn Single into Flowable
        }
    }
```

You should be able to make a similar conversion to `FlowableTransformer` for our `joinToString()` example as well.

You might consider creating separate static utility classes to store your `FlowableTransformers` and `ObservableTransformers` separately to prevent name clashes. Our `FlowableTransformer` and `ObservableTransformer` variants of `toImmutableList()` cannot exist in the same static utility class unless they have different method names. But it might be cleaner to put them in separate classes, such as `MyObservableTransformers` and `MyFlowableTransformers`. You could also have them in separate packages with the same class name, `MyTransformers`, one for Observables and the other for Flowables.

Avoiding shared state with Transformers

When you start creating your own Transformers and custom operators (covered later), an easy way to shoot yourself in the foot is to share states between more than one subscription. This can quickly create unwanted side effects and buggy applications and is one of the reasons you have to tread carefully as you create your own operators.

Say, you want to create an `ObservableTransformer<T, IndexedValue<T>>`, which pairs each emission with its consecutive index starting at 0. First, you create an `IndexedValue<T>` class to simply pair each `T` value with an `int index`:

```
static final class IndexedValue<T> {
    final int index;
    final T value;

    IndexedValue(int index, T value) {
        this.index = index;
        this.value = value;
    }

    @Override
    public String toString() {
```

```
                    return   index + " - " + value;
            }
        }
```

Then, you create an `ObservableTransformer<T,IndexedValue<T>>` that uses an `AtomicInteger` to increment and attach an integer to each emission. But there is something wrong with our implementation here:

```
static <T> ObservableTransformer<T,IndexedValue<T>> withIndex() {
    final AtomicInteger indexer = new AtomicInteger(-1);
    return upstream -> upstream.map(v -> new
IndexedValue<T>(indexer.incrementAndGet(), v));
 }
```

See anything wrong yet? Try to run this `Observable` operation, which has two Observers and uses this `withIndex()` Transformer. Look at the output carefully:

```
import io.reactivex.Observable;
import io.reactivex.ObservableTransformer;
import java.util.concurrent.atomic.AtomicInteger;

public class Launcher {

    public static void main(String[] args) {

        Observable<IndexedValue<String>> indexedStrings =
                Observable.just("Alpha", "Beta", "Gamma", "Delta",
"Epsilon")
                    .compose(withIndex());

        indexedStrings.subscribe(v ->
System.out.println("Subscriber 1: " + v));
        indexedStrings.subscribe(v ->
System.out.println("Subscriber 2: " + v));
    }

    static <T> ObservableTransformer<T,IndexedValue<T>>
withIndex() {
        final AtomicInteger indexer = new AtomicInteger(-1);
        return upstream -> upstream.map(v -> new
IndexedValue<T>(indexer.incrementAndGet(), v));
    }

    static final class IndexedValue<T> {
        final int index;
        final T value;

        IndexedValue(int index, T value) {
```

```
                        this.index = index;
                        this.value = value;
                    }

                    @Override
                    public String toString() {
                        return  index + " - " + value;
                    }
                }
            }
```

The output is as follows:

```
            Subscriber 1: 0 - Alpha
            Subscriber 1: 1 - Beta
            Subscriber 1: 2 - Gamma
            Subscriber 1: 3 - Delta
            Subscriber 1: 4 - Epsilon
            Subscriber 2: 5 - Alpha
            Subscriber 2: 6 - Beta
            Subscriber 2: 7 - Gamma
            Subscriber 2: 8 - Delta
            Subscriber 2: 9 - Epsilon
```

Note that a single instance of `AtomicInteger` was shared between both subscriptions, which means its state was shared as well. On the second subscription, instead of starting over at 0, it picks up at the index left by the previous subscription and starts at index 5 since the previous subscription ended at 4.

Unless you have some stateful behaviors you are deliberately implementing, this is probably an unwanted side-effect that can result in maddening bugs. Constants are usually fine, but a mutable shared state between subscriptions is often something you want to avoid.

A quick and easy way to create a new resource (such as `AtomicInteger`) for each subscription is to wrap everything in `Observable.defer()`, including the `AtomicInteger` instance. This way, a new `AtomicInteger` is created each time with the returned indexing operations:

```
        static <T> ObservableTransformer<T,IndexedValue<T>> withIndex() {
            return upstream -> Observable.defer(() -> {
                AtomicInteger indexer = new AtomicInteger(-1);
                return upstream.map(v -> new
        IndexedValue<T>(indexer.incrementAndGet(), v));
            });
        }
```

You can also create an `AtomicInteger` within `Observable.fromCallable()` and use `flatMap()` on it to the `Observable` that uses it.

In this particular example, you can also use `Observable.zip()` or `zipWith()` with `Observable.range()`. Since this is a pure Rx approach as well, no state will be shared between multiple subscribers, and this will also solve our problem:

```
static <T> ObservableTransformer<T,IndexedValue<T>> withIndex() {
    return upstream ->
        Observable.zip(upstream,
            Observable.range(0,Integer.MAX_VALUE),
            (v,i) -> new IndexedValue<T>(i, v)
        );
}
```

Again, inadvertent shared state and side-effects are dangerous in Rx! Whatever implementation you use to create your Transformer, it is better to rely on pure Rx factories and operators in your implementation if possible. Avoid creating imperative states and objects that risk being shared across subscriptions unless you are fulfilling some strange business requirement where a shared state is explicitly wanted.

Using to() for fluent conversion

On rare occasions, you may find yourself having to pass an `Observable` to another API that converts it into a proprietary type. This can be done simply by passing an `Observable` as an argument to a factory that does this conversion. However, this does not always feel fluent, and this is where the `to()` operator comes in.

For example, JavaFX has a `Binding<T>` type that houses a mutable value of type `T`, and it will notify affected user interface elements to update when it changes. RxJavaFX has `JavaFxObserver.toBinding()` and `JavaFxSubscriber.toBinding()` factories, which can turn an `Observable<T>` or `Flowable<T>` into a JavaFX `Binding<T>`. Here is a simple JavaFX `Application` that uses `Binding<String>` built-off `Observable<String>`, which is used to bind to a `textProperty()` operator of `label`:

```
import io.reactivex.Observable;
import io.reactivex.rxjavafx.observers.JavaFxObserver;
import io.reactivex.rxjavafx.schedulers.JavaFxScheduler;
import javafx.application.Application;
import javafx.beans.binding.Binding;
import javafx.scene.Scene;
import javafx.scene.control.Label;
import javafx.scene.layout.VBox;
```

```
import javafx.stage.Stage;

import java.util.concurrent.TimeUnit;

public final class JavaFxApp extends Application {

    @Override
    public void start(Stage stage) throws Exception {

        VBox root = new VBox();
        Label label = new Label("");

        // Observable with second timer
        Observable<String> seconds =
                Observable.interval(1, TimeUnit.SECONDS)
                        .map(i -> i.toString())
                        .observeOn(JavaFxScheduler.platform());

        // Turn Observable into Binding
        Binding<String> binding =
JavaFxObserver.toBinding(seconds);

        //Bind Label to Binding
        label.textProperty().bind(binding);

        root.setMinSize(200, 100);
        root.getChildren().addAll(label);

        Scene scene = new Scene(root);
        stage.setScene(scene);
        stage.show();
    }
}
```

Since we have gotten so used to fluent programming with RxJava, would it not be nice to make the conversion of the `Observable<String>` to a `Binding<String>` part of the `Observable` chain too? This way, we do not have to break our fluent style and save intermediary variables. That can be done with the `to()` operator, which simply accepts an `Function<Observable<T>,R>` to turn an `Observable<T>` into any arbitrary `R` type. In this case, we can turn our `Observable<String>` into a `Binding<String>`at the end of our `Observable` chain using `to()`:

```
import io.reactivex.Observable;
import io.reactivex.rxjavafx.observers.JavaFxObserver;
import io.reactivex.rxjavafx.schedulers.JavaFxScheduler;
import javafx.application.Application;
import javafx.beans.binding.Binding;
```

```
import javafx.scene.Scene;
import javafx.scene.control.Label;
import javafx.scene.layout.VBox;
import javafx.stage.Stage;
import java.util.concurrent.TimeUnit;

public final class JavaFxApp extends Application {

    @Override
    public void start(Stage stage) throws Exception {

        VBox root = new VBox();
        Label label = new Label("");

        // Turn Observable into Binding
        Binding<String> binding =
                Observable.interval(1, TimeUnit.SECONDS)
                        .map(i -> i.toString())
                        .observeOn(JavaFxScheduler.platform())
                        .to(JavaFxObserver::toBinding);

        //Bind Label to Binding
        label.textProperty().bind(binding);

        root.setMinSize(200, 100);
        root.getChildren().addAll(label);

        Scene scene = new Scene(root);
        stage.setScene(scene);
        stage.show();
    }
}
```

Simple but helpful, right? When you are dealing with proprietary non-Rx types that can be built off Rx Observabes and Flowables, this is a handy utility to maintain the fluent Rx style, especially when interoperating with binding frameworks.

Operators

Ideally, you will rarely get to a point where you need to build your own operator from scratch by implementing ObservableOperator or FlowableOperator. ObservableTransformer and FlowableTransformer will hopefully satisfy most cases where you can use existing operators to compose new ones, and this is usually the safest route. But on occasion, you may find yourself having to do something that the existing operators cannot do or not do easily. After you exhaust all other options, you may have to create an operator that manipulates each onNext(), onComplete(), and onError() event between the upstream and the downstream.

Before you go out and create your own operator, try to use existing operators first with compose() and a Transformer. After that fails, it is recommended that you post a question on StackOverflow and ask the RxJava community whether such an operator exists or can be composed easily. The RxJava community is very active on StackOverflow and they will likely provide a solution and only escalate the complexity of the solution as required.

 Note that David Karnok's *RxJava2Extensions* and Dave Moten's *RxJava2-Extras* have many useful Transformers and operators to augment RxJava as well. You should check out these libraries to see whether they fulfill your needs.

If it is determined that there are no existing solutions, then proceed carefully to build your own operator. Again, it is recommended that you solicit help from StackOverflow first. Building a native operator is no easy task, and getting insight and experience from an Rx expert is highly valuable and most likely necessary.

Implementing an ObservableOperator

Implementing your own ObservableOperator (as well as FlowableTransformer) is more involved than creating an ObservableTransformer. Instead of composing a series of existing operators, you intercept the onNext(), onComplete(), onError(), and onSubscribe() calls from the upstream by implementing your own Observer instead. This Observer will then logically pass the onNext(), onComplete(), and onError() events to the downstream Observer in a way that fulfills the desired operation.

Say, you want to create your own `doOnEmpty()` operator that will execute an `Action` when `onComplete()` is called and no emissions have occurred. To create your own `ObservableOperator<Downstream, Upstream>` (where `Upstream` is the upstream emission type and `Downstream` is the downstream emission type), you will need to implement its `apply()` method. This accepts an `Observer<Downstream>` observer argument and returns an `Observer<Upstream>`.

You can then use this `ObservableOperator` by calling it in the `lift()` operator in your `Observable` chain, as shown here:

```
import io.reactivex.Observable;
import io.reactivex.ObservableOperator;
import io.reactivex.Observer;
import io.reactivex.functions.Action;
import io.reactivex.observers.DisposableObserver;

public class Launcher {

    public static void main(String[] args) {

        Observable.range(1, 5)
                .lift(doOnEmpty(() ->
System.out.println("Operation 1 Empty!")))
                .subscribe(v -> System.out.println("Operation 1: "
+ v));


        Observable.<Integer>empty()
                .lift(doOnEmpty(() ->
System.out.println("Operation 2 Empty!")))
                .subscribe(v -> System.out.println("Operation 2: "
+ v));
    }

    public static <T> ObservableOperator<T,T> doOnEmpty(Action
action) {
        return new ObservableOperator<T, T>() {

            @Override
            public Observer<? super T> apply(Observer<? super T>
observer) throws Exception {
                return new DisposableObserver<T>() {
                    boolean isEmpty = true;

                    @Override
                    public void onNext(T value) {
                        isEmpty = false;
```

```
                    observer.onNext(value);
                }

                @Override
                public void onError(Throwable t) {
                    observer.onError(t);
                }

                @Override
                public void onComplete() {
                    if (isEmpty) {
                        try {
                            action.run();
                        } catch (Exception e) {
                            onError(e);
                            return;
                        }
                    }
                    observer.onComplete();
                }
            };
        }
    };
}
}
```

The output is as follows:

```
Operation 1: 1
Operation 1: 2
Operation 1: 3
Operation 1: 4
Operation 1: 5
Operation 2 Empty!
```

Inside `apply()`, you take the passed `Observer` that accepts events for the downstream. You create another `Observer` (in this case, we should use a `DisposableObserver` that handles disposal requests for us) to receive emissions and events from the upstream and relay them to the downstream `Observer`. You can manipulate the events to execute the desired logic as well as add any side-effects.

In this case, we simply passed the events from the upstream to the downstream untampered but track whether `onNext()` was called to flag if emissions were present. When `onComplete()` is called and no emissions are present, it will execute the user-specified action within `onComplete()`. It is usually a good idea to wrap any code that could throw runtime errors in `try-catch` and pass those captured errors to `onError()`.

With `ObservableOperator`, it may seem odd that you get the downstream as an input and have to produce an `Observer` for the upstream as the output. With the `map()` operator, for example, the function receives the upstream value and returns the value to be emitted toward the downstream. The reason for this is that code from an `ObservableOperator` gets executed at subscription time where the call travels from the end `Observer` (downstream) toward the source `Observable` (upstream).

Since it is a single abstract method class, you can also express your `ObservableOperator` implementation as a lambda, as shown here:

```
public static <T> ObservableOperator<T, T> doOnEmpty(Action action)
{
    return observer -> new DisposableObserver<T>() {
        boolean isEmpty = true;

        @Override
        public void onNext(T value) {
            isEmpty = false;
            observer.onNext(value);
        }

        @Override
        public void onError(Throwable t) {
            observer.onError(t);
        }

        @Override
        public void onComplete() {
            if (isEmpty) {
                try {
                    action.run();
                } catch (Exception e) {
                    onError(e);
                    return;
                }
            }
            observer.onComplete();
        }
    };
}
```

Just like `Transformers`, be mindful when creating custom operators to not share states between subscriptions unless you absolutely mean to. This is a relatively simple operator because it is a simple reactive building block, but operators can be made enormously complex. This is especially the case when the operators deal with concurrency (for example, `observeOn()` and `subscribeOn()`) or share states between subscriptions (for example, `replay()`). The implementations of `groupBy()`, `flatMap()`, and `window()` are complicated and intricate as well.

There are a couple of rules in the `Observable` contract you must follow when calling the three events. Never call `onComplete()` after `onError()` has occurred (or vice versa). Do not call `onNext()` after `onComplete()` or `onError()` is called, and do not call any events after disposal. Breaking these rules can have unintended consequences downstream.

Another thing that needs to be pointed out is that `onNext()`, `onComplete()`, and `onError()` calls can be manipulated and mixed as needed. For example, `toList()` does not pass an `onNext()` call downstream for every `onNext()` it receives from the upstream. It will keep collecting these emissions in an internal list. When `onComplete()` is called from the upstream, it will call `onNext()` on the downstream to pass that list before it calls `onComplete()`. Here, we implement our own `myToList()` operator to understand how `toList()` could work, even though in normal circumstances, we should use `collect()` or `toList()`:

```java
import io.reactivex.Observable;
import io.reactivex.ObservableOperator;
import io.reactivex.observers.DisposableObserver;
import java.util.ArrayList;
import java.util.List;

public class Launcher {

    public static void main(String[] args) {

        Observable.range(1, 5)
                .lift(myToList())
                .subscribe(v -> System.out.println("Operation 1: "
+ v));

        Observable.<Integer>empty()
                .lift(myToList())
                .subscribe(v -> System.out.println("Operation 2: "
+ v));
    }
```

```java
public static <T> ObservableOperator<List<T>,T> myToList() {
    return observer -> new DisposableObserver<T>() {

        ArrayList<T> list = new ArrayList<>();

        @Override
        public void onNext(T value) {
            //add to List, but don't pass anything downstream
            list.add(value);
        }

        @Override
        public void onError(Throwable t) {
            observer.onError(t);
        }

        @Override
        public void onComplete() {
            observer.onNext(list); //push List downstream
            observer.onComplete();
        }
    };
}
```

The output is as follows:

```
Operation 1: [1, 2, 3, 4, 5]
Operation 2: []
```

Before you start getting ambitious in creating your own operators, it might be good to study the source code of RxJava or other libraries, such as RxJava2-Extras. Operators can be difficult to implement correctly as you need to have a good understanding of how to build reactive patterns from imperative ones. You will also want to test the heck out of it (which we will cover in Chapter 10, *Testing and Debugging*) in order to ensure that it behaves correctly before putting it in production.

FlowableOperator

When you create your own ObservableOperator, you will most likely want to create a FlowableOperator counterpart as well. This way, your operator can be used for both Observables and Flowables. Thankfully, FlowableOperator is implemented in a similar manner to ObservableOperator, as shown here:

```java
import io.reactivex.Flowable;
```

```java
import io.reactivex.FlowableOperator;
import io.reactivex.functions.Action;
import io.reactivex.subscribers.DisposableSubscriber;
import org.reactivestreams.Subscriber;

public class Launcher {

    public static void main(String[] args) {

        Flowable.range(1, 5)
                .lift(doOnEmpty(() ->
System.out.println("Operation 1 Empty!")))
                .subscribe(v -> System.out.println("Operation 1: "
+ v));


        Flowable.<Integer>empty()
                .lift(doOnEmpty(() ->
System.out.println("Operation 2 Empty!")))
                .subscribe(v -> System.out.println("Operation 2: "
+ v));
    }

    public static <T> FlowableOperator<T,T> doOnEmpty(Action
action) {
        return new FlowableOperator<T, T>() {
            @Override
            public Subscriber<? super T> apply(Subscriber<? super
T> subscriber) throws Exception {
                return new DisposableSubscriber<T>() {
                    boolean isEmpty = true;

                    @Override
                    public void onNext(T value) {
                        isEmpty = false;
                        subscriber.onNext(value);
                    }

                    @Override
                    public void onError(Throwable t) {
                        subscriber.onError(t);
                    }

                    @Override
                    public void onComplete() {
                        if (isEmpty) {
                            try {
                                action.run();
```

```
                                    } catch (Exception e) {
                                        onError(e);
                                        return;
                                    }
                                }
                                subscriber.onComplete();
                            }
                        };
                    }
                };
            }
        }
```

Instead of Observers, we used Subscribers, which hopefully is not surprising at this point. The `Subscriber` passed via `apply()` receives events for the downstream, and the implemented `Subscriber` receives events from the upstream, which it relays to the downstream (just as we used `DisposableObserver`, we use `DisposableSubscriber` to handle disposal/unsubscription for us). Just like earlier, `onComplete()` will verify that no emissions occurred and run the specified action if that is the case.

And of course, you can express your `FlowableOperator` as a lambda too:

```java
public static <T> FlowableOperator<T,T> doOnEmpty(Action action) {
    return subscriber -> new DisposableSubscriber<T>() {
        boolean isEmpty = true;

        @Override
        public void onNext(T value) {
            isEmpty = false;
            subscriber.onNext(value);
        }

        @Override
        public void onError(Throwable t) {
            subscriber.onError(t);
        }

        @Override
        public void onComplete() {
            if (isEmpty) {
                try {
                    action.run();
                } catch (Exception e) {
                    onError(e);
                    return;
                }
            }
        }
```

```
                        subscriber.onComplete();
                    }
                };
            }
```

Again, be studious and thorough when you start implementing your own operators, especially as they pass a threshold of complexity. Strive to use existing operators to compose Transformers, and hit StackOverflow or the RxJava community to see whether others can point out an obvious solution first. Implementing operators is something you should be conservative about and only pursue when all other options have been exhausted.

Custom Transformers and operators for Singles, Maybes, and Completables

There are Transformer and operator counterparts for `Single`, `Maybe`, and `Completable`. When you want to create an `Observable` or `Flowable` operator that yields `Single`, you might find it easier to convert it back into an `Observable`/`Flowable` by calling its `toObservable()` or `toFlowable()` operators. This also applies to `Maybe`.

If on some rare occasion you need to create a Transformer or operator specifically to take a `Single` and transform it into another `Single`, you will want to use `SingleTransformer` or `SingleOperator`. `Maybe` and `Completable` will have counterparts with `MaybeTransformer`/`MaybeOperator` and `CompletableTransformer`/`CompletableOperator`, respectively. The implementation of `apply()` for all of these should largely be the same experience, and you will use `SingleObserver`, `MaybeObserver`, and `CompletableObserver` to proxy the upstream and downstream.

Here is an example of a `SingleTransformer` that takes `Single<Collection<T>>` and maps the emitted `Collection` to an unmodifable collection:

```java
import io.reactivex.Observable;
import io.reactivex.SingleTransformer;
import java.util.Collection;
import java.util.Collections;

public class Launcher {

    public static void main(String[] args) {
        Observable.just("Alpha","Beta","Gamma","Delta","Epsilon")
                .toList()
                .compose(toUnmodifiable())
```

```
                .subscribe(System.out::println);
        }

    public static <T>  SingleTransformer<Collection<T>,
Collection<T>> toUnmodifiable() {
        return singleObserver ->
singleObserver.map(Collections::unmodifiableCollection);
    }
  }
```

The output is as follows:

```
[Alpha, Beta, Gamma, Delta, Epsilon]
```

Using RxJava2-Extras and RxJava2Extensions

If you are interested in learning about additional operators beyond what RxJava provides, it may be worthwhile to explore the *RxJava2-Extras* and *RxJava2Extensions* libraries. While neither of these libraries are at a 1.0 version, useful operators, Transformers, and `Observable`/`Flowable` factories are continually added as an ongoing project.

Two useful operators are `toListWhile()` and `collectWhile()`. These will buffer emissions into a list or collection while they meet a certain condition. Because a `BiPredicate` passes both the list/collection and the next `T` item as lamda input parameters, you can use this to buffer items but cut off the moment something changes about the emissions. Here, we keep collecting strings into a list but push that list forward when the length changes (kind of like `distinctUntilChanged()`). We also will qualify a list being empty, as that is the start of the next buffer, as well as sample an item from the list to compare lengths with the next emission:

```
import com.github.davidmoten.rx2.flowable.Transformers;
import io.reactivex.Flowable;

public class Launcher {

    public static void main(String[] args) {


Flowable.just("Alpha","Beta","Zeta","Gamma","Delta","Theta","Epsilo
n")
                .compose(Transformers.toListWhile((list,next) ->
                    list.size() == 0 || list.get(0).length() ==
```

```
            next.length()
                            )).subscribe(System.out::println);
        }
    }
```

The output is as follows:

```
[Alpha]
[Beta, Zeta]
[Gamma, Delta, Theta]
[Epsilon]
```

Spend some quality time with RxJava2-Extras and RxJava2Extensions to learn about their custom operators. This way, you will not have to reinvent something that may already be done, and there are already many powerful factories and operators. One of my personal favorites is a resettable `cache()` operator, which works like the cache we studied in `Chapter 5`, *Multicasting*, but it can be cleared and then resubscribed to the source at any time. It can also clear the cache at fixed time intervals or periods of no activity, preventing stale caches from persisting.

Summary

In this chapter, we got our feet wet by creating our own operators. It is preferable to use `ObservableTransformer` and `FlowableTransformer` to compose existing operators together to create new ones, and even with that, you need to be cautious when introducing stateful resources that cause undesirable side-effects. When all else fails, you can create your own `ObservableOperator` or `FlowableOperator` and create an operator at a low level that intercepts and relays each emission and event. This can be tricky and you should exhaust all other options, but with careful study and testing, creating operators can be a valuable advanced skill to have. Just be careful to not reinvent the wheel and seek guidance from the Rx community as you start dabbling in custom operators.

If you truly are interested in implementing your own operators (at a low level, not with Transformers), definitely study existing operators in RxJava and other reputable RxJava extension libraries. It is easy to hack an operator together and believe nothing will go wrong, when in fact there are a lot of complications you can overlook. Your operator needs to be serialized, cancellable, concurrent, and handle re-entrancy (which occurs when an emission invokes a request on the same thread). Of course, some operators are simpler than others, but you should never assume without committed study first.

In the next chapter, we will learn about the different strategies to do unit testing against RxJava APIs and utilities. Whether you create your own custom operators or you have an Rx project at work, automated testing is something you will want to be proficient in. We will also learn how to debug RxJava applications, which is not always easy, but it can be done effectively.

10
Testing and Debugging

While unit testing is not a silver bullet to ensure that your code works properly, it is a good practice to strive for. This is especially true if your logic is highly deterministic and modular enough to isolate.

Testing with RxJava at first glance may not seem straightforward. After all, RxJava declares behaviors rather than states. So how do we test whether behaviors are working correctly, especially when most testing frameworks expect a stateful result? Fortunately, RxJava comes with several tools to aid testing, and you can use these tools with your favorite testing frameworks. There are many testing tools available on the market that can work with RxJava, but in this chapter, we will use JUnit.

We will also cover a few tips to effectively debug RxJava programs. One of the downsides of RxJava is that when bugs occur, traditional approaches to debugging are not always effective, particularly because the stack traces are not always helpful and breakpoints do not apply easily. But there is a benefit RxJava offers in debugging: with the right approach, you can walk through your entire reactive chain and find the operator that causes things to go wrong. The problem becomes very linear and a matter of isolating the bad link. This can simplify the debugging process significantly.

This chapter has a number of testing features to cover, so we will start with simpler naive approaches to cover basic blocking operators. Then, we will escalate to the more robust tools, such as `TestObserver`, `TestSubscriber`, and `TestScheduler`, which you will likely use in your applications.

In this chapter, we will cover the following topics:

- `blockingSubscribe()`
- Blocking operators
- `TestObserver` and `TestSubscriber`
- `TestScheduler`
- RxJava debugging strategies

Configuring JUnit

In this section, we will be using JUnit as our testing framework. Add the following dependency to your Maven or Gradle project.

Here is the configuration for Maven:

```
<dependency>
    <groupId>junit</groupId>
    <artifactId>junit</artifactId>
    <version>4.12</version>
</dependency>
```

Here is the configuration for Gradle:

```
dependencies {
    compile 'junit:junit:4.12'
}
```

To save yourself hassle, organize your code project to conform to the Maven Standard Directory layout. You might want to place your test classes in a `/src/test/java/` folder so Maven and Gradle will automatically recognize it as the test code folder. You also should put your production code in a `/src/main/java/` folder in your project. You can read more about the Maven Standard Directory layout at `https://maven.apache.org/guides/introduction/introduction-to-the-standard-directory-layout.html`.

Blocking subscribers

Remember how sometimes we have to stop the main thread from racing past an `Observable` or `Flowable` that operates on a different thread and keep it from exiting the application before it has a chance to fire? We often prevented this using `Thread.sleep()`, especially when we used `Observable.interval()`, `subscribeOn()`, or `observeOn()`.

The following code shows how we did this typically and kept an
`Observable.interval()` application alive for five seconds:

```
import io.reactivex.Observable;
import java.util.concurrent.TimeUnit;

public class Launcher {

    public static void main(String[] args) {
        Observable.interval(1, TimeUnit.SECONDS)
                .take(5)
                .subscribe(System.out::println);

        sleep(5000);
    }

    public static void sleep(int millis) {
        try {
            Thread.sleep(millis);
        } catch (InterruptedException e) {
            e.printStackTrace();
        }
    }
}
```

When it comes to unit testing, the unit test usually has to complete before it starts the next
one. This can become quite messy when we have an `Observable` or `Flowable` operation
that happens on a different thread. When a `test` method declares an asynchronous
`Observable` or `Flowable` chain operation, we need to block and wait for that operation to
complete.

Here, we create a test to ensure that five emissions are emitted from
`Observable.interval()`, and we increment `AtomicInteger` before validating that it
was incremented five times:

```
import io.reactivex.Observable;
import org.junit.Test;
import java.util.concurrent.TimeUnit;
import java.util.concurrent.atomic.AtomicInteger;
import static org.junit.Assert.assertTrue;

public class RxTest {

    @Test
    public void testBlockingSubscribe() {

        AtomicInteger hitCount = new AtomicInteger();
```

```
                    Observable<Long> source = Observable.interval(1,
        TimeUnit.SECONDS)
                                    .take(5);

                    source.subscribe(i -> hitCount.incrementAndGet());

                    assertTrue(hitCount.get() == 5);
            }
        }
```

We use the `@Test` annotation to tell `JUnit` that this is a test method. You can run it in Intellij IDEA by clicking on its green triangular *play* button in the gutter or by running the test task in Gradle or Maven.

There is a problem, though. When you run this test, the assertion fails. `Observable.interval()` is running on a computation thread and the main thread rushes past it. The main thread performs `assertTrue()` before the five emissions are fired and therefore finds `hitCount` to be 0 rather than 5. We need to stop the main thread until `subscribe()` finishes and calls `onComplete()`.

Thankfully, we do not have to get creative using synchronizers and other native Java concurrency tools. Instead, we can use `blockingSubscribe()`, which will block the declaring main thread until `onComplete()` (or `onError()`) is called. Once those five emissions are gathered, the main thread can proceed and perform the assertion successfully, as demonstrated here. The test should then pass:

```java
import io.reactivex.Observable;
import org.junit.Test;
import java.util.concurrent.TimeUnit;
import java.util.concurrent.atomic.AtomicInteger;
import static org.junit.Assert.assertTrue;

public class RxTest {

    @Test
    public void testBlockingSubscribe() {

        AtomicInteger hitCount = new AtomicInteger();

        Observable<Long> source = Observable.interval(1,
TimeUnit.SECONDS)
                    .take(5);

        source.blockingSubscribe(i -> hitCount.incrementAndGet());
```

```
                    assertTrue(hitCount.get() == 5);
        }
    }
```

As we will see in this chapter, there are better ways to test other than
blockingSubscribe(). But blockingSubscribe() is a quick and effective way to stop
the declaring thread and wait for the Observable or Flowable to finish before proceeding,
even if it is on a different thread. Just make sure that the source terminates at some point, or
the test will never finish.

> Be judicious in how you use blockingSubscribe() outside the context
> of testing and using it in production. There are definitely times it is a
> legitimate solution to interface with a non-reactive API. For example, it
> can be valid to use it in production to keep an application alive
> indefinitely and is an effective alternative to using Thread.sleep(). Just
> be careful to ensure the asynchronous benefits of RxJava are not
> undermined.

Blocking operators

In RxJava, there is a set of operators we have not covered yet called **blocking operators**.
These operators serve as an immediate proxy between the reactive world and the stateful
one, blocking and waiting for results to be emitted, but returned in a non-reactive way.
Even if the reactive operations are working on different threads, blocking operators will
stop the declaring thread and make it wait for the results in a synchronized manner, much
like blockingSubscribe().

Blocking operators are especially helpful in making the results of an Observable or
Flowable easily available for evaluation. However, you will want to avoid using them in
production because they encourage anti-patterns and undermine the benefits of reactive
programming. For testing, you will still want to prefer TestObserver and
TestSubscriber, which we will cover later. But here are the blocking operators if you ever
have a need for them.

blockingFirst()

The blockingFirst() operator will stop the calling thread and make it wait for the first value to be emitted and returned (even if the chain is operating on a different thread with observeOn() and subscribeOn()). Say we want to test an Observable chain that filters a sequence of string emissions for only ones that have a length of four. If we want to assert that the first emission to make it through this operation is Beta, we can test for it like this:

```
import io.reactivex.Observable;
import org.junit.Test;
import static org.junit.Assert.assertTrue;

public class RxTest {

    @Test
    public void testFirst() {
        Observable<String> source =
                Observable.just("Alpha", "Beta", "Gamma", "Delta",
"Zeta");

        String firstWithLengthFour = source.filter(s -> s.length()
== 4)
                .blockingFirst();

        assertTrue(firstWithLengthFour.equals("Beta"));
    }
}
```

Here, our unit test is called testFirst(), and it will assert that the first string emitted with a length of four is Beta. Note that instead of using subscribe() or blockingSubscribe() to receive the emissions, we use blockingFirst(), which will return the first emission in a non-reactive way. In other words, it returns a straight-up string and not an Observable emitting string.

This will block the declaring thread until the value is returned and assigned to firstWithLengthFour. We then use that saved value to assert that it is, in fact, Beta.

Looking at `blockingFirst()`, you may be tempted to use it in production code to save a result statefully and refer to it later. Try not to do that! While there are certain cases where you might be able to justify it (such as saving emissions into a `HashMap` for expensive computations and lookups), blocking operators can easily be abused. If you need to persist values, try to use `replay()` and other reactive caching strategies so that you can easily change its behaviors and concurrency policies down the road. Blocking will often make your code less flexible and undermine the benefits of Rx.

Note that the `blockingFirst()` operator will throw an error and fail the test if no emissions come through. However, you can provide a default value as an overload to `blockingFirst()` so it always has a value to fall back on.

A similar blocking operator to `blockingFirst()` is `blockingSingle()`, which expects only a single item to be emitted, but throws an error if there are more.

blockingGet()

`Maybe` and `Single` do not have `blockingFirst()` since there can only be one element at most. Logically, for a `Single` and `Maybe`, it is not exactly the *first* element, but rather the *only* element, so the equivalent operator is `blockingGet()`.

Here, we assert that all items of length four include only `Beta` and `Zeta`, and we collect them with `toList()`, which yields a `Single<List<String>>`. We can use `blockingGet()` to wait for this list and assert that it is equal to our desired result:

```java
import io.reactivex.Observable;
import org.junit.Test;
import java.util.Arrays;
import java.util.List;
import static org.junit.Assert.assertTrue;

public class RxTest {

    @Test
    public void testSingle() {
        Observable<String> source =
                Observable.just("Alpha", "Beta", "Gamma", "Delta",
"Zeta");

        List<String> allWithLengthFour = source.filter(s ->
s.length() == 4)
```

```
                    .toList()
                    .blockingGet();


        assertTrue(allWithLengthFour.equals(Arrays.asList("Beta","Zeta")));
            }
        }
```

blockingLast()

If there is `blockingFirst()`, it only makes sense to have `blockingLast()`. This will block and return the last value to be emitted from an `Observable` or `Flowable` operation. Of course, it will not return anything until `onComplete()` is called, so this is something you will want to avoid using with infinite sources.

Here, we assert that the last four-character string emitted from our operation is `Zeta`:

```
import io.reactivex.Observable;
import org.junit.Test;
import static org.junit.Assert.assertTrue;

public class RxTest {

    @Test
    public void testLast() {
        Observable<String> source =
                Observable.just("Alpha", "Beta", "Gamma", "Delta",
"Zeta");

        String lastWithLengthFour = source.filter(s -> s.length()
== 4)
                .blockingLast();

        assertTrue(lastWithLengthFour.equals("Zeta"));
    }
}
```

Just like `blockingFirst()`, `blockingLast()` will throw an error if no emissions occur, but you can specify an overload for a default value.

blockingIterable()

One of the most interesting blocking operators is `blockingIterable()`. Rather than returning a single emission like our previous examples, it will provide the emissions as they become available through `iterable<T>`. The `Iterator<T>` provided by the `Iterable<T>` will keep blocking the iterating thread until the next emission is available, and the iteration will end when `onComplete()` is called. Here, we iterate through each returned string value to ensure that its length is actually 5:

```
import io.reactivex.Observable;
import org.junit.Test;
import static org.junit.Assert.assertTrue;

public class RxTest {

    @Test
    public void testIterable() {
        Observable<String> source =
                Observable.just("Alpha", "Beta", "Gamma", "Delta",
"Zeta");

        Iterable<String> allWithLengthFive = source.filter(s ->
s.length() == 5)
                    .blockingIterable();

        for (String s: allWithLengthFive) {
            assertTrue(s.length() == 5);
        }
    }
}
```

The `blockingIterable()` will queue up unconsumed values until the `Iterator` is able to process them. This can be problematic without backpressure as you may run into `OutOfMemoryException` errors.

Unlike C#, note that Java's for-each construct will not handle cancellation, breaking, or disposal. You can work around this by iterating the `Iterator` from the iterable inside `try-finally`. In the `finally` block, cast the `Iterator` to a `disposable` so you can call its `dispose()` method.

The `blockingIterable()` can be helpful in quickly turning an `Observable` or `Flowable` into pull-driven functional sequence types such as a Java 8 Stream or Kotlin sequence, which can be built-off iterables. However, for Java 8 streams, you are likely better-off using David Karnok's RxJava2Jdk8Interop library (`https://github.com/akarnokd/RxJava2Jdk8Interop`), so that termination is handled more safely.

blockingForEach()

A more fluent way in which we can execute a blocking for each task is to use the `blockingForEach()` operator instead of `blockingIterable()`. This will block the declaring thread and wait for each emission to be processed before allowing the thread to continue. We can streamline our earlier example, where we iterated each emitted string and ensured that its length was five and specify the assertion as a lambda in the `forEach()` operator instead:

```
import io.reactivex.Observable;
import org.junit.Test;
import static org.junit.Assert.assertTrue;

public class RxTest {

    @Test
    public void testBlockingForEach() {
        Observable<String> source =
                Observable.just("Alpha", "Beta", "Gamma", "Delta",
"Zeta");

        source.filter(s -> s.length() == 5)
                .blockingForEach(s -> assertTrue(s.length() ==
5));
    }
}
```

A variant of `blockingForEach()` is `blockingForEachWhile()`, which accepts a predicate that gracefully terminates the sequence if the predicate evaluates to false against an emission. This can be desirable if all emissions are not going to be consumed and you want to gracefully terminate.

blockingNext()

The `blockingNext()` will return an iterable and block each iterator's `next()` request until the next value is provided. Emissions that occur after the last fulfilled `next()` request and before the current `next()` are ignored. Here, we have a source that emits every microsecond (1/1000th of a millisecond). Note that the iterable returned from `blockingNext()` ignored previous values it missed:

```
import io.reactivex.Observable;
import org.junit.Test;
import java.util.concurrent.TimeUnit;
```

```
public class RxTest {

    @Test
    public void testBlockingNext() {
        Observable<Long> source =
                Observable.interval(1, TimeUnit.MICROSECONDS)
                .take(1000);

        Iterable<Long> iterable = source.blockingNext();

        for (Long i: iterable) {
            System.out.println(i);
        }
    }
}
```

The output is as follows:

```
0
6
9
11
17
23
26
```

blockingLatest()

The iterable from `blockingLatest()`, on the other hand, does not wait for the next value, but requests the last emitted value. Any values before that which were not captured are forgotten. It will not reconsume the latest value if the iterator's `next()` consumed it previously and will block until the next one comes:

```
import io.reactivex.Observable;
import org.junit.Test;
import java.util.concurrent.TimeUnit;

public class RxTest {

    @Test
    public void testBlockingLatest() {
        Observable<Long> source =
                Observable.interval(1, TimeUnit.MICROSECONDS)
                .take(1000);

        Iterable<Long> iterable = source.blockingLatest();
```

```
        for (Long i: iterable) {
            System.out.println(i);
        }
    }
}
```

The output is as follows:

```
0
49
51
53
55
56
58
...
```

blockingMostRecent()

The `blockingMostRecent()` is similar to `blockingLatest()`, but it will re-consume the latest value repeatedly for every `next()` call from the iterator even if it was consumed already. It also requires a `defaultValue` argument so it has something to return if no value is emitted yet. Here, we use `blockingMostRecent()` against an `Observable` emitting every 10 milliseconds. The default value is −1, and it consumes each value repeatedly until the next value is provided:

```
import io.reactivex.Observable;
import org.junit.Test;
import java.util.concurrent.TimeUnit;

public class RxTest {

    @Test
    public void testBlockingMostRecent() {
        Observable<Long> source =
                Observable.interval(10, TimeUnit.MILLISECONDS)
                .take(5);

        Iterable<Long> iterable = source.blockingMostRecent(-1L);

        for (Long i: iterable) {
            System.out.println(i);
        }
    }
}
```

The output is as follows:

```
-1
-1
-1
...
0
0
0
...
1
1
1
...
```

As we finish covering blocking operators, it should be emphasized again that they can be an effective way to do simple assertions and provide means to block for results so they can be consumed easily by a testing framework. However, you will want to avoid using blocking operators for production as much as possible. Try not to give into the sirens of convenience, as you will find that they can quickly undermine the flexibility and benefits of reactive programming.

Using TestObserver and TestSubscriber

We've covered `blockingSubscribe()` and several blocking operators in this chapter so far. While you can use these blocking tools to do simple assertions, there is a much more comprehensive way to test reactive code than simply blocking for one or more values. After all, we should do more than test `onNext()` calls. We also have `onComplete()` and `onError()` events to account for! It also would be great to streamline testing other RxJava events, such as subscription, disposal, and cancellation.

So let's introduce the `TestObserver` and `TestSubscriber`, your two best friends in testing your RxJava applications.

`TestObserver` and `TestSubscriber` are a treasure trove of convenient methods to aid testing, many of which assert that certain events have occurred or specific values were received. There are also blocking methods, such as `awaitTerminalEvent()`, which will stop the calling thread until the reactive operation terminates.

`TestObserver` is used for `Observable`, `Single`, `Maybe`, and `Completable` sources, while `TestSubscriber` is used for Flowable sources. Here is a unit test showcasing several `TestObserver` methods, which also exist on `TestSubscriber` if you are working with Flowables. These methods perform tasks such as asserting that certain events have (or have not) occurred, awaiting terminations or asserting that certain values were received:

```java
import io.reactivex.Observable;
import io.reactivex.observers.TestObserver;
import org.junit.Test;
import java.util.concurrent.TimeUnit;

public class RxTest {

    @Test
    public void usingTestObserver() {

        //An Observable with 5 one-second emissions
        Observable<Long> source = Observable.interval(1,
TimeUnit.SECONDS)
                .take(5);

        //Declare TestObserver
        TestObserver<Long> testObserver = new TestObserver<>();

        //Assert no subscription has occurred yet
        testObserver.assertNotSubscribed();

        //Subscribe TestObserver to source
        source.subscribe(testObserver);

        //Assert TestObserver is subscribed
        testObserver.assertSubscribed();

        //Block and wait for Observable to terminate
        testObserver.awaitTerminalEvent();

        //Assert TestObserver called onComplete()
        testObserver.assertComplete();

        //Assert there were no errors
        testObserver.assertNoErrors();

        //Assert 5 values were received
        testObserver.assertValueCount(5);

        //Assert the received emissions were 0, 1, 2, 3, 4
```

```
                testObserver.assertValues(0L, 1L, 2L, 3L, 4L);
        }
    }
```

This is just a handful of many testing methods available, and they will make your unit tests in a much more comprehensive and streamlined manner. Most of the `TestObserver` methods return `TestObserver` so you can actually chain these assertions fluently (and this also applies to `TestSubscriber`).

 Note also that the `awaitTerminalEvent()` operator can accept a timeout argument that will throw an error if the source does not complete before that time.

Spend some time going through all these testing methods so you are aware of the different assertions you make. Prefer `TestObserver` and `TestSubscriber` over blocking operators as much as possible. This way, you can spend less time maintaining your tests and ensure that you cover the full spectrum of events in the life cycle of an `Observable` or `Flowable` operation.

`TestObserver` implements `Observer`, `MaybeObserver`, `SingleObserver`, and `CompetableObserver` to support all these reactive types. If you live test a long-running asynchronous source, you might want to use `awaitCount()` to wait for a minimum number of emissions to assert with and not wait for the `onComplete()` call.

Manipulating time with the TestScheduler

In our previous examples, did you notice that testing a time-driven `Observable` or `Flowable` requires that time to elapse before the test completes? In the last exercise, we took five emissions from an `Observable.interval()` emitting every 1 second, so that test took 5 seconds to complete. If we have a lot of unit tests that deal with time-driven sources, it can take a long time for testing to complete. Would it not be nice if we could simulate time elapses rather than experiencing them?

The `TestScheduler` does exactly this. It is a Scheduler implementation that allows us to *fast-forward* by a specific amount of elapsed time, and we can do any assertions after each *fast-forward* to see what events have occurred.

Here, we create a test against `Observable.interval()` that emits every minute and ultimately asserts that 90 emissions have occurred after 90 minutes. Rather than having to wait the entire 90 minutes in real time, we use `TestObserver` to artificially elapse these 90 minutes. This allows the test to run instantly:

```java
import io.reactivex.Observable;
import io.reactivex.observers.TestObserver;
import io.reactivex.schedulers.TestScheduler;
import org.junit.Test;

import java.util.concurrent.TimeUnit;

public class RxTest {

    @Test
    public void usingTestScheduler() {

        //Declare TestScheduler
        TestScheduler testScheduler = new TestScheduler();

        //Declare TestObserver
        TestObserver<Long> testObserver = new TestObserver<>();

        //Declare Observable emitting every 1 minute
        Observable<Long> minuteTicker =
                Observable.interval(1, TimeUnit.MINUTES,
testScheduler);

        //Subscribe to TestObserver
        minuteTicker.subscribe(testObserver);

        //Fast forward by 30 seconds
        testScheduler.advanceTimeBy(30, TimeUnit.SECONDS);

        //Assert no emissions have occurred yet
        testObserver.assertValueCount(0);

        //Fast forward to 70 seconds after subscription
        testScheduler.advanceTimeTo(70, TimeUnit.SECONDS);

        //Assert the first emission has occurred
        testObserver.assertValueCount(1);

        //Fast Forward to 90 minutes after subscription
        testScheduler.advanceTimeTo(90, TimeUnit.MINUTES);

        //Assert 90 emissions have occurred
```

```
                    testObserver.assertValueCount(90);
          }
    }
```

Cool, right? It is almost like time travel! We put `Observable.interval()` on our `TestScheduler`. This way, `TestScheduler` controls how the `Observable` interprets time and pushes emissions. We fast-forward 30 seconds using `advanceTimeBy()` and then assert that no emissions have happened yet. We then use `advanceTimeTo()` to jump 70 seconds after subscription occurred and assert that one emission did happen. Finally, we advance 90 minutes after subscription, and we assert that 90 emissions did, in fact, occur.

This all ran instantly rather than taking 90 minutes, showing that it is indeed possible to test time-driven `Observable`/`Flowable` operations without having to actually elapse that time. Carefully note that `advanceTimeBy()` will fast-forward the specified time interval relative to the *current* time, whereas `advanceTimeTo()` will jump to the exact time elapsed since the subscription has occurred.

In summary, use `TestScheduler` when you need to virtually represent time elapsing, but note that it is not a thread-safe Scheduler and should not be used with actual concurrency. A common pitfall is complicated flows that use many operators and Schedulers are not easily configurable to use `TestScheduler`. In this case, you can use `RxJavaPlugins.setComputationScheduler()` and similar methods that override the standard Schedulers and inject `TestScheduler` in its place.

There are two other methods to note in `TestScheduler`. The `now()` will return how much time has virtually elapsed in the unit you specify. The `triggerActions()` method will kick-off any actions that are scheduled to be triggered, but have not virtually been elapsed yet.

Debugging RxJava code

RxJava is not easy to debug at first glance, primarily due to the lack of debug tooling and the large stack traces it can produce. There are efforts in creating effective debugging tools for RxJava, most notably the Frodo library for Android (`https://github.com/android10/frodo`). We will not cover any debugging tools for RxJava as nothing has been standardized quite yet, but we will learn about an effective approach that you can take to debug reactive code.

A common theme in debugging RxJava operations is finding the bad link or the operator in the `Observable`/`Flowable` chain that is causing the problem. Whether an error is being emitted, `onComplete()` is never being called, or an `Observable` is unexpectedly empty, you often have to start at the beginning of the chain at the source and then validate each step downstream until you find the one not working correctly.

Say, we have an `Observable` pushing five strings containing numbers and alphabetic words separated by slashes "/". We want to break these up on the slashes "/", filter only for the alphabetic words, and capture them in `TestObserver`. However, run this operation and you will see that this test fails:

```java
import io.reactivex.observers.TestObserver;
import org.junit.Test;
import io.reactivex.Observable;

public class RxTest {

    @Test
    public void debugWalkthrough() {

        //Declare TestObserver
        TestObserver<String> testObserver = new TestObserver<>();

        //Source pushing three strings
        Observable<String> items =
                Observable.just("521934/2342/Foxtrot",
                        "Bravo/12112/78886/Tango",
                        "283242/4542/Whiskey/2348562");

        //Split and concatMap() on "/"
        items.concatMap(s ->
                Observable.fromArray(s.split("/"))
        )
         //filter for only alphabetic Strings using regex
         .filter(s -> s.matches("[A-Z]+"))

         //Subscribe the TestObserver
         .subscribe(testObserver);

        //Why are no values being emitted?
        System.out.println(testObserver.values());

        //This fails due to no values

        testObserver.assertValues("Foxtrot","Bravo","Tango","Whiskey");
    }
}
```

The output is as follows:

```
[]

java.lang.AssertionError: Value count differs; Expected: 4
[Foxtrot, Bravo, Tango, Whiskey],
    Actual: 0 [] (latch = 0, values = 0, errors = 0, completions =
1)

    at
io.reactivex.observers.BaseTestConsumer.fail(BaseTestConsumer.java:
163)
    at
io.reactivex.observers.BaseTestConsumer.assertValues(BaseTestConsum
er.java:485)
    at RxTest.debugWalkthrough(RxTest.java:32)
...
```

So what in the world went wrong? How do we debug this failing test? Well, remember that RxJava operations are a pipeline. The correct emissions are supposed to flow through and make it to the Observer. But no emissions were received instead. Let's get our plumber gear on and find out where the clog in the pipeline is. We will start at the source.

Place doOnNext() immediately after the source and before concatMap(), and print each emission. This gives us visibility into what is coming out of the source Observable. As shown here, we should see all the emissions from the source print, which shows that no emissions are being omitted and the source upstream is working correctly:

```
//Split and concatMap() on "/"
 items.doOnNext(s -> System.out.println("Source pushed: " + s))
        .concatMap(s ->
                Observable.fromArray(s.split("/"))
        )
```

The output is as follows:

```
Source pushed: 521934/2342/Foxtrot
Source pushed: Bravo/12112/78886/Tango
Source pushed: 283242/4542/Whiskey/2348562
[]

java.lang.AssertionError: Value count differs; Expected ...
```

Let's move downstream and look at `concatMap()` next. Maybe that is omitting emissions, so let's check. Move `doOnNext()` after `concatMap()` and print each emission to see whether all of them are coming through, as shown next:

```
//Split and concatMap() on "/"
items.concatMap(s ->
            Observable.fromArray(s.split("/"))
        )
    .doOnNext(s -> System.out.println("concatMap() pushed: " + s))
```

The output is as follows:

```
concatMap() pushed: 521934
concatMap() pushed: 2342
concatMap() pushed: Foxtrot
concatMap() pushed: Bravo
concatMap() pushed: 12112
concatMap() pushed: 78886
concatMap() pushed: Tango
concatMap() pushed: 283242
concatMap() pushed: 4542
concatMap() pushed: Whiskey
concatMap() pushed: 2348562
[]

java.lang.AssertionError: Value count differs; Expected ...
```

Okay, so `concatMap()` is working fine and all the emissions are going through. So nothing is wrong with the splitting operation inside `concatMap()`. Let's move on downstream and put `doOnNext()` after `filter()`. As shown, print each emission to see whether the ones we want come out of the `filter()`:

```
//filter for only alphabetic Strings using regex
.filter(s -> s.matches("[A-Z]+"))
.doOnNext(s -> System.out.println("filter() pushed: " + s))
```

The output is as follows:

```
[]

java.lang.AssertionError: Value count differs; Expected ...
```

Aha! No emissions were printed after `filter()`, which means nothing flowed through it. The `filter()` is the operator causing the problem. We intended to filter out the numeric strings and only emit the alphabetic words. But for some reason, all emissions were filtered out. If you know anything about regular expressions, note that we are only qualifying strings that are entirely uppercase. We actually need to qualify lowercase letters too, so here is the correction we need:

```
//filter for only alphabetic Strings using regex
 .filter(s -> s.matches("[A-Za-z]+"))
 .doOnNext(s -> System.out.println("filter() pushed: " + s))
```

The output is as follows:

```
filter() pushed: Foxtrot
filter() pushed: Bravo
filter() pushed: Tango
filter() pushed: Whiskey
[Foxtrot, Bravo, Tango, Whiskey]
```

Alright, it is fixed! Our unit test passed finally, and here it is in its entirety. Now that the problem is solved and we are finished debugging, we can remove `doOnNext()` and any print calls:

```
import io.reactivex.observers.TestObserver;
import org.junit.Test;
import io.reactivex.Observable;

public class RxTest {

    @Test
    public void debugWalkthrough() {

        //Declare TestObserver
        TestObserver<String> testObserver = new TestObserver<>();

        //Source pushing three strings
        Observable<String> items =
                Observable.just("521934/2342/Foxtrot",
                        "Bravo/12112/78886/Tango",
                        "283242/4542/Whiskey/2348562");

        //Split and concatMap() on "/"
        items.concatMap(s ->
                        Observable.fromArray(s.split("/"))
        )
        //filter for only alphabetic Strings using regex
        .filter(s -> s.matches("[A-Za-z]+"))
```

```
                    //Subscribe the TestObserver
                    .subscribe(testObserver);

                    //This succeeds

        testObserver.assertValues("Foxtrot","Bravo","Tango","Whiskey");
                }
            }
```

The output is as follows:

```
        [Foxtrot, Bravo, Tango, Whiskey]
```

In summary, when you have an Observable or Flowable operation that is emitting an error, the wrong items, or no items at all, start at the source and work your way downstream until you find the operator causing the problem. You can also put TestObserver at each step to get a more comprehensive report of what happened in that operation, but using operators such as doOnNext(), doOnError(), doOnComplete(), doOnSubscribe(), and so on are quick and easy ways to get an insight into what is happening in that part of the pipeline.

It may not be optimal that you have to modify code with doXXX() operators to debug it. If you are using Intellij IDEA, you can try to use breakpoints within lambdas, although I have only had mixed success with this approach. You can also research RxJava debugging libraries to get detailed logs without modifying your code. Hopefully, as RxJava continues to gain traction, more useful debugging tools will pop up and become standardized.

Summary

In this chapter, you learned how to test and debug RxJava code. When you create an application or an API that is built on RxJava, you may want to build unit tests around it in order to ensure that sanity checks are always enforced. You can use blocking operators to help perform assertions, but TestObserver and TestSubscriber will give you a much more comprehensive and streamlined testing experience. You can also use TestScheduler to simulate time elapses so that time-based Observables can be tested instantly. Finally, we covered a debugging strategy in RxJava, which often involves finding the *broken operator*, starting at the source, and moving downstream until it is found.

This chapter closes our journey covering the RxJava library, so congratulations if you got here! You now have a solid foundation of building reactive Java applications. In the final two chapters, we will cover RxJava in two specific domains: Android and Kotlin.

11
RxJava on Android

If there is one domain that reactive programming has taken by storm, it is definitely mobile apps. As discussed throughout this book, ReactiveX is highly useful for many domains. But mobile apps are becoming increasingly complex, and users have a short tolerance for apps that are unresponsive, slow, or buggy. Therefore, mobile applications were quick to be early adopters of ReactiveX to solve these problems. RxSwift has quickly become popular on iOS after RxJava got a foothold on Android. There are also RxAndroid and RxBinding libraries to integrate RxJava easily with the Android environment, which we will cover in this chapter.

One of the pain points that Android developers have coped with for some time is being stuck with Java 6. This means that many of the widely used versions of Android (KitKat, Lollipop, and Marshmallow) do not support Java 8 lambdas (although this changed in Android Nougat, which finally uses OpenJDK 8). At first glance, this means you are stuck using boilerplate-riddled anonymous classes to express your RxJava operators (refer to Appendix A for examples). However, by using Retrolambda, you can, in fact, use earlier versions of Android while using lambdas, which we will go through in this chapter. Another option you have is using the Kotlin language, which has become an increasingly popular platform for Android development. Kotlin is an arguably more modern and expressive language than Java and can compile to Java 6 bytecode. We will cover Kotlin with RxJava in the next chapter.

If you have no interest in Android development, feel free to skip this chapter. But the rest of you reading this book are most likely Android developers, so it is assumed that you have done some Android development already.

 If you have little or no experience with Android and would like to learn, a great book to get started is *Android Programming: The Big Nerd Ranch Guide* by Bill Phillips, Chris Stewart, and Kristin Marsicano (https://www.bigne rdranch.com/books/android-programming/). It is an excellent book to become thoroughly proficient in Android development quickly.

In this chapter, we will cover the following topics:

- Creating an Android project
- Configuring RxJava for Android
- Using RxJava and RxAndroid
- Using RxBinding
- Other Android Rx libraries

Creating the Android project

We are going to use Android Studio for the examples in this chapter, with Android 5.1 Lollipop as our platform target. Launch Android Studio and create a new project, as shown in the following figure:

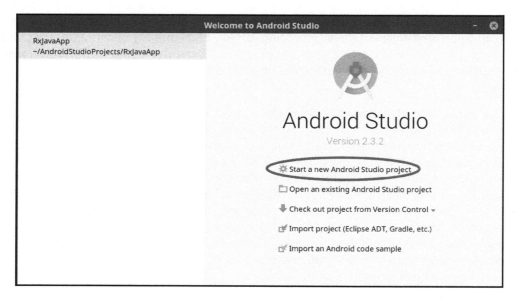

Figure 11.1: Creating a new Android project

In the next screen (shown in the following figure), name your project RxJavaApp with a **Company domain** of packtpub.com or whatever you prefer. Then, click on Next:

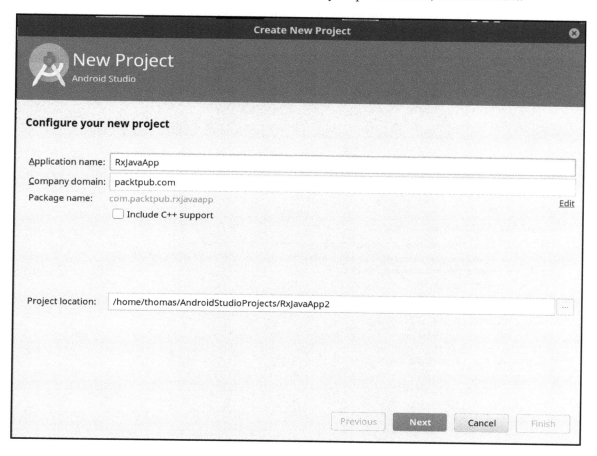

Figure 11.2

We are going to target **Phone and Tablet**. Since we may want our app to be compatible with devices running earlier versions of Android, let's select **Android 5.1 (Lollipop)** as our **Minimum SDK**. This will also give us an opportunity to practice using Retrolambda. After this, click on **Next**:

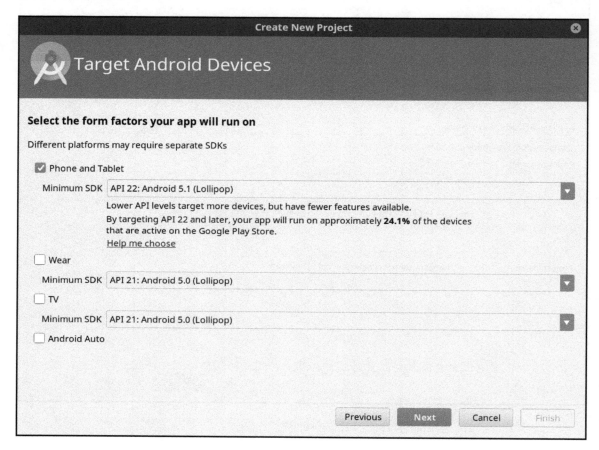

Figure 11.3

On the next screen, choose **Empty Activity** as our your template, as shown in the following figure. Then, click on **Next**. As you probably know, an activity is one interactive screen containing controls. For the examples in this chapter, we will use one activity:

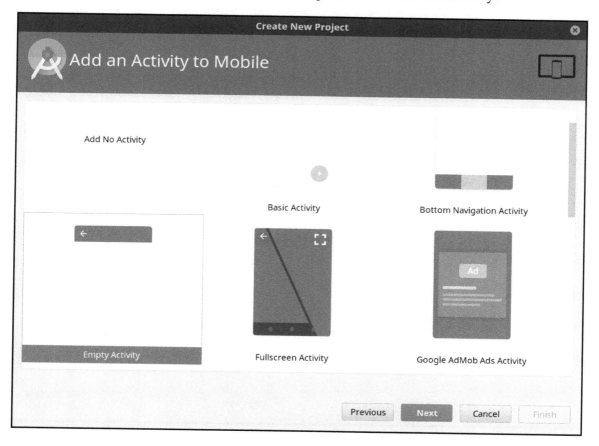

Figure 11.4

Finally, we come to the final screen to configure the Activity. Feel free to leave **Activity Name** as MainActivity and its corresponding **Layout Name** as activity_main. We will populate this Activity later. Then, click on **Finish**:

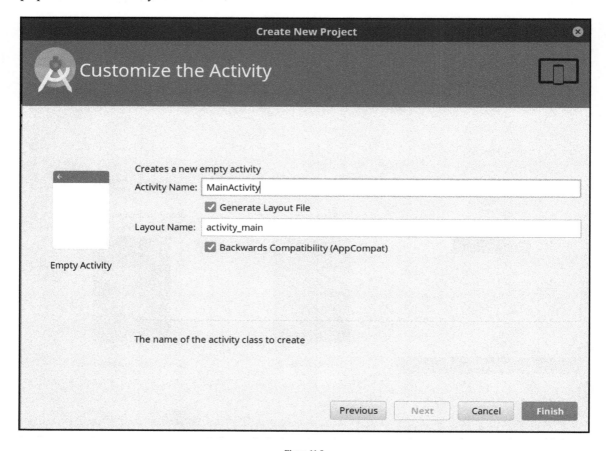

Figure 11.5

You should now come to a screen shortly with your entire Android project, and it should already be configured with Gradle. Open `build.gradle (Module: app)` so we can configure our required dependencies next, as shown in the following figure:

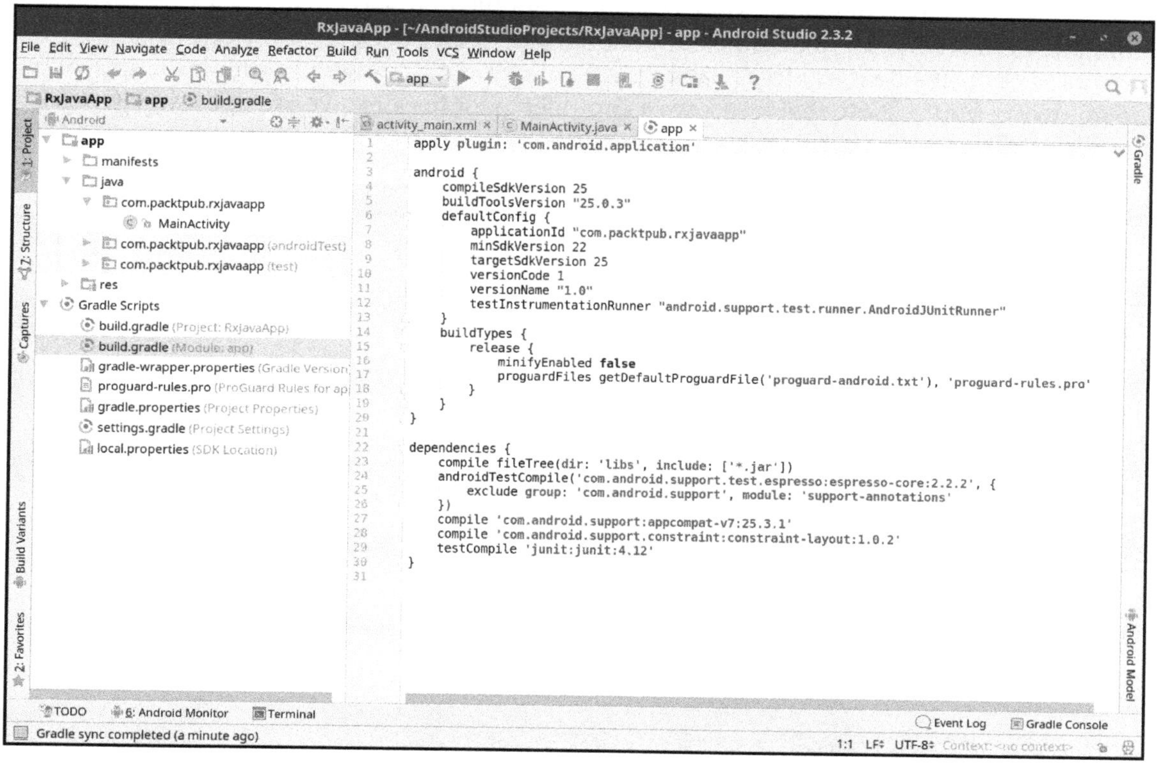

Figure 11.6

You will need to make a few changes to the `build.gradle` script targeting the app module so we can use RxJava and Retrolambda.

Configuring Retrolambda

First, let's get Retrolambda set up. We will also leverage a quick unit test to see whether it works correctly. Open the `ExampleUnitTest.java` file that was created with the project template. Remove the sample unit test method inside it and declare a new one called `lambdaTest()`. Inside it, try to declare a `Callable<Integer>` with a lambda, as shown in the following figure. Note that it throws a compiler error because we are not using Java 8 to support lambdas.

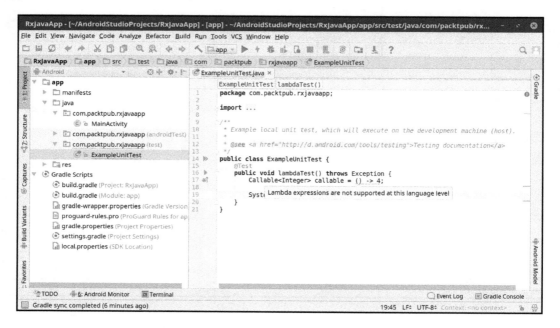

Figure 11.7 - Lambdas are not supported with this Android and Java version

We cannot use Java 8 if we are targeting Android Lollipop, so we need Retrolambda to save us from creating boilerplate-riddled anonymous inner classes. It will compile our lambdas to anonymous classes at the bytecode level, so it supports Java 6.

To get Retrolambda set up, we are going to use the gradle-retrolambda plugin to make the configuration process as seamless as possible. Go back to your `build.gradle (Module: app)` script and modify it like this:

```
buildscript {
    repositories {
        mavenCentral()
    }
```

```
    dependencies {
        classpath 'me.tatarka:gradle-retrolambda:3.6.1'
    }
}

apply plugin: 'com.android.application'
apply plugin: 'me.tatarka.retrolambda'

android {
    compileSdkVersion 25
    buildToolsVersion "25.0.2"
    defaultConfig {
        applicationId "com.packtpub.rxjavademo"
        minSdkVersion 22
        targetSdkVersion 25
        versionCode 1
        versionName "1.0"
        testInstrumentationRunner
"android.support.test.runner.AndroidJUnitRunner"
    }
    buildTypes {
        release {
            minifyEnabled false
            proguardFiles getDefaultProguardFile('proguard-
android.txt'), 'proguard-rules.pro'
        }
    }
    compileOptions {
        sourceCompatibility JavaVersion.VERSION_1_8
        targetCompatibility JavaVersion.VERSION_1_8
    }
}


dependencies {
    compile fileTree(dir: 'libs', include: ['*.jar'])

androidTestCompile('com.android.support.test.espresso:espresso-
core:2.2.2', {
        exclude group: 'com.android.support', module: 'support-
annotations'
    })
    compile 'com.android.support:appcompat-v7:25.3.1'
    compile 'com.android.support.constraint:constraint-
layout:1.0.2'
    testCompile 'junit:junit:4.12'
}
```

Click on the **Sync Now** prompt after you save the script to rebuild the project. The big change to note in the preceding code is that we added a buildscript { } block that brings in Retrolambda 3.6.1 as a dependency from `mavenCentral()`. We can then apply the retrolambda plugin. Finally, we add a `compileOptions` { } block inside the android { } one and set the source and target to be compatible with Java 8.

Run our unit test containing our lambda now. Score! As shown in the following figure, everything compiles and runs successfully, and we are now running lambdas on Java 6! Let's take a look:

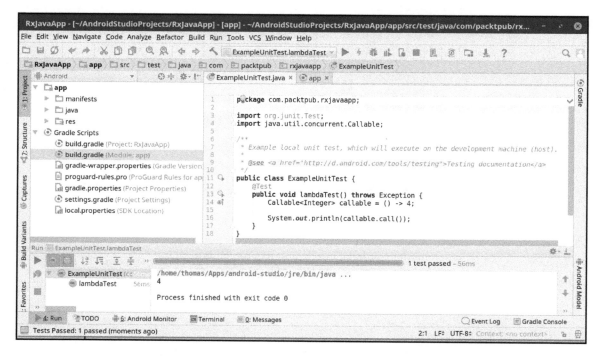

Figure 11.8 - We can now use lambdas with Java 6 on Android Lollipop with Retrolambda set up

Retrolambda is a brilliant tool for Android developers constrained to using Java 6. It cleverly compiles lambdas as traditional anonymous classes, and you can save yourself some terrible boilerplate work when using RxJava.

To learn more about Retrolambda and additional tweaks and configurations you can make, check out its GitHub page at `https://githu b.com/evant/gradle-retrolambda`. At the time of writing this, there are also upcoming lambda tools on Android Studio (`https://developer.and roid.com/studio/preview/features/java8-support.html`). These features may serve as an alternative to Retrolambda.

Configuring RxJava and friends

Now that the hard part is over and you have Retrolambda set up, all that is left for the configuration is bringing in RxJava and RxAndroid. Another set of libraries to add to your stack is Jake Wharton's RxBinding (`https://github.com/JakeWharton/RxBinding`), which streamlines RxJava usage for Android UI controls.

Add these three libraries to your dependencies { } block for your module (not the one inside the buildscript { } block!):

```
compile 'io.reactivex.rxjava2:rxjava:2.1.0'
compile 'io.reactivex.rxjava2:rxandroid:2.0.1'
compile 'com.jakewharton.rxbinding2:rxbinding:2.0.0'
```

So these should now be your full `build.gradle (Module: app)` contents:

```
buildscript {
    repositories {
        mavenCentral()
    }

    dependencies {
        classpath 'me.tatarka:gradle-retrolambda:3.6.1'
    }
}

apply plugin: 'com.android.application'
apply plugin: 'me.tatarka.retrolambda'

android {
    compileSdkVersion 25
    buildToolsVersion "25.0.2"
    defaultConfig {
        applicationId "com.packtpub.rxjavademo"
        minSdkVersion 22
        targetSdkVersion 25
        versionCode 1
        versionName "1.0"
```

```
                testInstrumentationRunner
    "android.support.test.runner.AndroidJUnitRunner"
        }
    buildTypes {
        release {
            minifyEnabled false
            proguardFiles getDefaultProguardFile('proguard-
android.txt'), 'proguard-rules.pro'
        }
    }
    compileOptions {
        sourceCompatibility JavaVersion.VERSION_1_8
        targetCompatibility JavaVersion.VERSION_1_8
    }
}


dependencies {
    compile fileTree(dir: 'libs', include: ['*.jar'])

androidTestCompile('com.android.support.test.espresso:espresso-
core:2.2.2', {
        exclude group: 'com.android.support', module: 'support-
annotations'
    })
    compile 'com.android.support:appcompat-v7:25.3.1'
    compile 'com.android.support.constraint:constraint-
layout:1.0.2'

    compile 'io.reactivex.rxjava2:rxjava:2.1.0'
    compile 'io.reactivex.rxjava2:rxandroid:2.0.1'
    compile 'com.jakewharton.rxbinding2:rxbinding:2.0.0'

    testCompile 'junit:junit:4.12'
}
```

Ensure that you click on the **Sync Now** prompt to rebuild the project with these dependencies in place. For the remainder of the chapter, we will touch on a few ways in which you can use RxJava, RxAndroid, and RxBinding together in your Android application. I could easily write a small book about different reactive features, bindings, and patterns you can use with Android, but in this chapter, we will take a minimalistic approach to focus on the core Rx features. We will touch on other libraries and resources you can research at the end of this chapter.

Using RxJava and RxAndroid

The primary feature of the RxAndroid library (`https://github.com/ReactiveX/RxAndroi d`) is that it has Android Schedulers to help your concurrency goals for your Android app. It has a Scheduler for the Android main thread as well as an implementation that can target any message Looper. Striving to be a core library, RxAndroid does not have many other features. You will need specialized reactive binding libraries for Android to do more than that, which we will explore later.

Let's start simple. We will modify `TextView` in the middle of our `MainActivity` (which already contains "`Hello World!`") to change to "`Goodbye World!`" after 3 seconds. We will do all of this reactively using `Observable.delay()`. Because this will emit on a computational Scheduler, we will need to leverage `observeOn()` to safely switch the emission to the Android main thread.

First, in the `res/layout/activity_main.xml` file, modify the `TextView` block to have an ID property called `my_text_view` (as shown in the following code). This way, we can refer to it from our app code in a moment:

```
<?xml version="1.0" encoding="utf-8"?>
<android.support.constraint.ConstraintLayout
    xmlns:android="http://schemas.android.com/apk/res/android"
    xmlns:tools="http://schemas.android.com/tools"
    xmlns:app="http://schemas.android.com/apk/res-auto"
    android:layout_width="match_parent"
    android:layout_height="match_parent"
    tools:context="com.packtpub.rxjavademo.MainActivity">

    <TextView
        android:id="@+id/my_text_view"
        android:layout_width="wrap_content"
        android:layout_height="wrap_content"
        android:text="Hello World!"
        app:layout_constraintBottom_toBottomOf="parent"
        app:layout_constraintLeft_toLeftOf="parent"
        app:layout_constraintRight_toRightOf="parent"
        app:layout_constraintTop_toTopOf="parent" />

</android.support.constraint.ConstraintLayout>
```

Finally, rebuild your project and go to the `MainActivity.java` file. In the `onCreate()` method implementation, we are going to look up our "`my_text_view`" component and save it to a variable called `myTextView` (and cast it to `TextView`).

Then, immediately, we are going to create an `Observable` emitting just the string `Goodbye World!` and delay it for 3 seconds. Because `delay()` will put it on a computational Scheduler, we will use `observeOn()` to put that emission back in `AndroidSchedulers.mainThread()` once it is received. Implement all this, as shown in the following code:

```
package com.packtpub.rxjavademo;

import android.support.v7.app.AppCompatActivity;
import android.os.Bundle;
import android.widget.TextView;
import java.util.concurrent.TimeUnit;
import io.reactivex.Observable;
import io.reactivex.android.schedulers.AndroidSchedulers;

public class MainActivity extends AppCompatActivity {

    @Override
    protected void onCreate(Bundle savedInstanceState) {
        super.onCreate(savedInstanceState);
        setContentView(R.layout.activity_main);

        TextView myTextView = (TextView)
findViewById(R.id.my_text_view);

        Observable.just("Goodbye World!")
                .delay(3, TimeUnit.SECONDS)
                .observeOn(AndroidSchedulers.mainThread())
                .subscribe(s -> myTextView.setText(s));
    }
}
```

Run this application either on an emulated virtual device or an actual connected device. Sure enough, you will get an app that shows "`Hello World!`" for 3 seconds and then changes to "`Goodbye World!`". Here, I run this app on a virtual Pixel phone, as shown in the following figure:

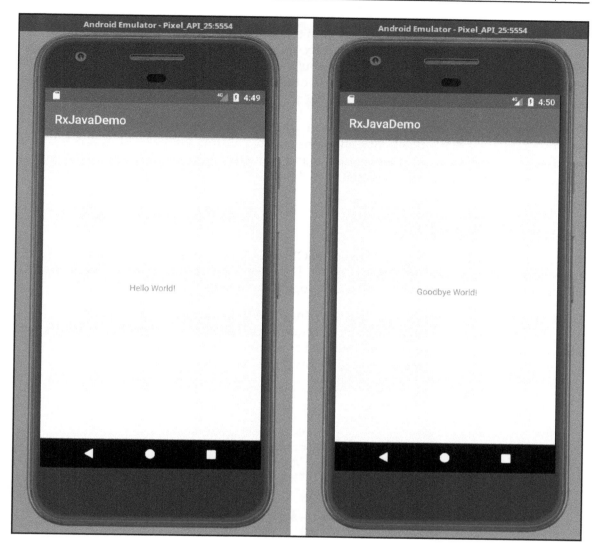

Figure 11.9 - An Android app that switches text from "Hello World!" to "Goodbye World!" after 3 seconds.

If you do not use this `observeOn()` operation to switch back to the Android `mainThread()`, the app will likely crash. Therefore, it is important to make sure any emissions that modify the Android UI happen on the `mainThread()`. Thankfully, RxJava makes this easy to do compared to traditional concurrency tools.

Pretty much everything you learned earlier in this book can be applied to Android development, and you can mix RxJava and RxAndroid with your favorite Android utilities, libraries, and design patterns. However, if you want to create Observables off of Android widgets, you will need to use RxBinding and other libraries to augment your Rx capabilities on Android.

There is also an `AndroidSchedulers.from()` factory that accepts an event Looper and returns a Scheduler that will execute emissions on any Android Looper. This will operate the `Observable/Flowable` on a new thread and emit results through `onNext()` on the thread running a background operation.

Using RxBinding

RxAndroid does not have any tools to create Observables off Android events, but there are many libraries that provide means to do this. The most popular library is RxBinding, which allows you to create Observables off of UI widgets and events.

There are many factories available in RxBinding. One static factory class you may use frequently is RxView, which allows you to create Observables off controls that extend View and broadcast different events as emissions. For instance, change your `activity_main.xml` to have a Button and TextView class, as follows:

```xml
<?xml version="1.0" encoding="utf-8"?>
<android.support.constraint.ConstraintLayout
    xmlns:android="http://schemas.android.com/apk/res/android"
    xmlns:tools="http://schemas.android.com/tools"
    android:layout_width="match_parent"
    android:layout_height="match_parent"
    tools:context="com.packtpub.rxjavademo.MainActivity">

    <LinearLayout
xmlns:android="http://schemas.android.com/apk/res/android"
        android:layout_width="wrap_content"
        android:layout_height="wrap_content"
        android:orientation="vertical"
        tools:layout_editor_absoluteY="8dp"
        tools:layout_editor_absoluteX="8dp">

    <Button
        android:id="@+id/increment_button"
        android:text="Increment"
        android:layout_width="wrap_content"
        android:layout_height="wrap_content" />
    <TextView
```

```
                  android:id="@+id/my_text_view"
                  android:layout_width="wrap_content"
                  android:layout_height="wrap_content"
                  android:text="0"/>
          </LinearLayout>

          </android.support.constraint.ConstraintLayout>
```

We saved `Button` and `TextView` to `increment_button` and `my_text_view` IDs, respectively. Now let's switch over to the `MainActivity.java` class and have the `Button` broadcast the number of times it was pressed to the `TextView`. Use the `RxView.clicks()` factory to emit each `Button` click as an Object and map it to a 1. As we did in `Chapter 3`, *Basic Operators*, we can use the `scan()` operator to emit a rolling count of emissions, as shown in the following code:

```java
package com.packtpub.rxjavademo;

import android.os.Bundle;
import android.support.v7.app.AppCompatActivity;
import android.widget.Button;
import android.widget.TextView;

import com.jakewharton.rxbinding2.view.RxView;

public class MainActivity extends AppCompatActivity {

    @Override
    protected void onCreate(Bundle savedInstanceState) {
        super.onCreate(savedInstanceState);
        setContentView(R.layout.activity_main);

        TextView myTextView = (TextView)
findViewById(R.id.my_text_view);
        Button incrementButton = (Button)
findViewById(R.id.increment_button);

        //broadcast clicks into a cumulative increment, and
display in TextView
        RxView.clicks(incrementButton)
                .map(o -> 1)
                .scan(0,(total, next) -> total + next)
                .subscribe(i -> myTextView.setText(i.toString()));
    }
}
```

Now run this app and press the button a few times. Each press will result in the number incrementing in the `TextView`, as shown in the following figure:

)

Figure 11.10 - Reactively turning Button clicks into a scan() emitting the number of times it was pressed.

Just in the RxView alone, there are dozens of factories to emit the states and events of a variety of properties on a View widget. Just to name a few, some of these other factories include `hover()`, `drag()`, and `visibility()`. There are also a large number of specialized factories for different widgets, such as `RxTextView`, `RxSearchView`, and `RxToolbar`.

There is so much functionality in RxBinding that it is difficult to cover all of it in this chapter. The most effective way to see what is available is to explore the RxBinding project source code on GitHub, which you can find at `https://github.com/JakeWharton/RxBinding/`.

Note that RxBinding has several "support" modules you can optionally bring in, including design bindings, RecyclerView bindings, and even Kotlin extensions. You can read more about these modules on GitHub README.

Other RxAndroid bindings libraries

If you are fully embracing the reactive approach in making Android apps, there are many other specialized reactive bindings libraries you can leverage in your apps. They often deal with specific domains of Android but can be helpful nonetheless if you work with these domains. Outside of RxBinding, here are some notable bindings libraries you can use reactively with Android:

- SqlBrite (`https://github.com/square/sqlbrite`): A SQLite wrapper that brings reactive semantics to SQL queries.
- RxLocation (`https://github.com/patloew/RxLocation`): A reactive location API
- rx-preferences (`https://github.com/f2prateek/rx-preferences`): A reactive SharedPreferences API
- RxFit (`https://github.com/patloew/RxFit`): Reactive fitness API for Android
- RxWear (`https://github.com/patloew/RxWear`): A reactive API for the Wearable library
- ReactiveNetwork (`https://github.com/pwittchen/ReactiveNetwork`): Reactively listens for the network connectivity state
- ReactiveBeacons (`https://github.com/pwittchen/ReactiveBeacons`): Reactively scans for **BLE (Bluetooth Low Energy)** beacons in proximity

As you can see, there is quite an RxJava ecosystem for Android, and you can view a fuller list on the RxAndroid wiki (`https://github.com/ReactiveX/RxAndroid/wiki`). Definitely leverage Google to see whether others exist for your specific task in mind. If you cannot find a library, there might be an OSS opportunity to start one!

Life cycles and cautions using RxJava with Android

As always, be deliberate and careful about how you manage the life cycle of your subscriptions. Make sure you do not rely on weak references in your Android app and assume reactive streams will dispose of themselves because they will not! So always call `dispose()` on your `disposables` when a piece of your Android application is no longer being used.

For instance, say you create a simple app that displays the number of seconds since it was launched. For this exercise, set up your layout like this in order to have `timer_field` in the `TextView` class:

```xml
<?xml version="1.0" encoding="utf-8"?>
<android.support.constraint.ConstraintLayout
xmlns:android="http://schemas.android.com/apk/res/android"
    xmlns:app="http://schemas.android.com/apk/res-auto"
    xmlns:tools="http://schemas.android.com/tools"
    android:layout_width="match_parent"
    android:layout_height="match_parent"
    tools:context="com.packtpub.rxjavaapp.MainActivity">

    <TextView
        android:id="@+id/timer_field"
        android:layout_width="wrap_content"
        android:layout_height="wrap_content"
        android:text="0"
        app:layout_constraintBottom_toBottomOf="parent"
        app:layout_constraintLeft_toLeftOf="parent"
        app:layout_constraintRight_toRightOf="parent"
        app:layout_constraintTop_toTopOf="parent" />

</android.support.constraint.ConstraintLayout>
```

We can use an `Observable.interval()` to emit every second to a `TextField`. But we need to decide carefully how and if this counter persists when the app is no longer active. When `onPause()` is called, we might want to dispose of this timer operation. When `onResume()` is called, we can subscribe again and create a new disposable, effectively restarting the timer. For good measure, we should dispose of it when `onDestroy()` is called as well. Here is a simple implementation that manages these life cycle rules:

```
package com.packtpub.rxjavaapp;

import android.support.v7.app.AppCompatActivity;
import android.os.Bundle;
import android.widget.TextView;

import java.util.concurrent.TimeUnit;

import io.reactivex.Observable;
import io.reactivex.android.schedulers.AndroidSchedulers;
import io.reactivex.disposables.Disposable;

public class MainActivity extends AppCompatActivity {

    private final Observable<String> timer;
    private Disposable disposable;

    MainActivity() {
        timer = Observable.interval(1, TimeUnit.SECONDS)
                .map(i -> Long.toString(i))
                .observeOn(AndroidSchedulers.mainThread());
    }

    @Override
    protected void onCreate(Bundle savedInstanceState) {
        super.onCreate(savedInstanceState);
        setContentView(R.layout.activity_main);
    }

    @Override
    protected void onPause() {
        super.onPause();
        disposable.dispose();
    }

    @Override
    protected void onResume() {
        super.onResume();
        TextView tv = (TextView) findViewById(R.id.timer_field);
        disposable = timer.subscribe(s -> tv.setText(s));
```

```
        }

        @Override
        protected void onDestroy() {
            super.onDestroy();
            if (disposable != null)
                disposable.dispose();
        }
    }
```

If you want to persist or save the state of your app, you may have to get creative and find a way to dispose of your reactive operations when `onPause()` is called while allowing it to pick up where it left when `onResume()` happens. In the following code, I statefully hold the last value emitted from my timer an `inAtomicInteger` and use that as the starting value in the event that a pause/resume occurs with a new subscription:

```
package com.packtpub.rxjavaapp;

import android.support.v7.app.AppCompatActivity;
import android.os.Bundle;
import android.widget.TextView;

import java.util.concurrent.TimeUnit;
import java.util.concurrent.atomic.AtomicInteger;

import io.reactivex.Observable;
import io.reactivex.android.schedulers.AndroidSchedulers;
import io.reactivex.disposables.Disposable;

public class MainActivity extends AppCompatActivity {

    private final Observable<String> timer;
    private final AtomicInteger lastValue = new AtomicInteger(0);
    private Disposable disposable;

    MainActivity() {
        timer = Observable.interval(1, TimeUnit.SECONDS)
                .map(i -> 1)

.startWith(Observable.fromCallable(lastValue::get))
                .scan((current,next) -> current + next)
                .doOnNext(lastValue::set)
                .map(i -> Integer.toString(i))
                .observeOn(AndroidSchedulers.mainThread());
    }

    @Override
```

```
    protected void onCreate(Bundle savedInstanceState) {
        super.onCreate(savedInstanceState);
        setContentView(R.layout.activity_main);
    }

    @Override
    protected void onPause() {
        super.onPause();
        disposable.dispose();
    }

    @Override
    protected void onResume() {
        super.onResume();
        TextView tv = (TextView) findViewById(R.id.timer_field);
        disposable = timer.subscribe(s -> tv.setText(s));

    }

    @Override
    protected void onDestroy() {
        super.onDestroy();

        if (disposable != null)
            disposable.dispose();
    }
}
```

So again, make sure you manage your reactive operations carefully and dispose of them deliberately with the life cycle of your app.

Also, make sure that you leverage multicasting for UI events when multiple Observers/Subscribers are listening. This prevents multiple listeners from being attached to widgets, which may not always be efficient. On the other hand, do not add the overhead of multicasting when there is only one Observer/Subscriber to a widget's events.

Summary

In this chapter, we touched on various parts of the rich RxAndroid ecosystem to build reactive Android applications. We covered Retrolambda so we can leverage lambdas with earlier versions of Android that only support Java 6. This way, we do not have to resort to anonymous inner classes to express our RxJava operators. We also touched on RxAndroid, which is the core of the reactive Android ecosystem, and it only contains Android Schedulers. To plug in your various Android widgets, controls, and domain-specific events, you will need to rely on other libraries, such as RxBinding.

In the next chapter, we will cover using RxJava with Kotlin. We will learn how to use this exciting new language, which has essentially become the Swift of Android, and why it works so well with RxJava.

12
Using RxJava for Kotlin New

In our final chapter, we will apply RxJava to an exciting new frontier on the **JVM**: the Kotlin language.

Kotlin was developed by JetBrains, the company behind Intellij IDEA, PyCharm, and several other major IDEs and developer tools. For some time, JetBrains used Java to build its products, but after 2010, JetBrains began to question whether it was the best language to meet their needs and modern demands. After investigating existing languages, they decided to build and open source their own. In 2016 (5 years later), Kotlin 1.0 was released. In 2017, Kotlin 1.1 was released to a growing community of users. Shortly afterward, Google announced Kotlin as an officially supported language for Android.

We will cover the following topics in this chapter:

- Why Kotlin?
- Configuring Kotlin
- Kotlin basics
- Extension operators
- Using RxKotlin
- Dealing with SAM ambiguity
- `let()` and `apply()`
- Tuples and data classes
- The future of ReactiveX and Kotlin

Why Kotlin?

Kotlin strives to be a pragmatic and industry-focused language, seeking a minimal (but legible) syntax that expresses business logic rather than boilerplate. However, it does not cut corners like many concise languages. It is statically typed and performs robustly in production and yet is speedy enough for prototyping. It also works 100% with Java libraries and source code, making it feasible for a gradual transition.

Android developers, who were stuck on Java 6 until recently, were quick to adopt Kotlin and effectively make it the "Swift of Android". Funnily, Swift and Kotlin have a similar feel and syntax, but Kotlin came into existence first. On top of that, a Kotlin community and ecosystem of libraries continued to grow quickly. In 2017, Google announced Kotlin as an officially supported language to develop Android apps. Due to JetBrains and Google's commitment, it is clear Kotlin has a bright future in the JVM.

But what does Kotlin have to do with RxJava? Kotlin has many useful language features that Java does not, and they can greatly improve the expressibility of RxJava. Also, more Android developers are using Kotlin as well as RxJava, so it makes sense to show how these two platforms can work together.

Kotlin is a language that can quickly be picked up by Java developers within a matter of days. If you want to learn Kotlin in detail, *Kotlin in Action* (`https://www.manning.com/book s/kotlin-in-action`) by Dmitry Jemerov and Svetlana Isakova is an excellent book. There is also the excellent online reference (`https://kotlinlang.org/docs/reference/`) provided by JetBrains. In this chapter, we will quickly go through some basic features of Kotlin to sell its pertinence in expressing RxJava more quickly.

Configuring Kotlin

You can use either Gradle or Maven to build your Kotlin project. You can create a new Kotlin project in Intellij IDEA without any build automation, but here is how to set up a Kotlin project for Gradle and Maven.

Configuring Kotlin for Gradle

To use the Kotlin language with Gradle, first add the following buildscript { } block to your `build.gradle` file:

```
buildscript {
    ext.kotlin_version = '<version to use>'

    repositories {
        mavenCentral()
    }

    dependencies {
        classpath "org.jetbrains.kotlin:kotlin-gradle-
        plugin:$kotlin_version"
    }
}
```

Then, you will need to apply the plugin, as shown in the following code, as well as the directories that will hold the source code.

Note that `src/main/kotlin` is already specified by default, but you would use the `sourceSets { }` block to specify a different directory if needed:

```
apply plugin: "kotlin"

sourceSets {
    main.kotlin.srcDirs += 'src/main/kotlin'
}
```

 You can learn more about the Kotlin Gradle configuration in detail on the Kotlin website at `https://kotlinlang.org/docs/reference/using-gradle.html`.

Configuring Kotlin for Maven

For Maven, define a `kotlin.version` property and the `Kotlin-stdlib` as a dependency in your POM, as shown in the following code. Then, build the project:

```
<properties>
    <kotlin.version>1.1.2-2</kotlin.version>
</properties>

<dependencies>
```

```
        <dependency>
            <groupId>org.jetbrains.kotlin</groupId>
            <artifactId>kotlin-stdlib</artifactId>
            <version>${kotlin.version}</version>
        </dependency>
    </dependencies>
```

You will also need to specify the source code directories and the kotlin-maven-plugin, as demonstrated in the following code:

```
    <build>

    <sourceDirectory>${project.basedir}/src/main/kotlin</sourceDirectory>

    <testSourceDirectory>${project.basedir}/src/test/kotlin</testSourceDirectory>
        <plugins>
            <plugin>
                <artifactId>kotlin-maven-plugin</artifactId>
                <groupId>org.jetbrains.kotlin</groupId>
                <version>${kotlin.version}</version>

                <executions>
                    <execution>
                        <id>compile</id>
                        <goals> <goal>compile</goal> </goals>
                    </execution>

                    <execution>
                        <id>test-compile</id>
                        <goals> <goal>test-compile</goal> </goals>
                    </execution>
                </executions>
            </plugin>
        </plugins>
    </build>
```

You can learn more about the Kotlin Maven configuration in detail on the Kotlin website at https://kotlinlang.org/docs/reference/using-maven.html.

Configuring RxJava and RxKotlin

In this chapter, we will also be using RxJava as well as an extension library called **RxKotlin**. For Gradle, add these two libraries as your dependencies like this:

```
compile 'io.reactivex.rxjava2:rxjava:2.1.0'
compile 'io.reactivex.rxjava2:rxkotlin:2.0.2'
```

For Maven, set them up like this:

```
<dependency>
    <groupId>io.reactivex.rxjava2</groupId>
    <artifactId>rxjava</artifactId>
    <version>2.1.0</version>
</dependency>
<dependency>
    <groupId>io.reactivex.rxjava2</groupId>
    <artifactId>rxkotlin</artifactId>
    <version>2.0.2</version>
</dependency>
```

Kotlin basics

Although Kotlin has a standalone compiler and can work with Eclipse, we are going to use Intellij IDEA.

A Kotlin project is structured much like a Java project. Following a standard Maven convention, you typically put your Kotlin source code in a `/src/main/kotlin/` folder instead of a `/src/main/java/` folder. The Kotlin source code is stored in text files with a `.kt` extension instead of `.java`. However, Kotlin files do not have to contain a class sharing the same name as the file.

Creating a Kotlin file

In Intellij IDEA, import your Kotlin project, if you haven't already. Right-click on the `/src/main/kotlin/` folder and navigate to **New** | **Kotlin File/Class**, as shown in the following figure:

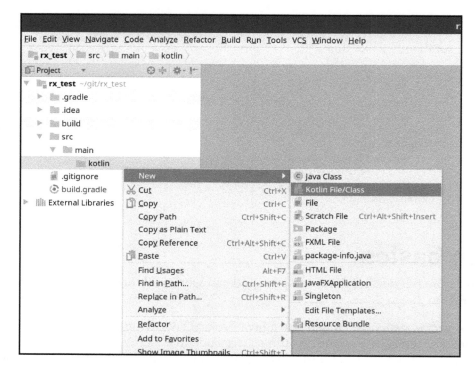

Figure 12.1: Creating a new Kotlin file

In the following dialog, name the file `Launcher` and then click on **OK**. You should now see the `Launcher.kt` file in the **Project** pane. Double-click on it to open the editor. Write the following "`Hello World`" Kotlin code, as shown here, and then run it by clicking on the **K** icon in the gutter:

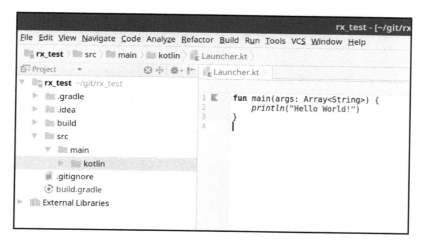

This is our first Kotlin application. Kotlin uses "functions" instead of methods, but it has a `main()` function just like Java has a `main()` method. Note that we do not have to house our `main()` function in a Java class. This is one benefit of Kotlin. Although it does compile to Java bytecode, you are not restricted to only object-oriented conventions and can be procedural or functional as well.

Assigning properties and variables

To declare a variable or property, you must decide whether to make it mutable or not. Preceding a variable declaration with a `val` will make it only assignable once, whereas `var` is mutable and can be reassigned a value multiple times. The name of the variable then follows with a colon separating it from the type. Then, you can assign a value if you have it on hand. In the following code, we assign a variable for an `Int` and a `String` and print them in an interpolated string:

```kotlin
fun main(args: Array<String>) {
    val myInt: Int = 5
    val myString: String = "Alpha"

    println("myInt=$myInt and myString=$myString")
}
```

The output is as follows:

```
myInt=5 and myString=Alpha
```

Kotlin's compiler is pretty smart and does not always have to have the type explicitly declared for variables and properties. If you assign it a value immediately, it will infer the type from that value. Therefore, we can remove the type declarations as follows:

```
fun main(args: Array<String>) {
    val myInt = 5 //infers type as `Int`
    val myString = "Alpha" //infers type as `String`

    println("myInt=$myInt and myString=$myString")
}
```

Extension functions

When you are doing RxJava work in Kotlin, something that is immensely helpful is creating extension functions. We will cover specifically how later, but here is a nonreactive example.

Say we want to add a convenient function to `LocalDate` in order to quickly compute the number of days to another `LocalDate`. Rather than invoking verbose helper classes to do this task repeatedly, we can quickly add an extension function to `LocalDate` called `numberOfDaysTo()`, as shown here. This does not extend `LocalDate` but rather lets the compiler resolve it as a static method:

```
import java.time.LocalDate
import java.time.temporal.ChronoUnit

fun main(args: Array<String>) {
    val startDate = LocalDate.of(2017,5,1)
    val endDate = LocalDate.of(2017,5,11)

    val daysBetween = startDate.numberOfDaysTo(endDate)

    println(daysBetween)
}

fun LocalDate.numberOfDaysTo(otherLocalDate: LocalDate): Long {
    return ChronoUnit.DAYS.between(this, otherLocalDate)
}
```

The output is as follows:

```
10
```

An extension function is just like a normal function in Kotlin, but you immediately declare the type you are adding the function to, followed by a dot, and then the extension function name (for example, fun `LocalDate.numberOfDaysTo()`). In the block that follows, it will treat the targeted `LocalDate` as `this`, just as if it was inside the class. But again, it resolves all this as a static method upon compilation. Kotlin magically abstracts this away for you.

This allows you to create a more fluent DSL (domain-specific language) that is streamlined for your particular business. As an added bonus, Intellij IDEA will show this extension function in the autocompletion as you work with `LocalDate`.

Since the body of this extension function is only one line, you can actually use the equals(=) syntax to declare a function more succinctly and omit the return keyword as well as the explicit type declaration, as shown in the following code:

```
fun LocalDate.numberOfDaysTo(otherLocalDate: LocalDate) =
        ChronoUnit.DAYS.between(this, otherLocalDate)
```

As we will see soon, Kotlin extension functions are a powerful tool to add new operators to Observables and Flowables, and they offer much more flexibility and convenience than `compose()` and `lift()`. But first, let's look at Kotlin lambdas.

Kotlin lambdas

I could spend a lot of time deconstructing lambdas in Kotlin, but in the interest of "getting to the point", I will show how they are expressed in the context of RxJava. You can learn about Kotlin lambdas in depth on the Kotlin reference site (`https://kotlinlang.org/docs/reference/lambdas.html`).

Kotlin offers a few more ways to express lambdas than Java 8, and it also uses curly brackets `{ }` instead of round brackets `( )` to accept lambda arguments into functions. The following is how we express an `Observable` chain emitting strings and then map and print their lengths:

```
import io.reactivex.Observable

fun main(args: Array<String>) {
```

```
                    Observable.just("Alpha", "Beta", "Gama", "Delta", "Epsilon")
                            .map { s: String -> s.length }
                            .subscribe { i: Int -> println(i) }
            }
```

The output is as follows:

```
            5
            4
            4
            5
            7
```

Note how we express our lambda arguments for map() and subscribe(). This feels weird at first, using the curly brackets { } to accept lambda arguments, but it does not take long before it feels pretty natural. They help make a distinction between stateful arguments and functional ones. You can put rounded brackets around them if you like, but this is messy and is only needed if you need to pass multiple lambda arguments (for operators such as collect()):

```
            import io.reactivex.Observable

            fun main(args: Array<String>) {

                Observable.just("Alpha", "Beta", "Gama", "Delta", "Epsilon")
                        .map( { s: String -> s.length } )
                        .subscribe( { i: Int -> println(i) } )
            }
```

As said earlier, the Kotlin compiler is smart when it comes to type inference. So most of the time, we do not need to declare our lambda s or i parameters as String and Int. The compiler can figure that out for us, as shown in the following code:

```
            import io.reactivex.Observable

            fun main(args: Array<String>) {

                Observable.just("Alpha", "Beta", "Gama", "Delta", "Epsilon")
                        .map { s -> s.length }
                        .subscribe { i -> println(i) }
            }
```

Even better, these are simple one-parameter lambdas, so we do not even have to name these parameters. We can omit them entirely and refer to them using the `it` keyword as shown next:

```
import io.reactivex.Observable

fun main(args: Array<String>) {

    Observable.just("Alpha", "Beta", "Gama", "Delta", "Epsilon")
            .map { it.length }
            .subscribe { println(it) }
}
```

Similar to Java 8, we can also use a function-reference syntax. If we are simply passing our arguments exactly in the same manner and order to a function or a constructor, we can use a double-colon :: syntax, as shown here. Note that we *do* use rounded brackets here:

```
import io.reactivex.Observable

fun main(args: Array<String>) {

    Observable.just("Alpha", "Beta", "Gama", "Delta", "Epsilon")
            .map(String::length)
            .subscribe(::println)
}
```

Something else that is interesting about Kotlin lambda arguments is that when you have multiple arguments where the last one is a lambda, you can put a lambda expression outside the rounded parentheses. In the following code, `scan()` emits the rolling total of string lengths and provides a seed value of 0. However, we can put the final lambda argument outside of the rounded parentheses ( ):

```
import io.reactivex.Observable

fun main(args: Array<String>) {

    Observable.just("Alpha", "Beta", "Gama", "Delta", "Epsilon")
            .map { s: String -> s.length }
            .scan(0) { total, next -> total + next }
            .subscribe {
                println("Rolling sum of String lengths is $it")
            }
}
```

Extension operators

As covered earlier, Kotlin provides extension functions. These can be an enormously helpful alternative to using just `compose()` and `lift()`.

For instance, we could not use Transformers and `compose()` to turn an `Observable<T>` into a `Single<R>`. But this is more than doable with Kotlin extension functions. In the following code, we create a `toSet()` operator and add it to `Observable<T>`:

```kotlin
import io.reactivex.Observable

fun main(args: Array<String>) {

    val source = Observable.just("Alpha", "Beta", "Gama", "Delta",
    "Epsilon")

    val asSet = source.toSet()

}

fun <T> Observable<T>.toSet() =
        collect({ HashSet<T>() }, { set, next -> set.add(next) })
        .map { it as Set<T> }
```

The `toSet()` returns a `Single<Set<T>>`, and it was called on an `Observable<T>`. In the extension function, the `collect()` operator is called on the invoked `Observable`, and then it cast the `HashSet` to a `Set` so the implementation is hidden. As you can see, it is easy to create new operators and make them easy to discover.

You can also make extension functions target only certain generic types. For example, I can create a `sum()` extension function that only targets `Observable<Int>` (`Int` is the Integer/int abstraction type in Kotlin). It will only be valid when used with an `Observable` emitting integers and can only compile or show up in autocomplete for that type:

```kotlin
import io.reactivex.Observable

fun main(args: Array<String>) {

    val source = Observable.just(100, 50, 250, 150)

    val total = source.sum()
}

fun Observable<Int>.sum() =
        reduce(0) { total, next -> total + next }
```

Using RxKotlin

There is a small library called RxKotlin (`https://github.com/ReactiveX/RxKotlin/`), which we made a dependency at the beginning of this chapter. At the time of writing this, it is hardly a complex library but rather a small collection of convenient extension functions for common reactive conversions. It also attempts to standardize some conventions when using RxJava with Kotlin.

For instance, there are the `toObservable()` and `toFlowable()` extension functions that can be invoked on iterables, sequences, and a few other sources. In the following code, instead of using `Observable.fromIterable()` to turn a `List` into an `Observable`, we just call its `toObservable()` extension function:

```kotlin
import io.reactivex.rxkotlin.toObservable

fun main(args: Array<String>) {

    val myList = listOf("Alpha", "Beta", "Gamma", "Delta",
    "Epsilon")

    myList.toObservable()
            .map(String::length)
            .subscribe(::println)
}
```

There are some other extensions in RxKotlin worth exploring, and you can view it all on the GitHub page. The library is deliberately small and focused since it is easy to clutter an API with every extension function for every task possible. But it holds the functionality for common tasks such as the preceding one.

RxKotlin also has useful helpers to get around the SAM problem that exists between Java and Kotlin (you might have noticed this issue if you have been experimenting already). We will cover this next.

Dealing with SAM ambiguity

At the time of writing this, there is a nuance when Kotlin invokes Java libraries with functional parameters. This problem especially rears its head in RxJava 2.0 when many parameter overloads are introduced. Kotlin does not have this issue when invoking Kotlin libraries but it does with Java libraries. When there are multiple argument overloads for different functional SAM types on a given Java method, Kotlin gets lost in its inference and needs help. Until JetBrains resolves this issue, you will need to work around this either by being explicit or using RxKotlin's helpers.

Here is a notorious example: The `zip()` operator. Try to do a simple zip here and you will get a compile error due to failed inference:

```
import io.reactivex.Observable

fun main(args: Array<String>) {

    val strings = Observable.just("Alpha", "Beta", "Gamma",
    "Delta")
    val numbers = Observable.range(1,4)

    //compile error, can't infer parameters
    val zipped = Observable.zip(strings, numbers) { s,n -> "$s $n"
}

    zipped.subscribe(::println)
}
```

One way to resolve this is to explicitly construct the SAM type with your lambda. In this case, we need to tell the compiler that we are giving it a `BiFunction<String, Int, String>`, as shown here:

```
import io.reactivex.Observable
import io.reactivex.functions.BiFunction

fun main(args: Array<String>) {

    val strings = Observable.just("Alpha", "Beta", "Gamma",
    "Delta")
    val numbers = Observable.range(1,4)

    val zipped = Observable.zip(strings, numbers,
            BiFunction<String,Int,String> { s,n -> "$s $n" }
    )
```

```
        zipped.subscribe(::println)
    }
```

Unfortunately, this is pretty verbose. Many use RxJava and Kotlin to have less code, not more, so this is not ideal. Thankfully, RxKotlin provides some utilities to work around this issue. You can use the Observables, Flowables, Singles, and Maybes utility classes to invoke implementations of the factories affected by the SAM problem. Here is our example using this approach:

```
import io.reactivex.Observable
import io.reactivex.rxkotlin.Observables

fun main(args: Array<String>) {

    val strings = Observable.just("Alpha", "Beta", "Gamma",
    "Delta")
    val numbers = Observable.range(1,4)

    val zipped = Observables.zip(strings, numbers) { s, n -> "$s
$n" }

    zipped.subscribe(::println)
}
```

There are also extension functions for non-factory operators affected by the SAM issue. The following is our example using a `zipWith()` extension function that successfully performs inference with our Kotlin lambda argument. Note that we have to import this extension function to use it:

```
import io.reactivex.Observable
import io.reactivex.rxkotlin.zipWith

fun main(args: Array<String>) {

    val strings = Observable.just("Alpha", "Beta", "Gamma",
    "Delta")
    val numbers = Observable.range(1,4)

    val zipped = strings.zipWith(numbers) { s, n -> "$s $n" }

    zipped.subscribe(::println)
}
```

It should also be pointed out that `subscribe()` on Single and Maybe is affected by the SAM ambiguity issue as well, so there are `subscribeBy()` extensions to cope with it, as shown next:

```
import io.reactivex.Observable
import io.reactivex.rxkotlin.subscribeBy

fun main(args: Array<String>) {

    Observable.just("Alpha", "Beta", "Gamma", "Delta", "Epsilon")
            .count()
            .subscribeBy { println("There are $it items") }
}
```

Try not to let the issue of SAM ambiguity deter you from trying Kotlin. It is a nuance when interoperating Kotlin lambdas with Java SAM types. The issue has been acknowledged by JetBrains and should be temporary. Also, there has been a discussion in the Kotlin community to create a ReactiveX implementation in pure Kotlin for other reasons, and we will touch on the future of RxKotlin at the end of this chapter.

Using let() and apply()

In Kotlin, every type has a `let()` and `apply()` extension function. These are two simple but helpful tools to make your code more fluent and expressive.

Using let()

`let()` simply accepts a lambda that maps the invoked object `T` to another object `R`. It is similar to how RxJava offers the `to()` operator, but it applies to any type `T` and not just Observables/Flowables. For example, we can call `let()` on a string that has been lowercased and then immediately do any arbitrary transformation on it, such as concatenating its `reversed()` string to it. Take a look at this operation:

```
fun main(args: Array<String>) {

    val str = "GAMMA"

    val lowerCaseWithReversed = str.toLowerCase().let { it + " " +
    it.reversed() }

    println(lowerCaseWithReversed)
}
```

The output is as follows:

```
gamma ammag
```

The `let()` comes in handy when you do not want to save a value to a variable just so you can refer to it multiple times. In the preceding code, we did not have to save the result of `toLowerCase()` to a variable. Instead, we just immediately called `let()` on it to do what we need.

In an RxJava context, the `let()` function can be helpful in quickly taking an `Observable`, forking it, and then recombining it using a combine operator. In the following code, we multicast an `Observable` of numbers to a `let()` operator, which creates a sum and a count, and then returns the result of the `zipWith()` operator that uses both to find the average:

```
import io.reactivex.Observable
import io.reactivex.rxkotlin.subscribeBy
import io.reactivex.rxkotlin.zipWith

fun main(args: Array<String>) {

    val numbers =
            Observable.just(180.0, 160.0, 140.0, 100.0, 120.0)

    val average = numbers.publish()
            .autoConnect(2)
            .let {
                val sum = it.reduce(0.0) { total, next -> total +
                next }
                val count = it.count()

                sum.zipWith(count) { s, c -> s / c }
            }

    average.subscribeBy(::println)
}
```

The output is as follows:

```
140.0
```

The last line in `let()` is what gets returned and does not require a return keyword.

In summary, `let()` is a powerful and simple tool to fluently convert an item into another item. Using it to fork an `Observable` or `Flowable` streams and then joining them again is one helpful application for it in RxJava.

Using apply()

A tool similar to `let()` is `apply()`. Instead of turning a `T` item into an `R` item, which `let()` does, `apply()` executes a series of actions against the `T` item instead, before returning the same `T` item itself. This is helpful in declaring an item `T` but doing tangential operations on it without breaking the declaration/assignment flow.

Here is a nonreactive example. We have a simple class, `MyItem`, which has a `startProcess()` function. We can instantiate `MyItem` but use `apply()` to call this `startProcess()` method before assigning `MyItem` to a variable, as shown in the following code:

```
fun main(args: Array<String>) {

    val myItem = MyItem().apply {
        startProcess()
    }

}

class MyItem {

    fun startProcess() = println("Starting Process!")
}
```

The output is as follows:

```
Starting Process!
```

In RxJava, `apply()` is helpful in adding an Observer or Subscriber in the middle of an `Observable`/`Flowable` chain but not breaking the flow from the primary task at hand. This can be helpful in emitting status messages to a separate stream.

In the following code, we emit five 1-second intervals and multiply each one. However, we create a `statusObserver` and subscribe to it within `apply()` right before the multiplication. We multicast before `apply()` as well so emissions are pushed to both destinations:

```
import io.reactivex.Observable
import io.reactivex.subjects.PublishSubject
import java.util.concurrent.TimeUnit

fun main(args: Array<String>) {

    val statusObserver = PublishSubject.create<Long>()
    statusObserver.subscribe { println("Status Observer: $it") }
```

```
Observable.interval(1, TimeUnit.SECONDS)
        .take(5)
        .publish()
        .autoConnect(2)
        .apply {
            subscribe(statusObserver)
        }
        .map { it * 100 }
        .subscribe {
            println("Main Observer: $it")
        }

    Thread.sleep(7000)
}
```

The output is as follows:

```
Status Observer: 0
Main Observer: 0
Status Observer: 1
Main Observer: 100
Status Observer: 2
Main Observer: 200
Status Observer: 3
Main Observer: 300
Status Observer: 4
Main Observer: 400
```

So again, `apply()` is helpful in taking a multicasted stream of emissions and pushing them to multiple Observers without having any intermediary variables.

Similiar to `apply()` is the extension function `run()`, which executes a series of actions but has a void return type (or in Kotlin-speak, Unit). There is also `with()`, which is identical to `run()` except than it is not an extension function. It accepts the targeted item as an argument.

Tuples and data classes

Kotlin supports Tuples to a small degree, but it also offers something even better with data classes. We will look at both of these in an RxJava context.

Kotlin supports the quick creation of a Pair containing two items (which can be of differing types). This is a simple two-value, but statically-typed, tuple. You can construct one quickly by putting the to keyword between two values. This is helpful in doing zip() operations between two streams, and you just want to pair the two items together.

In the following code, we zip a stream of string items with a stream of Int items and put each pair into Pair<String, Int>.

```
import io.reactivex.Observable
import io.reactivex.rxkotlin.Observables

fun main(args: Array<String>) {

    val strings = Observable.just("Alpha", "Beta", "Gamma",
    "Delta")
    val numbers = Observable.range(1,4)

    //Emits Pair<String, Int>
    Observables.zip(strings, numbers) { s, n -> s to n }
            .subscribe {
                println(it)
            }
}
```

The output is as follows:

```
(Alpha, 1)
(Beta, 2)
(Gamma, 3)
(Delta, 4)
```

An even better approach is to use a data class. A data class is a powerful Kotlin tool that works just like a class, but it automatically implements hashcode()/equals(), toString(), as well as a nifty copy() function that allows you to clone and modify properties onto a new instance of that class.

But for now, we will just use a data class as a cleaner approach than a Pair because we actually give each property a name instead of first and second. In the following code, we will create a StringAndNumber data class and use it to zip each pair of values:

```
import io.reactivex.Observable
import io.reactivex.rxkotlin.Observables

fun main(args: Array<String>) {

    val strings = Observable.just("Alpha", "Beta", "Gamma",
```

```
            "Delta")
            val numbers = Observable.range(1,4)

            data class StringAndNumber(val myString: String, val myNumber:
        Int)

            Observables.zip(strings, numbers) { s, n ->
        StringAndNumber(s,n) }
                    .subscribe {
                        println(it)
                    }
        }
```

The output is as follows:

```
        StringAndNumber(myString=Alpha, myNumber=1)
        StringAndNumber(myString=Beta, myNumber=2)
        StringAndNumber(myString=Gamma, myNumber=3)
        StringAndNumber(myString=Delta, myNumber=4)
```

Data classes (as well as just plain Kotlin classes) are quick and easy to declare, so you can use them tactically for even small tasks. Use them to make your code clearer and easier to maintain.

Future of ReactiveX and Kotlin

Kotlin is a powerful and pragmatic language. JetBrains put in a lot of effort not only to make it effective, but also compatible with existing Java code and libraries. Despite a few rough patches such as SAM lambda inference, they did a phenomenal job making Java and Kotlin work together. However, even with this solid compatibility, many developers become eager to migrate entirely to Kotlin to leverage its functionality. Named parameters, optional parameters, nullable types, extension functions, inline functions, delegates, and other language features make Kotlin attractive for exclusive use. Not to mention, JetBrains has successfully made Kotlin compilable to JavaScript and will soon support LLVM native compilation. Libraries built in pure Kotlin can potentially be compiled to all these platforms. To solidify Kotlin's position even further, Google officially established it as the next supported language for Android.

So this begs the question: would there the benefit in creating a ReactiveX implementation in pure Kotlin and not rely on RxJava? After all, the Kotlin language has a powerful set of features that could offer a lot to a ReactiveX implementation and bring it to multiple platforms Kotlin will compile to. It would also create a ReactiveX experience optimized for Kotlin, supporting nullable type emissions, extension operators, and coroutine-based concurrency.

Coroutines provide an interesting and useful abstraction to quickly (and more safely) implement concurrency into a Kotlin application. Because coroutines support task suspension, they provide a natural mechanism to support backpressure. In the event that a ReactiveX implementation in Kotlin is pursued, coroutines can play a huge part in making backpressure simple to implement.

 If you want to learn about how Kotlin coroutines can be leveraged to create a ReactiveX implementation in Kotlin, read Roman Elizarov's fascinating article at `https://github.com/Kotlin/kotlinx.coroutines /blob/master/reactive/coroutines-guide-reactive.md`.

So yes, there could be a lot to gain by making a ReactiveX implementation in pure Kotlin. At the time of writing this, this conversation is getting more traction in the Kotlin community. Keep an eye out as people continue to experiment and proof-of-concepts creep toward prototypes and then the official release.

Summary

In this chapter, we covered how to use RxJava for Kotlin. The Kotlin language is an exciting opportunity to express code on the JVM more pragmatically, and RxJava can leverage many of its useful features. Extension functions, data classes, RxKotlin, and functional operators such as `let()`/`apply()` allow you to express your reactive domain more easily. Although SAM inference can cause you to hit snags, you can leverage RxKotlin's helper utilities to get around this issue until JetBrains creates a fix. Down the road, it will be interesting to see if a ReactiveX implementation in pure Kotlin appears. Such an implementation would bring in a lot of functionality that Kotlin allows and Java does not.

This is the end! If you have covered this book cover-to-cover, congrats! You should have a strong foundation to leverage RxJava in your workplace and projects. Reactive programming is a radically different approach to problem solving, but it is radically effective too. Reactive programming will continue to grow in pertinence and shape the future of how we model code. Being on this cutting edge will make you not only marketable, but also a leader for the years to come.

Appendix

This appendix will walk you through lambda expressions, functional types, mixing object-oriented and reactive programming, and how schedulers work.

Introducing lambda expressions

Java officially supported lambda expressions when Java 8 was released in 2014. *Lambda expressions* are shorthand implementations for **single abstract method** (**SAM**) classes. In other words, they are quick ways to pass functional arguments instead of anonymous classes.

Making a Runnable a lambda

Prior to Java 8, you might have leveraged anonymous classes to implement interfaces, such as Runnable, on the fly as shown in the following code snippet:

```java
public class Launcher {

    public static void main(String[] args) {

        Runnable runnable = new Runnable() {
            @Override
            public void run() {
                System.out.println("run() was called!");
            }
        };

        runnable.run();
    }
}
```

The output is as follows:

```
run() was called!
```

To implement `Runnable` without declaring an explicit class, you had to implement its `run()` abstract method in a block immediately after the constructor. This created a lot of boilerplate and became a major pain point with Java development, and was a barrier to using Java for functional programming. Thankfully, Java 8 officially brought lambdas to the Java language. With lambda expressions, you can express this in a much more concise way:

```
public class Launcher {

    public static void main(String[] args) {

        Runnable runnable = () -> System.out.println("run() was
        called!");

        runnable.run();
    }
}
```

Awesome, right? That is a lot less code and boilerplate noise, and we will dive into how this works. Lambda expressions can target any interface or abstract class with one abstract method, which is called *single abstract method* types. In the preceding code, the `Runnable` interface has a single abstract method called `run()`. If you pass a lambda that matches the arguments and return type for that abstract method, the compiler will use that lambda for the implementation of that method.

Everything to the left of the `->` arrow is an argument. The `run()` method of `Runnable` does not take any arguments, so the lambda provides no arguments with the empty parenthesis `()`. The right side of the arrow `->` is the action to be executed. In this example, we are calling a single statement and printing a simple message with `System.out.println("run() was called!");`.

Java 8 lambdas can support multiple statements in the body. Say we have this `Runnable` anonymous inner class with multiple statements in its `run()` implementation, as shown in the following code snippet:

```
public class Launcher {
    public static void main(String[] args) {

        Runnable runnable = new Runnable() {
            @Override
            public void run() {
                System.out.println("Message 1");
```

```
                System.out.println("Message 2");
            }
        };

        runnable.run();
    }
}
```

You can move both `System.out.println()` statements to a lambda by wrapping them in a multiline `{ }` block to the right of the arrow `->`. Note that you need to use semicolons to terminate each line within the lambda, shown in the following code snippet:

```
public class Launcher {
    public static void main(String[] args) {

        Runnable runnable = () -> {
            System.out.println("Message 1");
            System.out.println("Message 2");
        };

        runnable.run();
    }
}
```

Making a Supplier a lambda

Lambdas can also implement methods that return items. For instance, the `Supplier` class introduced in Java 8 (and originally introduced in Google Guava) has an abstract `get()` method that returns a `T` item for a given `Supplier<T>`. If we have a `Supplier<List<String>>` whose `get()` returns `List<String>`, we can implement it using an old-fashioned anonymous class:

```
import java.util.ArrayList;
import java.util.List;
import java.util.function.Supplier;

public class Launcher {

    public static void main(String[] args) {

        Supplier<List<String>> listGenerator = new
Supplier<List<String>>() {
            @Override
            public List<String> get() {
                return new ArrayList<>();
```

```
            }
        };
        List<String> myList = listGenerator.get();
    }
}
```

But we can also use a lambda, which can implement `get()` much more succinctly and yield `List<String>`, shown as follows:

```
import java.util.ArrayList;
import java.util.List;
import java.util.function.Supplier;

public class Launcher {

    public static void main(String[] args) {

        Supplier<List<String>> listGenerator = () -> new
ArrayList<>
        ();

        List<String> myList = listGenerator.get();
    }
}
```

When your lambda is simplify invoking a constructor on a type using the `new` keyword, you can use a double colon `::` lambda syntax to invoke the constructor on that class. This way, you can leave out the symbols `()` and `->`, shown as follows:

```
import java.util.ArrayList;
import java.util.List;
import java.util.function.Supplier;

public class Launcher {

    public static void main(String[] args) {

        Supplier<List<String>> listGenerator = ArrayList::new;

        List<String> myList = listGenerator.get();
    }
}
```

RxJava does not have Java 8's Supplier but rather a Callable, which accomplishes the same purpose.

Making a Consumer a lambda

Consumer<T> accepts a T argument and performs an action with it but does not return any value. Using an anonymous class, we can create a Consumer<String> that simply prints the string as shown in the following code snippet:

```
import java.util.function.Consumer;

public class Launcher {

    public static void main(String[] args) {

        Consumer<String> printConsumer = new Consumer<String>() {
            @Override
            public void accept(String s) {
                System.out.println(s);
            }
        };

        printConsumer.accept("Hello World");
    }
}
```

The output is as follows:

```
Hello World
```

You can implement this as a lambda. We can choose to call the String parameter s on the left-hand side of the lambda arrow -> and print it on the right-hand side:

```
import java.util.function.Consumer;

public class Launcher {

    public static void main(String[] args) {

        Consumer<String> printConsumer = (String s) ->
        System.out.println(s);

        printConsumer.accept("Hello World");
    }
}
```

The compiler can actually infer that s is a String type based on the Consumer<String> you are targeting. So you can leave that explicit type declaration out, as shown in the following code:

```
import java.util.function.Consumer;

public class Launcher {

    public static void main(String[] args) {

        Consumer<String> printConsumer = s ->
System.out.println(s);

        printConsumer.accept("Hello World");
    }
}
```

For a simple single method invocation, you can actually use another syntax to declare the lambda using a double colon : :. Declare the type you are targeting on the left-hand side of the double-colon and invoke its method on the right-hand side of the double colon. The compiler will be smart enough to figure out you are trying to pass the String argument to System.out::println:

```
import java.util.function.Consumer;

public class Launcher {

    public static void main(String[] args) {

        Consumer<String> printConsumer = System.out::println;

        printConsumer.accept("Hello World");
    }
}
```

Making a Function a lambda

Lambdas can also implement single abstract methods that accept arguments and return an item. For instance, RxJava 2.0 (as well as Java 8) has a Function<T,R> type that accepts a T type and returns an R type. For instance, you can declare a Function<String,Integer>, whose apply() method will accept a String and return an Integer. Here, we implement apply() by returning the string's length in an anonymous class, as shown here:

```
import java.util.function.Function;

public class Launcher {

    public static void main(String[] args) {

        Function<String,Integer> lengthMapper = new
Function<String,
Integer>() {
            @Override
            public Integer apply(String s) {
                return s.length();
            }
        };

        Integer length = lengthMapper.apply("Alpha");

        System.out.println(length);
    }
}
```

You can make this even more concise by implementing Function<String,Integer> with a lambda, as shown here:

```
import java.util.function.Function;

public class Launcher {

    public static void main(String[] args) {

        Function<String,Integer> lengthMapper = (String s) ->
s.length();

        Integer length = lengthMapper.apply("Alpha");

        System.out.println(length);
    }
}
```

We have a couple of syntaxes we can alternatively use to implement
`Function<String,Integer>`.

Java 8's compiler is smart enough to see that our parameter s is a `String` based on the
`Function<String,Integer>` type we are assigning it to. Therefore, we do not need to
explicitly declare s as a `String` because it can infer it:

```
Function<String,Integer> lengthMapper = (s) -> s.length();
```

We do not need to wrap our s in parentheses `(s)` either, as those are not needed for a single
argument (but are needed for multiple arguments, as we will see later):

```
Function<String,Integer> lengthMapper = s -> s.length();
```

If we are simply calling a method or property on the incoming item, we can use the double
colon `::` syntax to call the method on that type:

```
Function<String,Integer> lengthMapper = String::length;
```

`Function<T,R>` is heavily used in RxJava as `Observable` operators often to transform
emissions. The most common example is the `map()` operator, which turns each T emission
into an R emission and derives an `Observable<R>` from an `Observable<T>`.:

```
import io.reactivex.Observable;

public class Launcher {
    public static void main(String[] args) {
        Observable.just("Alpha","Beta","Gamma")
                .map(String::length) //accepts a Function<T,R>
                .subscribe(s -> System.out.println(s));
    }
}
```

Note that there are other flavors of `Function`, such as `Predicate` and `BiFunction`, which
accept two arguments, not one. The `reduce()` operator accepts a `BiFunction<T,T,T>`
where the first T argument is the rolling aggregation, the second T is the next item to put
into the aggregation, and the third T is the result of merging the two. In this case, we use
`reduce()` to add all the items using a rolling total:

```
import io.reactivex.Observable;

public class Launcher {
    public static void main(String[] args) {
        Observable.just("Alpha","Beta","Gamma")
                .map(String::length)
                .reduce((total,next) -> total + next) //accepts a
```

```
                           BiFunction<T,T,T>
                           .subscribe(s -> System.out.println(s));
                    }
            }
```

Functional types

Here are all the functional types available in RxJava 2.0 at the time of writing this, and you can find them in the `io.reactivex.functions` package. You may recognize many of these functional types as being almost identical to those in Java 8 (in `java.util.function`) or Google Guava. However, they were somewhat copied in RxJava 2.0 to make them available for use in Java 6 and 7. A subtle difference is that RxJava's implementations throw checked exceptions. This eliminates a pain point from RxJava 1.0 where checked exceptions had to be handled in lambdas that yielded them.

The RxJava 1.0 equivalents are listed as well, but note that the single abstract method (SAM) column corresponds to the RxJava 2.0 type. RxJava 1.0 functions implement `call()` and do not support primitives. RxJava 2.0 implemented a few functional types with primitives to reduce boxing overhead where reasonably possible:

RxJava 2.0	RxJava 1.0	SAM	Description
Action	Action0	run()	Executes an action, much like Runnable
Callable<T>	Func0<T>	get()	Returns a single item of type T
Consumer<T>	Action1<T>	accept()	Performs an action on a given T item but returns nothing
Function<T,R>	Func1<T,R>	apply()	Accepts a type T and returns a type R

`Predicate<T>`	`Func1<T,Boolean>`	`test()`	Accepts a `T` item and returns a primitive `boolean`
`BiConsumer<T1,T2>`	`Action2<T1,T2>`	`accept()`	Performs an action on a `T1` and `T2` item but returns nothing
`BiFunction<T1,T2,R>`	`Func2<T1,T2,R>`	`apply()`	Accepts a `T1` and `T2` and returns a type `R`
`BiPredicate<T1,T2>`	`Func2<T1,T2,Boolean>`	`test()`	Accepts a `T1` and `T2` and returns a primitive `boolean`
`Function3<T1,T2,T3,R>`	`Func3<T1,T2,T3,R>`	`apply()`	Accepts three arguments and returns an `R`
`BooleanSupplier`	`Func0<Boolean>`	`getAsBoolean()`	Returns a single primitive `boolean` value
`LongConsumer`	`Action1<Long>`	`accept()`	Performs an action on a given `Long` but returns nothing
`IntFunction`	`Func1<T>`	`apply()`	Accepts a primitive `int` and returns an item of type `T`

Not every primitive equivalent for a functional type has been implemented in RxJava 2.0. For example, currently, there is no `IntSupplier` like there is in Java 8's standard library. This is because RxJava 2.0 does not need it to implement any of its operators.

Mixing object-oriented and reactive programming

As you start applying your RxJava knowledge to real-world problems, something that may not immediately be clear is how to mix it with object-oriented programming. Leveraging multiple paradigms such as object-oriented and functional programming is becoming increasingly common. Reactive programming and object-oriented programming, especially in a Java environment, can definitely work together for the greater good.

Obviously, you can emit any type T from an Observable or any of the other reactive types. Emitting objects built off your own classes is one way object-oriented and reactive programming work together. We have seen a number of examples in this book. For instance, Java 8's LocalDate is a complex object-oriented type, but you can push it through an Observable<LocalDate>, as shown in the following code:

```
import io.reactivex.Observable;
import java.time.LocalDate;

public class Launcher {

    public static void main(String[] args) {

        Observable<LocalDate> dates = Observable.just(
                LocalDate.of(2017,11,3),
                LocalDate.of(2017,10,4),
                LocalDate.of(2017,7,5),
                LocalDate.of(2017,10,3)
        );

        // get distinct months
        dates.map(LocalDate::getMonth)
        .distinct()
        .subscribe(System.out::println);
    }
}
```

The output is as follows:

```
NOVEMBER
OCTOBER
JULY
```

As we have seen in several examples throughout the book, a number of RxJava operators provide adapters to take a stateful, object-oriented item and turn it into a reactive stream. For instance, there is the `generate()` factory for `Flowable` and `Observable` to build a series of emissions off a mutable object that is updated incrementally. In the following code, we emit an infinite, consecutive sequence of Java 8 LocalDates but take only the first 60 emissions. Since `LocalDate` is immutable, we wrap the seed `LocalDate` of `2017-1-1` in an `AtomicReference` so it can be mutably replaced with each increment:

```java
import io.reactivex.Emitter;
import io.reactivex.Flowable;
import java.time.LocalDate;
import java.util.concurrent.atomic.AtomicReference;

public class Launcher {

    public static void main(String[] args) {

        Flowable<LocalDate> dates =
                Flowable.generate(() -> new AtomicReference<>
(LocalDate.of(2017,1,1)),
                (AtomicReference<LocalDate> next, Emitter<LocalDate>
emitter) ->
                emitter.onNext(next.getAndUpdate(dt ->
dt.plusDays(1)))
                        );
        dates.take(60)
                .subscribe(System.out::println);
    }
}
```

The output is as follows:

```
2017-01-01
2017-01-02
2017-01-03
2017-01-04
2017-01-05
2017-01-06
. . .
```

So again, RxJava has many factories and tools to adapt your object-oriented, imperative operations and make them reactive. Many of them are covered throughout this book.

But are there cases for a class to return an Observable, Flowable, Single, or Maybe from a property or method? Certainly! When your object has properties or methods whose results are dynamic and change over time and represent an event(s) or a sizable sequence of data, they are candidates to be returned as a reactive type.

Here is an abstract example: say, you have a DroneBot type that represents a flying drone. You could have a property called getLocation() that returns an Observable<Point> instead of Point. This way, you can get a live feed that pushes a new Point emission every time the drone's location changes:

```java
import io.reactivex.Observable;

public class Launcher {

    public static void main(String[] args) {
        DroneBot droneBot = null; // create DroneBot

        droneBot.getLocation()
          .subscribe(loc ->
            System.out.println("Drone moved to " + loc.x + "," +
loc.y));
    }

    interface DroneBot {
        int getId();
        String getModel();
        Observable<Location> getLocation();
    }

    static final class Location {
        private final double x;
        private final double y;
        Location(double x, double y) {
            this.x = x;
            this.y = y;
        }
    }
}
```

This `DroneBot` example shows another way in which you can mix object-oriented and reactive programming effectively. You can easily get a live feed of that drone's movements by returning an `Observable`. There are many use cases for this pattern: stock feeds, vehicle locations, weather station feeds, social networks, and so on. However, be careful if the properties are infinite. If you wanted to manage the location feeds of 100 drones, flat mapping all their infinite location feeds together into a single stream is likely not going to produce anything meaningful, apart from a noisy sequence of locations with no context. You will likely subscribe to each one separately, in a UI that populates a `Location` field in a table displaying all the drones, or you will use `Observable.combineLatest()` to emit a snapshot of the latest locations for all drones. The latter can be helpful in displaying points on a geographic map live.

Having reactive class properties is useful when they are finite as well. Say you have a list of warehouses, and you want to count the total inventory across all of them. Each `Warehouse` contains an `Observable<ProductStock>`, which returns a finite sequence of the product stocks currently available. The `getQuantity()` operator of `ProductStock` returns the quantity of that product available. We can use `reduce()` on the `getQuantity()` values to get a sum of all the available inventory, as shown here:

```java
import io.reactivex.Observable;
import java.util.List;

public class Launcher {

    public static void main(String[] args) {
        List<Warehouse> warehouses = null; // get warehouses

        Observable.fromIterable(warehouses)
            .flatMap(Warehouse::getProducts)
            .map(ProductStock::getQuantity)
            .reduce(0, (total,next) -> total + next)
            .subscribe(i -> System.out.println("There are " + i + "
            units in inventory"));
    }

    interface Warehouse {
        Observable<ProductStock> getProducts();
    }
    interface ProductStock {
        int getId();
        String getDescription();
        int getQuantity();
    }
}
```

So, finite Observables like the ones returned from `getProducts()` on `Warehouse` can be helpful too and are especially helpful for analytical tasks. But note that this particular business case decided that `getProducts()` would return the products available at that moment, not an infinite feed that broadcasts the inventory every time it changes. This was a design decision, and sometimes, representing snapshot data in a cold manner is better than a hot infinite feed. An infinite feed would have required `Observable<List<ProductStock>>` (or `Observable<Observable<ProductStock>>`) to be returned so logical snapshots are emitted. You can always add a separate `Observable` that emits notifications of changes and then uses `flatMap()` on your `getProducts()` to create a hot feed of inventory changes. This way, you create basic building blocks in your code model and then compose them together reactively to accomplish more complex tasks.

Note that you can have methods that return reactive types accept arguments. This is a powerful way to create an `Observable` or `Flowable` catered to a specific task. For instance, we could add a `getProductsOnDate()` method to our `warehouse` that returns an `Observable` emitting product stock from a given date, as shown in the following code:

```
interface Warehouse {
    Observable<ProductStock> getProducts();
    Observable<ProductStock> getProductsOnDate(LocalDate date);
}
```

In summary, mixing reactive and object-oriented programming is not only beneficial, but also necessary. When you design your domain classes, think carefully what properties and methods should be made reactive and whether they should be cold, hot, and/or infinite. Imagine how you will be using your class and whether your candidate design will be easy or difficult to work with. Be sure to not make every property and method reactive for the sake of being reactive either. Only make it reactive when there is usability or performance benefit. For example, you should not make a `getId()` property for your domain type reactive. This ID on that class instance is unlikely to change, and it is just a single value, not a sequence of values.

Materializing and Dematerializing

Two interesting operators we did not cover are `materialize()` and `dematerialize()`. We did not cover them in Chapter 3, *Basic Operators*, with all the other operators because it might have been confusing at that point in your learning curve. But hopefully, the point at which you are reading this, you understand the `onNext()`, `onComplete()`, and `onError()` events well enough to use an operator that abstractly packages them in a different way.

The `materialize()` operator will take these three events, `onNext()`, `onComplete()`, and `onError()`, and turn all of them into emissions wrapped in a `Notification<T>`. So if your source emits five emissions, you will get six emissions where the last one will be `onComplete()` or `onError()`. In the following code, we materialize an `Observable` emitting five strings, which are turned into six `Notification` emissions:

```
import io.reactivex.Observable;

public class Launcher {

    public static void main(String[] args) {

        Observable<String> source =
                Observable.just("Alpha", "Beta", "Gamma", "Delta",
"Epsilon");

        source.materialize()
                .subscribe(System.out::println);

    }
}
```

The output is as follows:

```
OnNextNotification[Alpha]
OnNextNotification[Beta]
OnNextNotification[Gamma]
OnNextNotification[Delta]
OnNextNotification[Epsilon]
OnCompleteNotification
```

Each `Notification` has three methods, `isOnNext()`, `isOnComplete()`, and `isOnError()`, to determine what type of event `Notification` is. There is also `getValue()`, which will return the emission value for `onNext()` but will be null for `onComplete()` or `onError()`. We leverage these methods on `Notification`, as shown in the following code, to filter out the three events to three separate Observers:

```
import io.reactivex.Notification;
import io.reactivex.Observable;

public class Launcher {

    public static void main(String[] args) {

        Observable<Notification<String>> source =
                Observable.just("Alpha", "Beta", "Gamma", "Delta",
"Epsilon")
```

```
                              .materialize()
                              .publish()
                              .autoConnect(3);

          source.filter(Notification::isOnNext)
                    .subscribe(n -> System.out.println("onNext=" +
      n.getValue())));

          source.filter(Notification::isOnComplete)
                    .subscribe(n -> System.out.println("onComplete"));

          source.filter(Notification::isOnError)
                    .subscribe(n -> System.out.println("onError"));
        }
      }
```

The output is as follows:

```
onNext=Alpha
onNext=Beta
onNext=Gamma
onNext=Delta
onNext=Epsilon
onComplete
```

You can also use `dematerialize()` to turn an `Observable` or `Flowable` emitting notifications back into a normal `Observable` or `Flowable`. It will produce an error if any emissions are not `Notification`. Unfortunately, at compile time, Java cannot enforce operators being applied to Observables/Flowables emitting specific types such as Kotlin:

```
import io.reactivex.Observable;

public class Launcher {

    public static void main(String[] args) {

        Observable.just("Alpha", "Beta", "Gamma", "Delta",
    "Epsilon")
                    .materialize()
                    .doOnNext(System.out::println)
                    .dematerialize()
                    .subscribe(System.out::println);
        }
    }
```

The output is as follows:

```
OnNextNotification[Alpha]
Alpha
OnNextNotification[Beta]
Beta
OnNextNotification[Gamma]
Gamma
OnNextNotification[Delta]
Delta
OnNextNotification[Epsilon]
Epsilon
OnCompleteNotification
```

So what exactly would you use `materialize()` and `dematerialize()` for? You may not use them often, which is another reason why they are covered here in the appendix. But they can be handy in composing more complex operators with transformers and stretching transformers to do more without creating low-level operators from scratch. For instance, RxJava2-Extras uses `materialize()` for a number of its operators, including `collectWhile()`. By treating `onComplete()` an emission itself, `collectWhile()` can map it to push the collection buffer downstream and start the next buffer.

Otherwise, you will likely not use it often. But it is good to be aware that it exists if you need it to build more complex transformers.

Understanding Schedulers

You will likely not use schedulers like this in isolation as we are about to do in this section. You are more likely to use them with `observeOn()` and `subscribeOn()`. But here is how they work in isolation outside of an Rx context.

A Scheduler is RxJava's abstraction for pooling threads and scheduling tasks to be executed by them. These tasks may be executed immediately, delayed, or repeated periodically depending on which of its execution methods are called. These execution methods are `scheduleDirect()` and `schedulePeriodicallyDirect()`, which have a few overloads. Below, we use the computation Scheduler to execute an immediate task, a delayed task, and a repeated task as shown below:

```
import io.reactivex.Scheduler;
import io.reactivex.schedulers.Schedulers;

import java.util.concurrent.TimeUnit;
```

```
public class Launcher {

    public static void main(String[] args) {

        Scheduler scheduler = Schedulers.computation();

        //run task now
        scheduler.scheduleDirect(() -> System.out.println("Now!"));

        //delay task by 1 second
        scheduler.scheduleDirect(() ->
System.out.println("Delayed!"), 1, TimeUnit.SECONDS);

        //repeat task every second
        scheduler.schedulePeriodicallyDirect(() ->
System.out.println("Repeat!"), 0, 1, TimeUnit.SECONDS);

        //keep alive for 5 seconds
        sleep(5000);
    }

    public static void sleep(long millis) {
        try {
            Thread.sleep(millis);
        } catch (InterruptedException e) {
            e.printStackTrace();
        }
    }
}
```

Your output will likely be the following:

```
Now!
Repeat!
Delayed!
Repeat!
Repeat!
Repeat!
Repeat!
Repeat!
```

The scheduleDirect() will only execute a one-time task, and accepts optional overloads to specify a time delay. schedulePeriodicallyDirect() will repeat infinitely. Interestingly, all of these methods return a Disposable to allow cancellation of the task it is executing or waiting to execute.

These three methods will automatically pass tasks to a `Worker`, which is an abstraction that wraps around a single thread that sequentially does work given to it. You can actually call the Scheduler's `createWorker()` method to explicitly get a Worker and delegate tasks to it directly. Its `schedule()` and `schedulePeriodically()` methods operate just like Scheduler's `scheduleDirect()` and `schedulePeriodicallyDirect()` respectively (and also return disposables), but they are executed by the specified worker. When you are done with a worker, you should dispose it so it can be discarded or returned to the `Scheduler`. Here is an equivalent of our earlier example using a `Worker`:

```
import io.reactivex.Scheduler;
import io.reactivex.schedulers.Schedulers;

import java.util.concurrent.TimeUnit;

public class Launcher {

    public static void main(String[] args) {

        Scheduler scheduler = Schedulers.computation();
        Scheduler.Worker worker = scheduler.createWorker();

        //run task now
        worker.schedule(() -> System.out.println("Now!"));

        //delay task by 1 second
        worker.schedule(() -> System.out.println("Delayed!"), 1,
TimeUnit.SECONDS);

        //repeat task every second
        worker.schedulePeriodically(() ->
System.out.println("Repeat!"), 0, 1, TimeUnit.SECONDS);

        //keep alive for 5 seconds, then dispose Worker
        sleep(5000);
        worker.dispose();
    }

    public static void sleep(long millis) {
        try {
            Thread.sleep(millis);
        } catch (InterruptedException e) {
            e.printStackTrace();
        }
    }
}
```

This is the output you may get:

```
Now!
Repeat!
Repeat!
Delayed!
Repeat!
Repeat!
Repeat!
Repeat!
```

Of course, every Scheduler is implemented differently . A Scheduler may use one thread or several threads. It may cache and reuse threads, or not reuse them at all. It may use an Android thread or a JavaFX thread (as we have seen with RxAndroid and RxJavaFX in this book). But that is essentially how schedulers work, and you can perhaps see why they are useful in implemeting RxJava operators.

Index

A

action operators
  about 101
  doOnComplete() 101
  doOnDispose() 104
  doOnError() 101
  doOnNext() 101
  doOnSubscribe() 104
  doOnSuccess() 105
Akka 8
all() operator 86
ambiguous 121, 122, 123
Android programming
  reference 307
Android project
  creating 308, 310, 311, 312, 313
any() operator 87
apply()
  using 348
AsyncSubject 161
autoConnect() operator 143, 145
automatic connection
  about 142
  autoConnect() operator 143, 145
  refCount 146
  share() 146

B

backpressure
  about 231, 232
  example 233
  Flowable 235
  using 237
BackpressureStrategy
  BUFFER 247
  DROP 247
  ERROR 247
  LATEST 247
  MISSING 247
  using 246
BehaviorSubject 159
bindings libraries, RxAndroid
  ReactiveBeacons 325
  ReactiveNetwork 325
  rx-preferences 325
  RxFit 325
  RxLocation 325
  RxWear 325
  SqlBrite 325
blocking operators 289
blockingFirst() operator 290, 291
blockingForEach() operator 294
blockingGet() operator 291
blockingIterable() operator 293
blockingLast() operator 292
blockingLatest() operator 295
blockingMostRecent() 296
blockingNext() operator 294
boundary-based buffering 211, 212
boundary-based windowing 215
buffer() operator 206
buffering
  about 206
  boundary-based buffering 211, 212
  fixed-size buffering 206, 208
  time-based buffering 209, 210

C

caching 148, 153, 154
cast() operator 75
Central Repository
  reference 12
classes 8

cold Observables
  about 35, 36, 38
  versus hot Observables 35
collect() operator 93, 94
collection operators
  about 88
  collect() 93
  toList() 89
  toMap() 90, 91
  toMultiMap() 90, 91
  toSortedList() 90
combine latest
  about 125
  withLatestFrom() operator 127
CompositeDisposable
  using 61
concatenation
  about 117
  concatMap() 120
  Observable.concat() 118
  Observable.concatWith() 118
concatMap() operator 120
concurrency
  about 167
  fundamentals 168, 169
  significance 168
ConnectableObservable 40, 42
Consumer
  lambda, making 357, 358
contains() operator 88
coroutines 352
count() operator 84
custom transformers 281

D

data class 350
defaultIfEmpty() operator 77
delay() operator 80
dematerializing 367, 370
Disposable
  handling, within Observer 59
Disposal
  handling, with Observable.create() 62
disposing 58
distinct() operator 70

distinctUntilChanged() operator 72
doOnComplete() 101
doOnDispose() operator 104
doOnError() operator 101
doOnNext() operator 101
doOnSubscribe() operator 104
doOnSuccess() operator 105

E

elementAt() operator 73, 74
error recovery operators
  about 94
  onErrorResumeNext() 97
  onErrorReturn() 95
  onErrorReturnItem() 95
  retry() 99
extension operators, Kotlin 342

F

filter() operator 66
fixed-size buffering 206, 208
fixed-size windowing 212
flatMap() 112
Flowable If...
  using 238
Flowable.create()
  using 246
Flowable.generate()
  using 255, 256
Flowable
  about 235, 239
  creating 245, 246
  Observable, turning into 248
  turning, into Observable 248
FlowableOperator
  implementing 278
FlowableTransformer 266
fluent conversion
  to(), using for 270
Friends
  configuring 317
Frodo library
  reference 301
Function
  lambda, making 359

functional types 361

G

Google Guava
  reference 94
Gradle
  Kotlin, configuring for 333
  reference 13
  using 13, 14
grouping 128

H

hot Observables
  about 38, 40
  versus cold Observables 35

J

JUnit
  configuring 286

K

keystrokes
  grouping 226, 228
Kotlin file
  creating 336, 337
Kotlin Gradle configuration
  reference 333
Kotlin in Action
  reference 332
Kotlin lambdas
  about 339
  reference 339
Kotlin Maven configuration
  reference 334
Kotlin
  basics 335
  configuring 332
  configuring, for Gradle 333
  configuring, for Maven 333
  extension functions 338, 339
  extension operators 342
  future 351
  need for 332
  properties, assigning 337

reference 332
variables, assigning 337

L

lambda expressions 353
Lambdas
  shorthand Observers, using with 32
let()
  using 346

M

map() operator 74
materializing 367, 370
Maven Standard Directory layout
  reference 286
Maven
  Kotlin, configuring for 333
  using 15
merging
  about 108
  flatMap() 112
  Observable.merge() 108
  Observable.mergeWith() 108
multicasting
  about 41, 134
  usage 140, 141
  working, with operators 135, 136, 139, 140
multithreading 167, 168

O

object-oriented, and reactive programming
  mixing 363, 364, 365, 366
objects 8
Observable contract
  reference 25
Observable If...
  using 238
Observable sources 42
Observable.combineLatest() factory 125, 126, 127
Observable.concat() 118
Observable.concatWith() 118
Observable.create()
  Disposal, handling with 62
  using 24, 26
Observable.defer() 50, 51

Observable.empty() 48
Observable.error() 49
Observable.fromCallable() 53
Observable.future() 47
Observable.interval() 44, 45
Observable.just() method
  using 28, 29
Observable.merge() operator 108
Observable.mergeWith() operator 108
Observable.never() 49
Observable.range() 42, 43
Observable
  about 23
  Completable 57
  Flowable, turning into 248
  MayBe 55
  onComplete() 24
  onError() event 24
  onNext() event 24
  Single 54
  turning, into Flowable 248
  working 24
ObservableOperator
  implementing 273, 274, 277
ObservableTransformer 262, 263
observeOn()
  about 189
  nuances 195
  using, for UI event threads 193
Observer interface
  about 30
  Disposable, handling within 59
  implementing 31
  subscribing to 31
onBackPressureBuffer()
  using 250
onBackPressureDrop()
  using 254
onBackPressureLatest()
  using 253
onBackpressureXXX() operators
  using 250
onErrorResumeNext() operator 97
onErrorReturn() operator 95
onErrorReturnItem() operator 95

operators
  about 273
  FlowableOperator 278
  for Completables 281
  for Maybes 281
  for Singles 281
  ObservableOperator 273, 274

P

parallel computing 196
parallelism 169, 196
parallelization 169, 196
PublishSubject 154, 155

R

Reactive Extensions 8
Reactive Streams
  reference 11
ReactiveBeacons
  reference 325
ReactiveNetwork
  reference 325
ReactiveX
  future 352
  history 8
reduce() operator 85
reducing operators
  about 84
  all() 86
  any() 87
  contains() 88
  count() 84
  reduce() 85
refCount() operator 146
repeat() operator 81
replay() operator 148
replaying 148
ReplaySubject 160
Retrolambda
  about 316
  configuring 314
  reference 316
retry() operator 99
Runnable
  lambda, making 353, 354

rx-preferences
  reference 325
RxAndroid
  bindings libraries 325
  reference 8, 193, 319
  using 319
RxBinding
  reference 317, 325
  using 322
RxFit
  reference 325
RxGroovy 8
RxJava 1.0
  versus RxJava 2.0 20
RxJava code
  debugging 301, 302, 304, 305
RxJava concurrency
  about 170, 171, 174
  application, keeping alive 176
RxJava, with Android
  cautions 326
  lifecycles 326
RxJava-JDBC libraries 37
RxJava-JDBC
  reference 8, 37
RxJava2-Extras
  using 282
RxJava2Extensions
  using 282
RxJava2Jdk8Interop library
  reference 293
RxJava
  about 10
  Central Repository, navigating 12
  configuring 317
  history 8
  leveraging 16, 18
  setting up 11
  using 21, 319
RxJavaFX
  reference 8, 193
RxKotlin
  about 8
  configuring 335
  reference 343

  using 343
RxNetty
  reference 8
RxScala 8
RxSwing
  reference 193
RxWear
  reference 325

S

SAM ambiguity
  dealing with 344, 346
scan() operator 82
schedulers
  about 178, 370
  computation 179
  ExecutorService 181
  IO tasks 179
  new thread 180
  shutting down 182
  single thread 180
  starting 182
  trampoline 180
share() operator 146
shared state
  avoiding, with transformers 267, 270
shorthand Observers
  using, with Lambdas 32
single abstract method (SAM) 353
skip() operator 68
skipWhile() operator 69, 70
Sodium 8
sorted() operator 78, 79, 80
SqlBrite
  about 325
  reference 325
SQLite JDBC 37
startWith() operator 75
Subjects
  about 154
  AsyncSubject 161
  BehaviorSubject 159
  issues 157
  PublishSubject 154, 155
  ReplaySubject 160

serializing 158
UnicastSubject 162
using 155
subscribeOn() operator
about 182, 183, 186
nuances 187
Subscriber
about 240
blocking 286
creating 240
implementing 241
Supplier
lambda, making 355
suppressing operators
about 66
distinct() 70
distinctUntilChanged() 72
elementAt() 73, 74
filter() 66
skip() 68
skipWhile() 69, 70
take() 67
takeWhile() 69, 70
switchIfEmpty() operator 77
switching 221, 222, 223

T

take() operator 67
takeWhile() operator 69, 70
TestObserver
using 297, 299
TestScheduler
time, manipulating with 299, 300
TestSubscriber
using 297, 299
thread pool 169
threads 169
throttle() operators 216
throttleFirst() operator 219
throttleLast() operator 218
throttleWithTimeout() operator 220
throttling 216
time-based buffering 209, 210
time-based windowing 214
time

manipulating, with TestScheduler 299, 300
to()
using, for fluent conversion 270
toList() operator 89
toMap() operator 91
toMultiMap() operator 91
toSortedList() operator 90
transformers
about 261
FlowableTransformer 266
ObservableTransformer 262, 263
shared state, avoiding with 267, 270
transforming operators
about 74
cast() 75
defaultIfEmpty() 77
delay() 80
map() 74
repeat() 81
scan() 82
sorted() 78, 79, 80
startWith() 75
switchIfEmpty() 77
Tuples 349

U

UI event threads
observeOn(), using for 193
UnicastSubject 162
unsubscribeOn() 201

V

volatile keyword 168

W

window() operators 212
windowing
about 212
boundary-based windowing 215
fixed-size windowing 212
time-based windowing 214
withLatestFrom() operator 127

Z

zipping
    about 123, 124

Lightning Source UK Ltd.
Milton Keynes UK
UKHW032033151218
333979UK00005B/315/P

9 781787 120426